Waters of Discord

WAITING FOR BLOCKADE RUNNERS.
Both the blockade runner and the blockading vessel
required men with sharp eyes and a good glass.
Men aboard blockading ships encountered long days of
boredom punctuated by brief periods of excitement and intense
activity when a blockade runner appeared.
(Massachusetts Commandery Military Order of the Loyal Legion
and the U.S. Army Military History Institute.)

Waters of Discord

THE UNION BLOCKADE OF TEXAS DURING THE CIVIL WAR

Rodman L. Underwood

McFarland & Company, Inc., Publishers
Jefferson, North Carolina, and London

ALSO BY RODMAN L. UNDERWOOD
AND FROM MCFARLAND

Stephen Russell Mallory: A Biography of the Confederate Navy Secretary and United States Senator (2005)

The present work is a reprint of the illustrated case bound edition of Waters of Discord: The Union Blockade of Texas During the Civil War, *first published in 2003 by McFarland.*

LIBRARY OF CONGRESS CATALOGUING-IN-PUBLICATION DATA

Underwood, Rodman L., 1930–
Waters of discord : the Union blockade of Texas during the Civil War / Rodman L. Underwood.
p. cm.
Includes bibliographical references and index.

ISBN 978-0-7864-3776-4
softcover : 50# alkaline paper ∞

1. United States—History—Civil War, 1861–1865—Blockades.
2. Texas—History—Civil War, 1861–1865—Blockades.
3. Blockade—Texas—History—19th century.
4. Texas—History—Civil War, 1861–1865—Naval operations.
5. United States—History—Civil War, 1861–1865—Naval operations.
6. United States. Navy—History—Civil War, 1861–1865.
7. Confederate States of America. Navy—History.
8. United States—Politics and government—1861–1865.   I. Title.

E600.U53W38 2008   973.7'5—dc22   2003017402

British Library cataloguing data are available

©2003 Rodman L. Underwood. All rights reserved

No part of this book may be reproduced or transmitted in any form or by any means, electronic or mechanical, including photocopying or recording, or by any information storage and retrieval system, without permission in writing from the publisher.

On the cover: Captain Raphael Semmes CSS *Alabama*, August 1863 (Naval Historical Foundation); blockade runner *Denbigh*, painting by Thomas C. Healy, July 29, 1864, Mobile

Manufactured in the United States of America

McFarland & Company, Inc., Publishers
Box 611, Jefferson, North Carolina 28640
www.mcfarlandpub.com

To my wife,
Carol Jeanne Hale Underwood

My gratitude for everything

Contents

Preface 1
Some Notes on the Texas Coastline 5

1. Blockade Genesis 11
2. Blockade Growth 39
3. Blockade Running and Blockade Evasion 49
4. Moves and Countermoves 77
5. A Snarl: Cotton, Politics, and Foreign Involvement ... 103
6. The Rio Grande Expedition 125
7. The Confederacy Collapses 135
8. Blockade Revisited: An Evaluation 147
9. Epilogue 167

Appendix I. Blockade Proclamation 171
Appendix II. Excerpted Report of the Blockade Strategy Board 173
Notes 175
Bibliography 187
Index 193

Preface

During the Civil War, more attention was paid to fighting by Texas troops in the Eastern Theater than to military operations in the Lone Star State. Actions in the East were of a larger scale than those in Texas and were more accessible to reporting by Eastern newspapers which had the largest national circulation. Most combat in Texas took place on the Gulf of Mexico coast, as well as on open Gulf waters, but individual actions were small and widely dispersed over the approximately 325-mile coastline. The fact that these engagements tended to be small and isolated does not suggest they were unimportant. They were imbued with the same enthusiasm and intensity as was demonstrated in larger battles and engagements east of the Mississippi River.

Limited national interest in Civil War Texas was due to the state's being separated geographically from the rest of the Confederacy and its further isolation after the Federal government gained control of the Mississippi River. The Lone Star State was viewed by most as the "Wild West," the frontier's edge, a place where federal and state troops dealt with the "Indian problem." A young woman who came to Texas as a refugee from her Louisiana plantation after the fall of Vicksburg in 1863 wrote in her diary that she had found "the dark corner of the Confederacy." Since it did not evoke the romantic imagery associated with stately mansions bathed in the scent of magnolias, Texas often was not viewed as a "real" Southern state. This was due in part to the fact it had been in the Union only 16 years when the war erupted. Texas was overshadowed by important events in the East; furthermore, some popular maps of the era showed Texas as extending no farther west than Galveston.

In much of the literature about the Civil War in Texas, with the exception of a few major engagements, battles are covered with minimal acknowledgment or discussion of the strategies behind them. In most instances, there is little analysis of how tactics employed by Union and Confederate forces in specific engagements contributed to or detracted from strategic concerns. For example, much action on land is examined with scant attention to how this fighting furthered blockade goals. Similarly, naval activity associated with the Union blockade of Texas is usually discussed without any information on supporting land action. In truth, all army and navy operations were closely intertwined, because either directly or indirectly they were associated with the primary strategic goal in the area: constructing and maintaining the Union blockade. To properly evaluate strategy and tactics, land and sea actions must be examined together.

Military histories of Texas tend to limit their coverage of the blockade to army action. The seminal contribution can be found in *Confederate Military History*, Clement A. Evans, editor, which was published in Atlanta in 1899. Oran Milo Roberts, former Texas Supreme Court chief justice and governor, relates the role of the Lone Star State in the Civil War in Volume XI. A more recent contribution is *Texas and Texans in the Civil War* (1995), written by retired history professor Ralph A. Wooster. Other scholarly works relating to the Civil War blockade tend to concentrate on Atlantic coast activities. These books include James R. Soley's *The Blockade and the Cruisers* (1903); Francis B. C. Bradlee's *Blockade Running during the Civil War and the Effect of Land and Water Transportation on the Confederacy* (1925); Frank L. Owsley's *King Cotton Diplomacy: Foreign Relations of the Confederate States of America* (1935); and, more recently, Virgil C. Jones's three-volume work, *The Civil War at Sea* (1990). Another interesting book written by a former officer of the Confederate Navy is J. Thomas Scharf's *History of the Confederate States Navy*. The author presents an overview of C.S.A. Navy activities and devotes Chapter XVII to coverage of east Texas waters, particularly Galveston and Sabine Pass.

Robert Warren Glover, in his May 1974 Ph.D. dissertation entitled "The West Gulf Blockade, 1861-1865: An Evaluation," offers a sound overview of various aspects of the blockade. In 1988, Stephen R. Wise devoted a portion of his book *Lifeline of the Confederacy: Blockade Running During the Civil War* to blockade running activities in Texas. Another contribution is Ivan Musicant's 1995 book *Divided Waters: The Naval History of the Civil War*, but it too gives limited attention to naval activity off the Texas coast. Otherwise, a broad examination directed specifically toward the blockade of Texas has not been published. This effort is intended to fill that void.

The thesis of this book is that nearly all land and sea actions in and around Texas were directed toward strengthening the Union blockade and diminishing the effectiveness of the Southern war machine. In contrast to the Civil War from the Mississippi River eastward, there was little effort by the Union to destroy the Confederate army because no sizable force remained in the Lone Star State. Moreover, the Federal government had little interest in permanently occupying portions of Texas beyond those necessary to support the blockade effort.

Many writers have evaluated the blockade's effectiveness without considering its goals. This book examines the effectiveness of the blockade in connection with evolving Union blockade goals. These objectives initially reflected the president's vision of closing specific ports. Later, they represented a much broader operational conceptualization developed by the Navy secretary that involved blockading the entire Southern coast. Overall, Union strategy and tactics in and near Texas are examined; special attention is paid to army and navy interdependence in meeting blockade goals. Defensive measures employed by Texans to blunt these threats are also examined.

We review, with fresh perspective, major related activities that have received attention in the past, such as the Battle of Galveston, the Sabine Pass expeditions, and the Rio Grande campaign. Other affairs that have received little notice are covered as well. These include the Bagdad blockade evasion route, relationships with the French in Mexico, the activities of a shadowy Confederate agent named "Superviele," blockade successes and failures, and the snarl of cotton and politics. Finally, much of the literature on the blockade and blockade running is surveyed and analyzed. Emphasis is placed upon clearly identifying and enunciating primary and secondary objectives of the blockade in order to properly evaluate blockade efficacy.

Some Notes on the Texas Coastline

The Texas coast extends for about 325 nautical miles. Most of it is guarded by a series of barrier islands that may be located several hundred yards or so from the coast in some areas, and up to five miles from the coast in other areas. They serve as protection for the coastline from major storms, and are made up of sand, interrupted by breaks in the land called passes. Due to wind, storms, and currents, such passages are constantly changing—new passes open while old passages close suddenly. Consequently, navigational and topographical details that were accurate during the Civil War may not be accurate today because of these shifting sand bars and swash channels. Innumerable rivers and creeks drain the coastal plain into the gulf. Water between the coast and the barrier islands is often calm and beautiful, but for shipping, it can be treacherous. Knowledge of local waters and their attendant channels is necessary for safe navigation; inland waterways and bays vary in depth and can become dangerously shallow. Winds affect the depths in bays as water may pile up during an onshore breeze and empty out due to the influence of an offshore breeze. Tides usually vary by a foot or so.

To the east, the Sabine Pass, Sabine Lake, and the Sabine River separate Texas from Louisiana. To the south, Texas lies on the Rio Grande and has a common border with Mexico. Beginning in the east, the Texas coast gradually curves southward until it reaches the Rio Grande. Going west along the coast for 55 miles from the Sabine Pass brings us to the town of Galveston. In 1860, Galveston was the chief maritime city of Texas and had 8,117 inhabitants. It is located on Galveston Island, a barrier island that is connected to the mainland by a peninsula. During the war, major access to the mainland was by a peninsular railroad. Water depth at the Galveston Bay main channel was 12 feet at low tide over a shifting sand bar, and there were four smaller side channels or swashes to the east

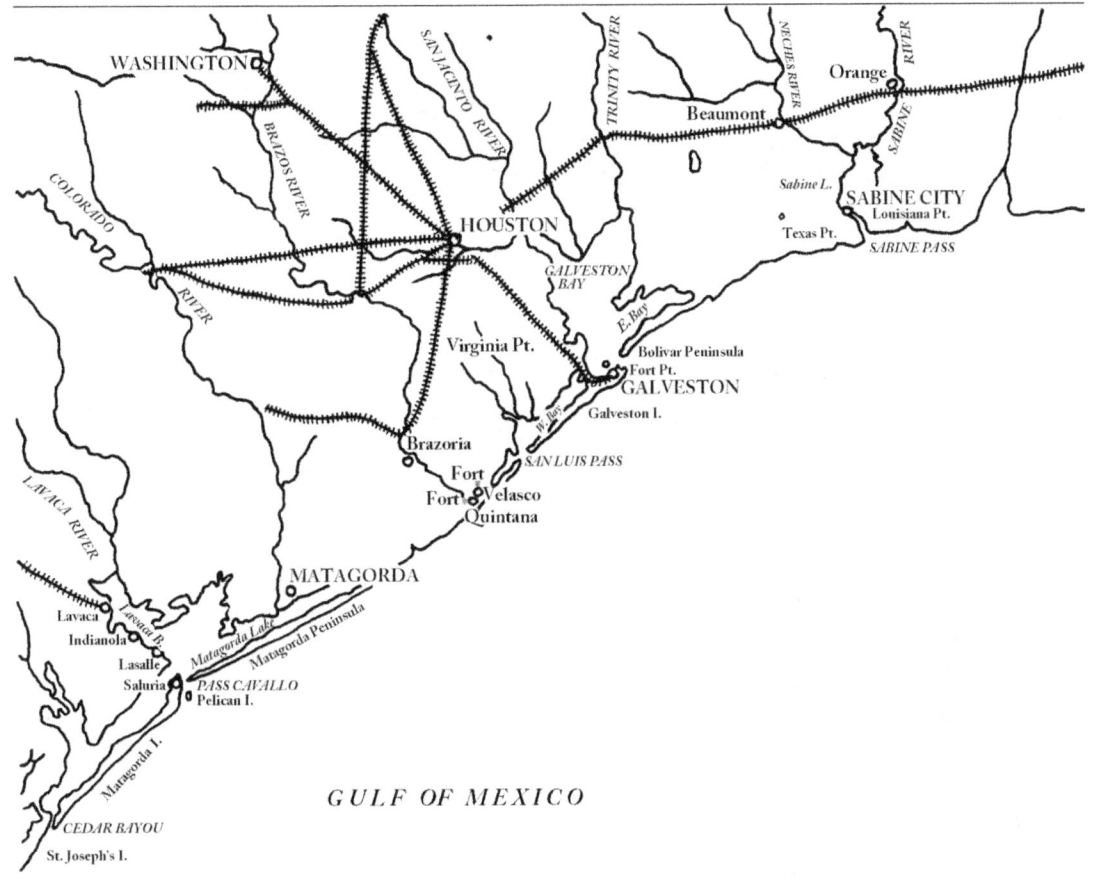

Opposite and above: Map of Texas Coast.

and west. Toward the interior is Trinity Bay, fed by the Trinity River; small steamers traded up and down Trinity and Galveston bays.

Proceeding down West Bay is the Brazos River, which was heavily used for transporting cotton and other staples from the interior in exchange for European military and civilian goods. During the war, it carried a water depth of eight feet at low tide. Velasco was the area's principal port; it was located on the east side of the Brazos River, four miles from the gulf. Nearby is another important drainage, Caney Creek, which was used for the same purposes. Matagorda Island fronting Matagorda Bay is the next prominent feature on the coastline. Due to the importance of Indianola and Port Lavaca as major trading centers, this area was a magnet for U.S. naval action. Entry to Matagorda Bay was gained through Pass Cavallo and during the war a major Confederate stronghold—Fort Esperanza—guarded this pass. The inlet at this point had a water depth of ten feet on the bar, which prevented vessels larger than gunboats from entering the bay.

The next barrier island down the coast is St. Joseph Island (also known as San Jose Island); it is about 21 miles long and five miles wide. St. Joseph Island is separated on the north from Matagorda Island by Cedar Bayou and on the south from Mustang Island by the Aransas Pass. The Aransas Pass was important

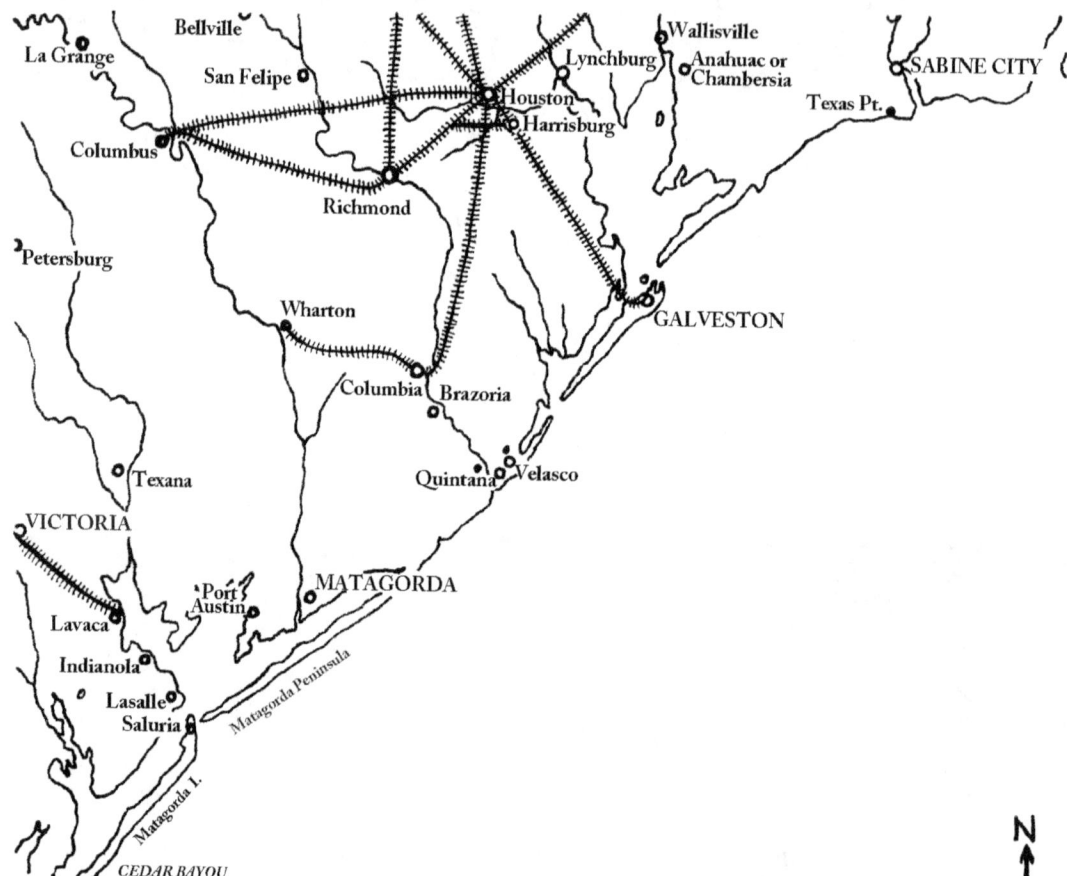

Detail of East Texas Coast from Sabine Pass to Cedar Bayou

during the war because it was a means of access to the gulf. With a water depth of nine feet, it provided an entry into Aransas Bay. Corpus Christi Bay is nearby; however, mud flats separated it from the Aransas Pass. Corpus Christi was a major commercial center during the Civil War but it did not have convenient access to the ocean. Therefore it was more significant as an intracoastal commerce fairway.

Below Corpus Christi is a lengthy lagoon named Laguna Madre that is protected by Padre Island. This island is a long, narrow sandbar that resembles a shoestring and is from one to five miles offshore. Padre Island terminates just north of Brazos Island and the passage between the two is named Brazos Santiago Pass. On the mainland side of this pass is Point Isabel with its important dockage (its name was changed to Port Isabel in the 1930s). During the Civil War, wharves were located on the lagoon side of Brazos Island at the port of Brazos Santiago. Sandbars at the Rio Grande mouth carried too little water to enable ocean vessels to proceed upriver and required that cargo be dropped off at Brazos Santiago port. These goods were then conveyed by lighters (barge-like vessels) to Point Isabel

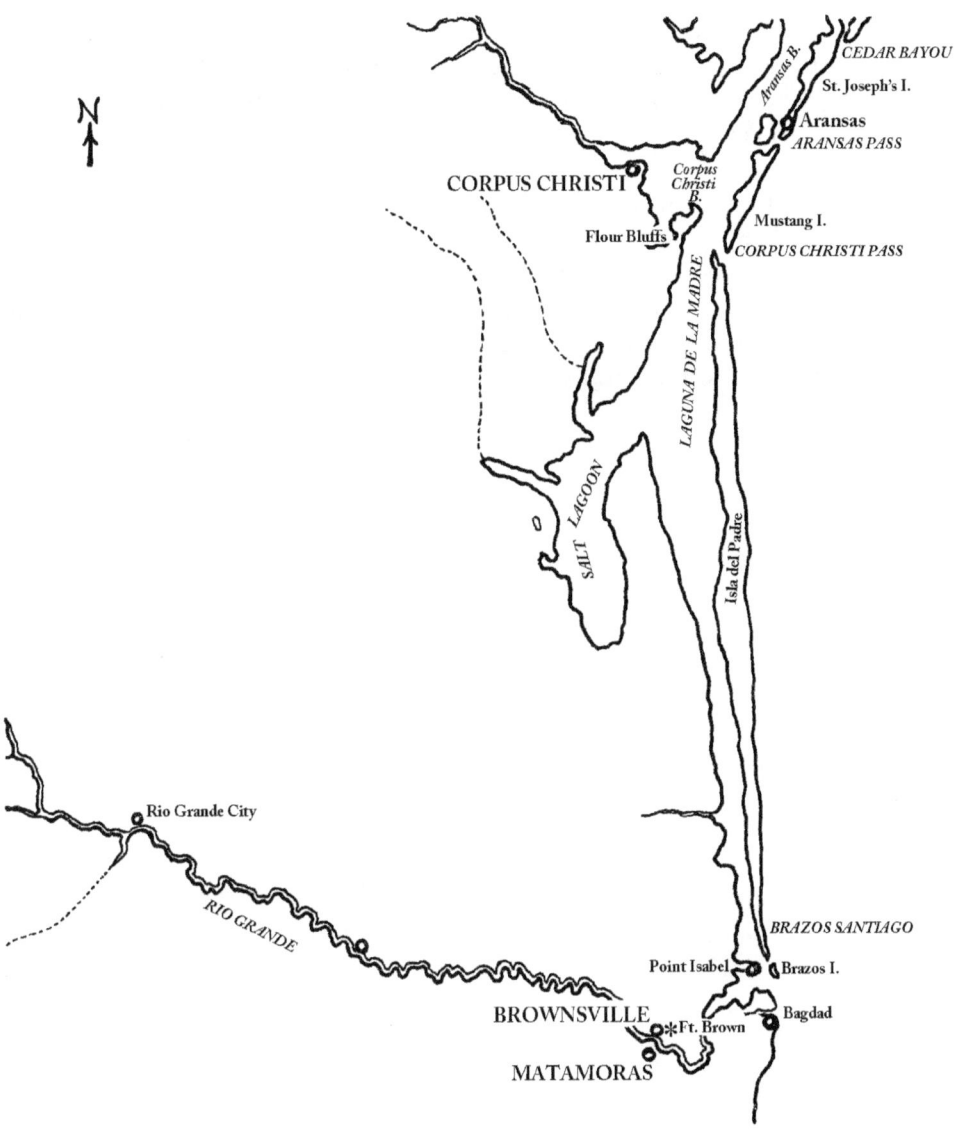

Detail of South Texas Coast from Cedar Bayou to the Rio Grande

and then usually transported by oxcart to their destinations. Early in the war, this area experienced blockade activity.

The Rio Grande empties into the Gulf of Mexico at the southern tip of Brazos Island; this location is named Boca Chica. Because of numerous sandbars at the entrance of the river, all but shallow draft vessels were prevented from entering either Texas or Mexico by way of the Rio Grande. Most traffic went through Brazos Santiago and Point Isabel. The Rio Grande itself was something of a wild, uncontrolled river, flooding often and sometimes shifting course. Upstream thirty miles or so are the twin cities of Brownsville, Texas, and Matamoros, Mexico.

Much of the Civil War–era Texas coastline has fallen victim to storms and progress. Storms have closed old passes, opened new ones, and have contributed to shifting sand bars. Many locales that were nearly deserted in the last half of the nineteenth century are now heavily populated. One good example is South Padre Island, which has become a recreational mecca. Dredging and man-made channels have transformed many waterways. The intracoastal waterway has been developed and shipping channels now provide Brownsville and a dozen other Texas cities with access to the gulf. Nevertheless, the Civil War scholar can still benefit by driving along the coast and traversing coastal waters. It is necessary to actually see the land and water on which many battles, skirmishes, and engagements were fought to fully understand and appreciate them.

Chapter 1

Blockade Genesis

In November 1860, twenty-year-old Sallie McNeill was living in Brazoria, Texas, south of Houston, on the plantation of her grandfather, Levi Jordan. She had graduated in 1858 from Baylor University and had recently returned to the 2,222-acre plantation to share responsibilities with her grandmother and mother as plantation mistress. Sallie began writing a diary. An entry dated November 12, 1860, is her first reference to the Civil War:

> Stirring news! Lincoln is elected doubtless, but there will be bloody struggles ere he reaches Washington.... Oh, I am just beginning to realize the possibility of a Civil War with all its horrors. God forbid that our glorious Union should be dissolved.... Our worst foes are in our midst. Negro insurrections will be constant and bloody under the guidance of abolitionists.... I have always pshawed and hooted at the idea of disunion, but I can no longer close my eyes to stubborn facts. It is terrible the thought of fighting against one's own, for we are one people.... Southerners will not allow interference with their peculiar institutions. We can hope.[1]

At about the same time, Abraham Lincoln was probably thinking some of these same thoughts. He had received no votes in Texas because he was not on the ballot; nevertheless, he was preparing to assume his national responsibilities. In the meantime, the slide toward secession began and in late December, South Carolina withdrew from the Union. Both Lincoln and General Winfield Scott in Washington were alarmed about the secession of the Palmetto State because of Federal fortifications in Charleston harbor. The president-elect was in contact with General Scott about those fortifications and he asked the general to be prepared to hold or retake Fort Sumter (should that be necessary) on or after his inauguration in March 1861.

Texas was in a similar state of turmoil. In the summer of 1860, a series of incidents that were referred to as "Texas Troubles" played a major role in fanning the flames of secession fever. The atmosphere was tense and organized secessionists around the state did not let up on the pressure. A secession convention met on January 28, 1861, passed a motion to secede from the Union, and on February 1 passed an ordinance of secession. The secession question was submitted to state citizens for a popular vote. In the meantime, the convention formed a Committee of Public Safety that was empowered to seize Federal property. Over 1,000 state troops representing the committee collected at the Federal armory on February 18 and demanded that the commanding general, David E. Twiggs, turn over his troops and property to the Texas troops. Following negotiations, General Twiggs surrendered his 2,600 troops that were scattered at 19 posts or forts throughout the state (they represented about fifteen percent of the regular army). In addition, he relinquished Federal property valued at $1,300,000 that included 15,000 stands of arms, 80 pieces of ordnance, mules, horses and other materiel of war. Texas citizens went to the polls on February 23 and voted for separation from the Union by better than a three-to-one margin. On March 2, 1861, the secession convention met to announce the results of the public referendum and three days later reorganized the state government and took the necessary steps to join the Confederate States of America.

Similar seizures of U.S.A. property were taking place in all seceding states in the months before Lincoln's inauguration, but lame duck President James Buchanan was content to maintain the military status quo so as not to start a war. On March 5, 1861, the day after his inauguration, President Lincoln found a report on his desk indicating that the commander at Fort Sumter had sufficient supplies on hand for a mere six weeks. Both sides began moving toward a collision course.

Fort Sumter was a man-made granite island situated at Charleston Harbor. Major Robert Anderson, commander of Fort Sumter, received four envoys sent by C.S.A. Brigadier General Pierre Gustav Beauregard in the early morning hours of April 12, 1861, demanding that he evacuate the fortification and surrender his command. He refused and the envoys announced that Beauregard would open fire on Fort Sumter "in one hour from this time." It was 3:20 a.m. and the Confederate general had his forty-seven howitzers and mortars trained on the Union fort. The C.S.A. secretary of war had instructed Beauregard to get Anderson to give a definite time for surrender or "reduce the fort." That is precisely what Beauregard had in mind. The honor of firing the first shot was afforded Roger Pryor, who declined, saying, "I could not fire the first gun of the war." An old-line secessionist, Edmund Ruffin, said he could and would fire the gun. "At 4:30 he pulled a lanyard; the first shot of the war drew a red parabola against the sky and burst with a glare, outlining the dark pentagon of Fort Sumter."[2] The war had begun.

Things moved rapidly. Newspapers fanned flames of war. The North believed it was fighting for flag and country and this theme was taken up by the *Indianapolis Daily Journal* when it proclaimed, "We must fight now, not because we want to subjugate the South ... but because we *must*, ... The Nation has been defied" (emphasis in the original). The *Chicago Journal* said that the South had "outraged the Constitution, set at defiance all law, and trampled under the foot that flag which has been the glorious and consecrated symbol of American Liberty."³ In the South, C.S.A. Vice President Alexander H. Stephens spoke for many Southerners when he said, "We fight for our homes, our fathers and mothers, our wives, brothers, sisters, sons, and daughters! ... We can call out a million of peoples if need be, and when they are cut down we can call another, and another, until the last man of the South finds a bloody grave." Confederate President Jefferson Davis, speaking on April 29, reinforced the defensive posture of the C.S.A. cause when he said that the South would meet the challenge launched by Lincoln (in calling up men) and added, "All we ask is to be left alone."⁴ President Davis had called for 100,000 volunteers on March 6, 1861; five weeks later, President Lincoln issued a similar call for 75,000 men. Virginia passed an ordinance of secession two days later and that same day Jefferson Davis invited Southern ships to take out letters of marque to prey on American commerce. Lincoln responded by declaring the ports of all seceded states to be under blockade. The Virginia militia moved to minimize the barrier by capturing the United States Navy Yard at Norfolk on April 20. Virginia organized for war and joined the Confederacy on April 25. The states of Arkansas, North Carolina and Tennessee seceded within the next five weeks. By July 1861, General Beauregard had 22,000 men near the vital railroad junction of Manassas and a small creek called Bull Run, outside Washington. President Lincoln and his generals were well aware of this assembly of rebels and the threat it posed to the Union capital. Meanwhile, their eyes were cast upon the Confederate capital of Richmond, Virginia, just 100 miles down the road.

For the North, the goal was to restore the Union. This meant it would have to invade the South, destroy the Confederacy's capacity to wage war, and crush the Southern people's will to resist. The Union knew it would need to move aggressively into the South and bring rebel states back into the Union at bayonet point. The North recognized that not only would it have to attack the South physically, but if it were a long war, it also would be required to deal with the South's dependence on foreign imports. This meant doing something to discourage these overseas goods coming into Confederate ports along a nearly 3,600-mile coastline. At the same time, however, Northern planners were aware of military opportunities offered by this long coast. It was honeycombed with various river highways such as the Tennessee, Cumberland, and Mississippi rivers that penetrated deeply into the Confederacy's interior. This fact made the South vulnerable to attack by combined Army-Navy forces.

On the other hand, the Confederacy, through sustained defensive action, could win by extending war long enough to cause the North to determine that combat, if continued, would be too costly in terms of money or lives lost. The South's basic strategy would be to assume a defensive posture to protect herself from anticipated attacks from her antagonist, while at the same time seizing offensive opportunities if there was good reason to believe that the United States Army could be destroyed. The seceding states expected at least to hold the North at bay until Great Britain or France (or both) came to the aid of the

Confederacy, or the Union lost the will to fight.[5] Both sides were interested in going on the offensive, when possible, as opposed to defensive action, since this strategy had worked well in the recently concluded war with Mexico. They took a long, hard look at each others' capitals with the view that a quick capture of those choice targets would bring a swift conclusion to a war that many expected would last no longer than 90 days.

The two sides were quite different in their capacity to wage war. The South had a strong agrarian economy and a cadre of young men with military training acquired through Southern academies such as the Virginia Military Institute in Lexington, Virginia, The Citadel at Charleston, South Carolina, and, not to be overlooked, the U.S. Military Academy at West Point as well. Southerners were proud, strong willed and determined. However, they had problems that would affect the war's outcome. The South had a shortage of capital and manufacturing capacity. Her wealth was connected primarily with land and slaves and she produced less than ten percent of the manufactured goods in the United States. She had but one major iron works (Tredegar Iron Works in Richmond) and her railroad system was of different gauges, which would hinder rapid transit of troops and supplies throughout the Deep South during the war. Her political system emphasized rights of individual states; lack of a strong central government would handicap her in her efforts to wage effective warfare. The South, however, had thousands upon thousands of brave, committed, and courageous young men. Northerners would come to respect that Southern character as manifested in the rebel yell.

The North had a substantial edge in the number of men who could be sacrificed for the cause. In the end, the North's capability and willingness to sacrifice more men than the South was an important factor in its winning this war. Additionally, the North had an edge in wealth accumulating through her growing industrialized society, a vastly superior manufacturing capability, and a strong centralized government. Her railway system was superior to that of the South and would contribute mightily to the war's conduct. She lagged behind the South in terms of military leadership—nearly a third of her officers resigned their United States commissions to go South, and they were some of the best—but she quickly gained ground. The North entered the conflict in a dangerously weakened position with a tiny army, much of which was widely scattered at frontier outposts west of the Mississippi River (and General Twiggs in Texas had already surrendered part of the regular army). Further, the Northern army had nothing resembling a strategic plan and did not even have accurate maps of the South. For example, a year into the war, General Henry W. Halleck wanted maps of Southern regions and had to buy them from a St. Louis bookstore.[6] The United States Navy was in no better position. She had only forty-two warships at the outset and most of them were in foreign waters. Only about a dozen were available nearby. However, she did have a large merchant marine and an expansive shipbuilding capacity.

So this is how it was to start. The Confederacy had an army near Washington in a defensive position to protect Richmond, and it was ready to go on the offense should that opportunity present itself. The Yankees nervously scrutinized this force and took steps to protect Washington, while deciding how it would wage war against the South and bring her back into the Union. The North needed a sound strategic plan as quickly as possible and this preparation would fall to the Army and Navy. Earlier, Secretary of State William H. Seward had been concerned about the North's strategy in the event war should break out. He sent a memorandum dated April 1, 1861, to President Lincoln with the subject "Some Thoughts for the President's Consideration." In this document Seward wrote, "For the West. I would simultaneously defend and reinforce all the Forts in the Gulf, and have the Navy recalled from foreign stations to be prepared for a blockade."[7]

Seventy-four-year-old Winfield Scott was general in chief of the Union army. He had been a hero of the War of 1812 and the war with Mexico, but now was old, sick, and overweight. It was said he suffered from "Dropsy, vertigo, and amebic dysentery picked up in Mexico years earlier."[8] What he had, however, was abundant experience and a brilliant mind that could consider alternatives and come up with sound planning. On the Union side, there was stable leadership in Secretary of the Navy Gideon Welles, an excellent administrator. He appointed as his Assistant Secretary Gustavus V. Fox, who was a superb planner.

In spite of being physically frail, General Winfield Scott conceived the long-range strategy that eventually would defeat the South and allow the North to prevail. It was named the "Anaconda Plan" after the boa constrictor that wraps its muscular body around its victim and squeezes until all life is gone. This was exactly what General Scott had in mind: he envisioned applying pressure to the Confederacy from all sides until she no longer had the resources with which to wage war.

When President Lincoln issued his blockade proclamation on April 19, 1861, it was in direct response to President Davis's proclamation on April 17 that invited applications for letters of marque and reprisal to be granted by the Confederate States of America against ships and property of the United States of America. On May 6, 1861, the Confederate congress passed legislation providing that United States vessels might be captured and "brought into some port of the Confederate States, or of a nation or State in amity with the Confederate States, and shall be proceeded against before a competent tribunal; and after condemnation and forfeiture thereof, shall belong to the owners, officers, and crew of the vessel capturing the same, and be distributed as before provided." On May 14, the Confederate congress passed legislation pertaining to distribution of prize money.[9] The letters of marque constituted legal authority given by the C.S.A. to a private individual or individuals to fit out an armed vessel (privateer) to capture enemy merchant shipping. This act forced Lincoln's hand since he needed to protect the North's merchant fleet from such pillage.

In Lincoln's blockade proclamation, states that were members of the Confederacy are identified. Virginia is not named, although she had passed a secession ordinance on April 17, because she did not join the Confederacy until April 25.

UNION GENERAL IN CHIEF WINFIELD SCOTT. During April and May 1861, General in Chief Scott conceived the basic strategy for the Federal blockade. (National Archives and Records Administration.)

North Carolina was the next to last state to join the Confederacy. An amendment to the proclamation was issued on April 25 extending the barrier to Virginia and North Carolina. The proclamation follows the definition in international law of what legally constitutes an "official" blockade. The administration had also considered issuing a domestic law covering "closing of ports" instead of a blockade administered under international law. A blockade was chosen because it gave the United States certain rights that otherwise would not be available. Specifically, these rights involved stopping and searching neutral shipping on the high seas and seizing vessels that were found to be carrying specified contraband (forbidden goods or merchandise).

The Lincoln administration consulted with foreign dignitaries, particularly British Ambassador Lord Lyons, who made it clear that England would not honor a port closure but that a blockade would be respected. The administration feared the port closure procedure would be too limiting, could lead to war with England, and probably would be ineffective.[10] Furthermore, Lincoln believed a blockade would encourage England and France to remain neutral and not enter the war on the side of the Confederacy. Secession was of great interest to these nations because rebellion potentially exposed the United States to being split up as spoils of war to European powers should the Confederacy—with these nations as its allies—prevail.[11] Thus, Lincoln opted for a blockade after determining this was a practical solution for him. He recognized that some would claim the impossibility of barricading one's own country, while others would say that the proclamation implied recognition of the Confederacy as a belligerent state.

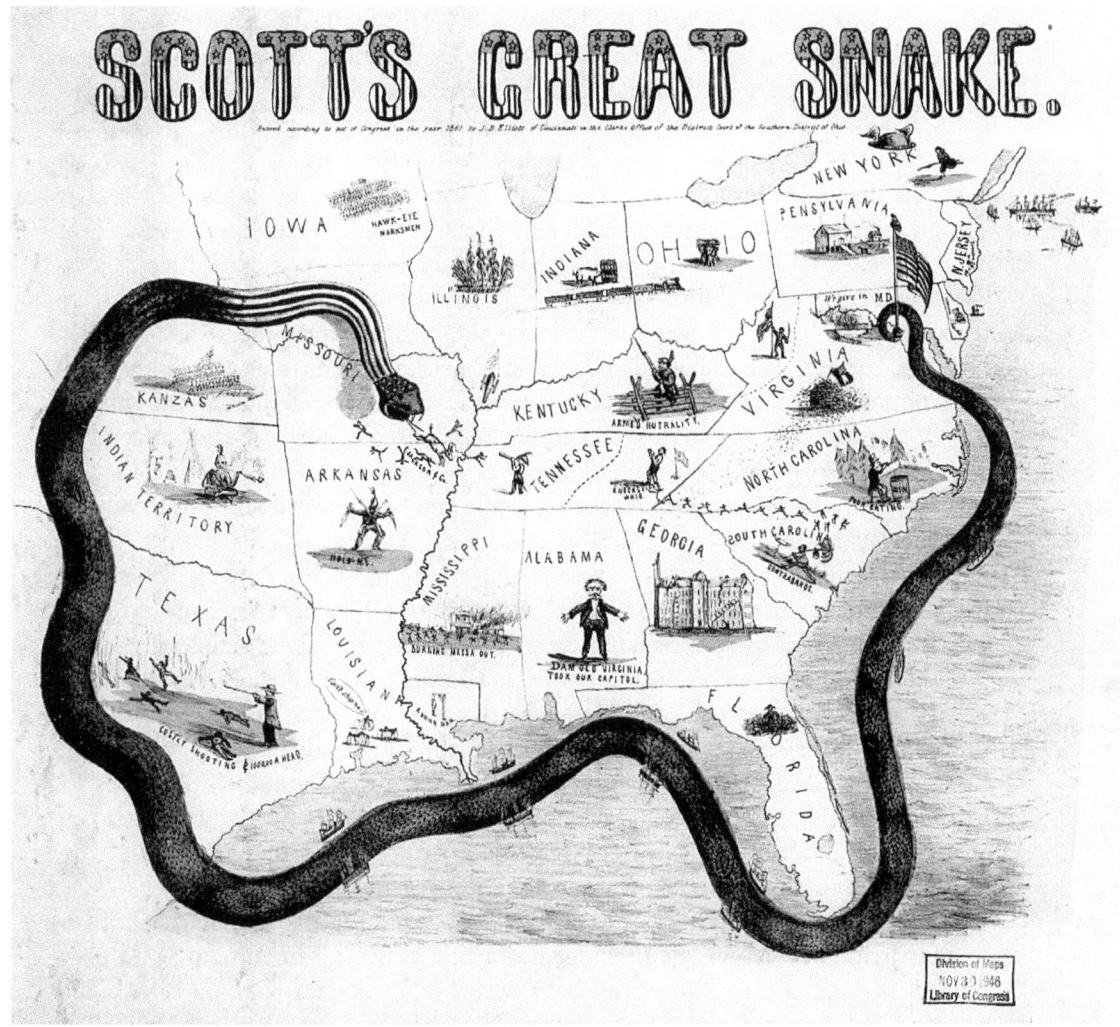

SCOTT'S GREAT SNAKE. A cartoon map published in 1861 illustrating General Winfield Scott's plan to economically crush the Confederacy. It is sometimes called the "Anaconda Plan." (Library of Congress, Geography and Map Division.)

The president was not too concerned about those risks or about strictly constructed legalities, although they presented some problems for him. In the ordinary sense, a blockade is considered to be an act of war. The crux of the problem was that a blockade could only be imposed between two nations at war with one another. Lincoln always maintained the Southern states were in a state of rebellion, were not a nation, and remained a part of the United States of America. Therefore, in a strict legal sense, a blockade could not apply to the C.S.A. The president, however, consistently maintained that the Southern movement was an insurrection and not a war. He would not acknowledge that a war existed, for in so doing he would have to admit that the Union was not perpetual and that secession was legal. Although the blockade for all practical purposes was a belligerent declaration, Lincoln maintained the legal fiction that the rebellion was not a war because a nation cannot declare war against herself.[12] He insisted, however, that the blockade was necessary to maintain the Constitution and laws of the land. In other words, to keep foreign shipping from aiding the Confederacy, and to really make the Anaconda "squeeze" effective, it was necessary to keep that shipping out of Southern ports by closing the ports and seizing foreign vessels on the high seas that were bound for an embargoed port. In his July 1861 message to Congress, Lincoln explained how he would prosecute the war "without excessive respect to constitutional niceties." He explained that certain measures, whether fully legal or not, were demanded as a public necessity in a time of such great crisis. Congress agreed and gave him the leeway he needed to pursue the war effort.[13]

In any case, the international community eventually honored the barrier, but in at least one instance, the Confederacy was recognized as a belligerent state. On May 13, 1861, England recognized the blockade and ordered British ships to respect it. That government steered a careful middle line by declaring England's "determination to maintain a strict and impartial neutrality in the contest ... between the Government of the United States and certain States styling themselves the Confederate States of America." This recognition of the C.S.A. belligerent status bothered some people and Secretary of State Seward was incensed. President Lincoln toned down Seward's intemperate responsive note to the British. In all this turmoil, almost everyone failed to notice that the British also issued an order on June 1 "forbidding British and imperial port authorities to admit prize ships."[14] This had the effect of enervating rebel privateering because ships and cargo taken as prizes could not be as easily delivered to a prize court. Consequently, the Confederacy had to destroy many of the prize ships it had captured.

Against this backdrop, General Scott began developing the Anaconda Plan so that it might become a full-fledged strategic planning document. The plan evolved through a series of three letters with Major General George B. McClellan, commanding the Ohio Volunteers. On April 27, 1861, General McClellan initiated the interchange by sending a letter to General Scott. His letter was composed of several plans, but they all proposed taking the pressure off Washington. He suggested controlling the junction of the Ohio and Mississippi rivers by occupying Cairo, Illinois, and then strengthening the line of the Ohio River. McClellan would then cross the Ohio near Gallipolis and move up the Great Kanawha Valley in western Virginia toward Richmond. A second plan he had in mind was to amass an army of 80,000 men near Cincinnati, march upon Nashville, and then move toward Montgomery, Alabama, and Charleston, South Carolina. Afterwards he would branch out toward Pensacola, Mobile, and New Orleans.

This letter, with Scott's comments, was submitted to the president on May 2. In his comments to Lincoln, General Scott said he did not know where 80,000 men were going to come from at this time; he did not want a march toward Richmond that might cause a revolt in western Virginia (he thought they might come into the Union on their own); he was concerned about minimal use of water transportation; he did not like the notion of subduing seceding states in a piecemeal fashion and; finally, he wanted to envelop "them all (nearly) at once by a cordon of posts on the Mississippi to its mouth from its junction with the Ohio, and by blockading ships of war on the seaboard."[15]

Scott wrote back to McClellan on May 3. He indicated that a complete blockade of the Atlantic and gulf ports was contemplated and he anticipated a strong move down the Mississippi to the ocean and occupation of New Orleans "so as to envelop the insurgent States." This would take place after training of troops was completed around mid–November. He said the greatest danger was that others would insist upon "instant and vigorous action" and not be content to wait for proper preparation. Scott preferred not to proceed with volunteers whose three-month tour of duty would soon expire. Instead, he chose to wait until those men who had been called up for a three-year term became available.[16] It is reasonable to assume that Lincoln had approved the general outline of this letter since the two of them were meeting daily.

Scott's last letter to McClellan was dated May 21 and began with a rebuke to him for apparently attempting to exceed his authority. He then specified how he would like to see training camps set up for the new three-year enlistees. Finally, General Scott detailed his plan for securing the Mississippi to the Gulf of Mexico and asked for McClellan's input regarding specific strong points along the way, and on the type and tonnage of craft that might be needed for a two pronged effort by water and land.[17] Apparently, the Anaconda Plan was now well developed; Scott had sketched the outline of the strategy that would be implemented over the next four years to defeat the South.

In his May 3 letter, General Scott anticipated that the Northern populace might be too impatient to tolerate the delayed gratification involved with the Anaconda Plan. He was right. Northerners watched General McClellan advance his troops up the Kanawha Valley in western Virginia in July 1861 and began to see a quick end to the "ninety-day war." On the heels of this advance came Horace Greeley's *New York Tribune* headline "Forward to Richmond! Forward to Richmond," urging that the Southern capital be taken before the C.S.A. Congress could convene on July 20. This fever for instant action grew more heated, but Lincoln supported the plan proposed by Scott. As a westerner, Lincoln always appreciated the importance of the Mississippi River as an artery in the heartland and correctly anticipated its importance to the C.S.A. The clamor of the people, however, was for immediate action and subjugation of the South without a lengthy preparation. The matter came to a head in June when Union Brigadier General Irvin McDowell, who was not concerned with broad strategy, formulated a plan for defeating General Beauregard's Southern forces at Manassas Junction, thirty miles away. It probably was a good plan, as plans go, with no grandiose ideas about going on to Richmond with his inexperienced men. General Scott did not like the idea; he saw it as a piecemeal approach during which the Federal armies might be destroyed. He preferred squeezing life out of the Confederacy through his boa constrictor–like technique. However, that approach was too long range for most people who were swept up in a frenzy to win the war immediately. McDowell's plan was approved when the president and his cabinet were persuaded to see strengths in that point of view. Time was of the essence because terms of service for the ninety-day regiments were about to expire. The battle commenced on July 21, and that evening a thoroughly defeated and panicked Yankee army raced toward the safety of Washington. Victorious rebel forces were unable to move on Washington because their soldiers were too inexperienced and exhausted.

Later that night General Scott and his staff, along with the president and his cabinet, assessed the damage. The folly of a piecemeal approach to war was apparent to all. Lincoln was despondent about the outcome of this first major battle of the war, but he remained determined to get on with it. The president's primary task was to make sure Washington was adequately fortified and secure. After assuring himself that the capital was protected, he wrote a note. The memorandum outlined his strategy for prosecuting the war and the first item said, "1. Let the plan for making the Blockade effective be pushed forward with all possible despatch."[18] Anaconda once more was in the forefront.

Abraham Lincoln had a self-deprecating wit that disarmed his opponents. While developing his legal position for the blockade message of April 19, he was painfully aware that such a barrier is an instrument of war between two or more parties engaged in warfare. He knew that through such action he was running the risk of implicit recognition of the Confederacy as a belligerent, rather than as a group of rebellious states. Thaddeus Stevens, the leader of Pennsylvania Republicans, ridiculed Lincoln because, he insisted, the Blockade Proclamation in legal terms meant, "we are blockading ourselves." When he confronted Lincoln on this "great blunder and absurdity," the president replied, "I don't know anything about the law of nations, and I thought it was all right."

"As a lawyer, Mr. Lincoln," Stevens remarked, "I should have supposed you would have seen the difficulty at once."

"Oh well," the president replied, "I'm a good enough lawyer in a Western law court, I suppose, but we don't practice the law of nations up there, and I supposed Seward knew all about it, and I left it to him. But it's done now and can't be helped so we must get along as well as we can."[19]

Lincoln's statement to Stevens is not as flippant as it may appear, because the president was indeed concerned with legalities. He took care to ensure that his actions were legal and within the scope of the Constitution when his message to a special session of Congress was read by a clerk on July 5, 1861. In this missive, he summarized actions he had taken at Sumter and steps he took in the weeks thereafter. The president defended his actions to sustain the Union, saying they were necessary because of the current situation, and he delineated how he would prosecute the war in the future. He stressed that extraordinary powers must be invested in the office of president in order to deal with the crisis at hand. He enumerated the specific activities he had conceptualized and requested that Congress sanction these actions. Lincoln identified a host of issues. Suspension of writ of habeas corpus was the most sensitive of the lot because it connected with the authority of both the legislative and judicial branches of government, and had been the subject of a recent Supreme Court decision. Both Congress and the country greeted the message with enthusiasm and acceptance. Congress moved immediately to pass bills retroactively, approving nearly all of Lincoln's actions and clarifying that they were legal and constitutional. The matter of habeas corpus drew only muted dissent. The "legal niceties" had been disposed of on the home front and now it was time to turn to the international scene.

Secretary of State Seward and the president had carefully worked together on the matter of a blockade, and they had considered and discarded the notion of port closures. The president consciously chose to impose a blockade in spite of the problem of implicit recognition of the Confederacy as a belligerent. Undoubtedly, Seward made Lincoln aware of the Treaty of Paris, which produced a declaration respecting maritime law that was signed on April 16, 1856. This was a guiding document signed by six nations (the United States was not a signatory) pertaining to respect for neutral commerce. The president and Secretary Seward wished to acknowledge these principles in order to insure foreign acceptance of, and respect for, the American blockade. These four articles were adopted: "1. Privateering is, and remains, abolished; 2. the neutral flag covers enemy's goods, with the exception of contraband of war; 3. neutral goods, with the exception of contraband of war, are not liable to capture under the enemy's flag; 4. blockades, in order to be binding, must be effective, that is to say, maintained by a force sufficient to prevent access to the coast of the enemy."[20]

The president and secretary of state issued the Blockade Proclamation on April 19, 1861. (See Appendix I.) The operative section of the proclamation is as follows:

> [Lincoln has] further deemed it advisable to set on foot a *blockade of the ports within the States aforesaid* [emphasis added].... For this purpose a competent force will be posted so as to prevent entrance and exit of vessels from the ports aforesaid. If, therefore, with a view to violate such blockade, a vessel shall approach, or shall attempt to leave either of the said ports, she will be duly warned by the Commander of one of the blockading vessels, who will endorse on her register the fact and date of such warning, and if the same vessel shall again attempt to enter or leave the blockaded port, she will be captured and sent to the nearest convenient port, for such proceedings against her and her cargo as prize, as may be deemed advisable.[21]

To impose a legally effective blockade, the United Stated needed to station ships near enough to a port to make entry appear to be dangerous; it was required that a competent force be stationed and present near specified port entrances. Any breach of the barrier might subject the intruding vessel to search and seizure and any contraband of war was subject to confiscation. Vessels or goods so confiscated were defined as a "prize." In order to convey the title of the prize to the captor, the case had to be brought to a prize court, located in the country of the captor, for adjudication. Following adjudication, the prize was conveyed to the captor to be used in any way he chose. As previously noted, Lincoln had convinced Congress to acknowledge the legality of the blockade and had now attended to the "nicety of law" with the international community. The legal stage had been set for imposition of the obstruction and, pointedly, Lincoln was enabling the Union to "get along as well as we can."

Strictly speaking, only part of the blockade had been instituted. The nations of the world and the Confederate States of America had been formally notified by a widely published proclamation of the existence of a blockade. This was somewhat irregular. Ordinarily, the public announcement of a blockade is accompanied by the presence of a force at or near designated ports to be embargoed. In this case, the essential part of the blockade was missing: forces were not present at or near ports to be embargoed. The blockade technically was not binding because there was no U.S. Navy present to prevent movement of foreign or C.S.A. shipping. Confederate sources pointed out this deficiency from the outset, but Great Britain did not wish to become entangled in foreign complications and practiced strict neutrality. Making the barrier more than a "paper blockade" required two things: an organizational plan and a navy to enforce the plan. The United States moved quickly to correct the situation.

With the legal stage set, it was time to implement a plan of action. When the war opened, U.S. Secretary of the Navy Gideon Welles (and later Assistant Secretary of the Navy Gustavus V. Fox) took steps to deploy a navy and develop a plan. In April and May 1861, the Navy and War departments began deluging the U.S. Coast Survey with requests for charts and maps of the rebel coastline that the blockading fleet would be patrolling. The superintendent of the Coast Survey, Alexander D. Bache, quickly realized the haphazard nature of the requests and appreciated the need for an organized and disciplined approach. He believed a committee could be helpful in this regard and in late May he began contacting trusted friends suggesting that a "blockade board" or "commission of conference" be formed to condense all the information available for use of the blockade. Not only did he envision the board becoming a clearinghouse for information, but also a body that would develop strategic military planning. Superintendent Bache selected the members of this board and gained Secretary Welles's approval. Between June 20 and June 26, Welles issued appropriate letters to the selected men and the "blockade board" first met on June 27, 1861, at Bache's office at the Smithsonian castle in Washington.[22] This ad hoc committee came to be known as the Blockade Strategy Board and it was composed of the following men: Captain Samuel F. DuPont, U.S. Navy, chairman, Professor Alexander D. Bache, Superintendent of the U.S. Coast Survey, Major John G. Barnard, U.S. Corps of Engineers, and Commander Charles H. Davis, U.S. Navy, recording secretary.

At the beginning of the blockade, it was recognized that coastal America had many different characteristics and the execution of the plan necessarily would vary according to area requirements. The Blockade Strategy Board therefore rendered its report in six discrete parts responding to specific geographical areas. These reports are dated July 5, July 16, July 26, August 9, September 3, and September 19, 1861.[23] They have in common descriptive features of particular coastlines with precise details of harbors and passes of principal ports that point out problems and promises associated with the barrier. The complexity of the data was almost overwhelming, and the challenge facing the board was development of clear guidelines for successful implementation of the naval plan. A high level of detail was required because the Southern coast spanned nearly 3,600 miles and included approximately 200 river mouths, bays, inlets, and harbors as well as hundreds of inner channels.

The ad hoc committee issued its first communication on July 5, 1861, and it dealt with establishing a depot for purposes of coaling, warehousing provisions and common stores, developing a harbor of refuge, and making it fleet headquarters for the Southern Atlantic coast. Fernandina, Florida, is discussed in detail as the most desirable location for such a station. Bache, DuPont and the others began their deliberations dealing with the important problem of establishing coaling stations at strategic locations to meet the fueling needs of the steamer fleet and minimize their time off station.

SECRETARY OF U.S. NAVY GIDEON WELLES. Secretary of the U.S. Navy Welles played a primary role in implementing and maintaining the blockade. (Library of Congress, Prints and Photographs Division, Civil War Photographs.)

The second report of the Blockade Strategy Board, dated July 16, recommends that, for organizational purposes, the Atlantic coast of the United States be divided into two sections. In this report, while there is emphasis on principal ports, there begins a shift in strategic thinking to extend the blockade to the entire coastline. The board recognized that this coastline was interlaced with bays, sounds, inlets and other large inland waters in which there was extensive local transportation of goods as well as foreign commerce with the West Indies. This report states, "It is an important object in the present war that this trade, home and foreign, should be interrupted, and for this purpose it is desirable to adopt some general method by which the approaches from the sea and the channels inside from sound to sound may be shut up."[24] This represented a significant shift in planning. Lincoln had originally erected a barrier to commerce at specific ports in the Confederate states. The board was now broadening this concept to erecting a barrier around the entire coastline and organizationally dividing the Atlantic Blockading Squadron into two sections, which would limit the span of control of local commanders for better operational management. Later, the Gulf Blockading Squadron was similarly divided.

The third conference report of July 26, 1861, pertains to the southernmost section of the Southern Atlantic blockade. It is rich in detail of that coastline and suggests that if the blockade is to be effective, attention must be paid the numerous interior channels and bays. The fourth document is dated August 9 and concentrates upon Florida and the important port of New Orleans, Louisiana, and its approaches. It concludes that both a blockade and army action may be necessary to take the city. The report concludes with a discussion of the port of Mobile, Alabama.

The fifth conference report of September 3, 1861, is of paramount concern because of its discussion of Texas; it will be covered in detail. This document is titled "Second report conference for the consideration of measures for effectually blockading the coast bordering on the Gulf of Mexico," and one section is titled "Coast of part of Louisiana and the whole coast of Texas, from Grande Pass, Vermilion Bay, to the Rio Grande del Norte."[25] (See Appendix II.) This section focuses on Galveston since it is the only deep-water port in Texas. It is located fifty-five miles from the Texas-Louisiana border at the Sabine River and 270 miles from the Rio Grande. The Galveston entrance has a depth of twelve feet at low water over a sand bar that usually shifts according to tides, currents, and storms. The report states that small steamers trade from Galveston northward to the Trinity River, as well as to myriad coastal rivers and bays. The following statement is of particular importance: "An efficient blockade of Galveston is, in fact, the blockade of the coast of Texas." This is so because the six other entrances in Texas have insufficient water depths for successful passage by ocean-going vessels. The report recommends that an efficient blockade can be maintained by perhaps four vessels. One of these ships should be of shallow draft in order to interrupt small commerce traversing interior sounds between Galveston and the Rio Grande. The committee further recommends that vessels be assigned to recover moveable United States property that had been seized or obtain indemnity for these seizures. Interestingly, the committee notes incompleteness of the coastal charts and recommends that a Coast Survey vessel be attached to the blockading squadrons so that detailed surveys might be completed.

It should be noted that planning for the Texas blockade concentrated almost entirely upon Galveston and it was considered prudent to assign only one vessel to interrupt interior shipping. Likewise, in other gulf blockade planning, a great deal more attention was paid to New Orleans and Mobile than was paid to interior commerce. Later experience would show the need to increase the effort to intercept shallow draft vessels evading the blockade by traversing interior sounds, passes and channels.

The sixth report of the Blockade Strategy Board is dated September 19, 1861, and constitutes an addendum to the fourth report regarding the approaches to New Orleans. Close attention was paid to this port because of its importance and in anticipation of its seizure early in the war. These reports were reviewed and approved by General Winfield Scott and President Lincoln and his cabinet on July 25 and 26, 1861.[26] The concept of a strategic shift from blockading ports to blockading the entire southern coastline was finalized in an order issued by Navy Secretary Gideon Welles on August 3, 1861. The order states, "The invasion and occupation of the seacoasts of the States in rebellion, as proposed by the Navy Department, [has] been accepted by the Government."[27]

Acting upon the report of the Blockade Strategy Board, the U.S. Navy first organized itself into the Atlantic Blockading Squadron based at Hampton Roads, Virginia, and the Gulf Blockading Squadron based at Key West, Florida. This flotilla was further subdivided into four blockading units on the following dates: North Atlantic and South Atlantic on October 29, 1861, and East Gulf and West Gulf on February 20, 1862.

President Lincoln's blockade proclamation focused narrowly upon specific ports within the Confederacy where the barrier was to be erected. The Blockade Strategy Board reports provided an overview not only of specific ports, but also of the entire Southern coastline. Secretary of the Navy Gideon Welles broadened the blockade's scope. Welles enunciated specific objectives in his annual report to Congress dated December 2, 1861. He set forth these goals: "1. The closing of all the insurgent ports along a coast of nearly three thousand miles, in the form and under the exacting regulations of an international blockade. ... 2. The organization of combined naval and military expeditions to operate in force against various points of the Southern coast, rendering efficient naval cooperations with the position and movements of such expeditions when landed. ... 3. The active pursuit of piratical cruisers which might escape the vigilance of the blockading force."[28] In his report, Secretary Welles had enunciated an enormous task for his navy; he clearly recognized the urgency of intercepting enemy shipping adjacent to coastlines and on the high seas. Furthermore, he accepted the challenge of using his forces in combined coastal operations with the army in a supporting role of landing troops. Obviously, blockading activity had been transformed into a considerably more expansive, ambitious, and difficult operation than originally had been formulated. This was the broad strategy that was implemented by Union naval and army forces.

Organizing a blockade and securing the ships to put it into operation are two different matters. In this era, steam had begun to supplant sail as the source

SECRETARY OF C.S.A. NAVY STEPHEN R. MALLORY. Confederate States of America Navy Secretary Stephen R. Mallory did an outstanding job of building a Southern navy from scratch. (Library of Congress, Prints and Photographs Division, Civil War Photographs.)

of power for propelling ships, and frequently vessels used both sources of power. As time went on, the sailing ship began to be replaced by the paddle-wheel steamer and then by screw-driven vessels. Concomitantly, there was a surge in development of armament for war ships. Guns became more powerful: calibers were increased, guns were adapted to fire shells projected from rifled barrels, and breech-loaders came into use. Finally, ideas of protecting the sides of vessels with armor—chains, tin, iron, and steel—became the vogue.

When Lincoln proclaimed a blockade in mid–April 1861, the United States was woefully unprepared to undertake such a gargantuan task. The Federal Navy "had only 90 vessels and 7000 men on its rolls. Of these, a mere 41 ships were in serviceable condition—and the majority of them were on foreign station." All that was immediately available for imposing a blockade were seven steamers (two at Pensacola, two at New York, one at Washington, D.C., and two on their way home from Veracruz, Mexico), five sailing ships (two at Pensacola, two returning from Veracruz, and a store-ship), and a tender at Washington Navy Yard.[29] The Federal Navy, reacting with alacrity to the president's proclamation, recalled most of its fleet from around the world and began chartering or purchasing nearly anything that would float, including merchant steamers and ferryboats. New York ferryboats especially were sought because they could "steam in either direction and had decks already strengthened to carry heavy loads." These vessels were armed in a fashion suitable to blockade enforcement. At the same time, the U.S. Navy began contracting with private shipbuilders to build vessels and it laid keels of new warships at its own eight yards.[30] The Federal fleet was quickly enlarged: by August 1861 the Navy had doubled to 180 vessels and by the end of 1861 it had grown to 264 vessels. By the end of the war, the Navy Department had purchased 313 steamers and 105 sailing craft and had commissioned a total of 670 warships, about 500 of which were on blockade duty. In time, blockade runners were captured and added to the blockading fleet since they were suitable for pursuing Southern shipping.[31] However, in 1861, the blockade was still inadequate for required action, but strong enough to begin meeting technical requirements of the Treaty of Paris.

The United States Navy expanded so rapidly that it encountered a number of problems associated with its new fleet. Some of the blockading ships were old and had not been properly cared for in the past. This led to breakdowns in equipment or engine problems, requiring frequent absences of these ships from their stations to return to a port for repairs. Other vessels had been constructed for use in protected waters; they had inadequate speed or other poor seagoing qualities that did not serve them well when forced to operate in stormy Atlantic waters. As use of coal burning steamships increased, so did the necessity for vessels to return to coaling stations; that would remove them temporarily from assigned positions in the blockade. Alternatively, ships could be re-supplied with coal at sea. Sometimes, however, the fuel situation became critical when a coaling station did not have an adequate supply of the fuel on hand. As early as 1862, blockading ships required three thousand tons of coal per week; this demand increased as more steamers were added to the fleet.[32] Lack of coal caused one commander of a blockading squadron to write this to his subordinate off New Inlet, North Carolina, in September 1863: "Economize fuel all you can for the present; until more vessels come, you may find it expedient not to keep more than one of the little vessels moving about at a time, even at night."[33] Commanders kept calling for additional ships to replace those that had to return to shore for fuel, water, stores, and repairs, but they were not always available.

Before war started, The Confederate States of America anticipated the need to develop a navy as part of its defensive strategy. Stephen R. Mallory was appointed Secretary of the C.S.A. Navy on February 21, 1861, and he served in that capacity until the end of the war.[34] Mallory turned out to be one of President Davis's finest appointments and he created a navy from scratch. He was well suited for the task. He served as a U.S. senator from Florida from 1851 to 1861 and during this period he was on the Committee on Naval Affairs (he was its chairman from 1855). From the beginning, Mallory defined the role of the Southern navy as being one of defending harbors and rivers, not attacking blockading ships. This definition of the role of the navy dovetailed with President Davis's defensive strategy. However, he did challenge the blockade by using cruisers (such as *Alabama* and *Florida*) to divert Union ships from the blockade, thus attempting to weaken the barrier.[35]

At the time of Mallory's appointment, a Confederate navy was virtually nonexistent since it consisted of only "six revenue cutters, a steam tender, a few coastwise steamers, and two Coast Survey steamers seized by the various states when they seceded."[36] By August 1861, however, Secretary Mallory had already contracted for several ironclads. The South's shipbuilding capacity was small in comparison to the North's extensive and well-established private shipbuilding industry. The C.S.A.'s best shipyard by far was New Orleans, where there were five yards, and five others were located elsewhere in Louisiana. Unfortunately, the South lost this important port in April 1862, but before this, at least 30 warships had been built or converted there.[37]

The industrial output of the North swamped that of the South and the rebels had limited capacity for production of engines, propeller shafts, armor, and armament. For example, in 1860 only the Tredegar Ironworks at Richmond, Virginia, could cast guns. Establishment of a foundry at Selma, Alabama, remedied this later. In spite of this disadvantage, Secretary Mallory moved swiftly. State forces had seized the Pensacola navy yard in Florida before the war. Although it was primarily a ship refitting facility, the Southerners did build some warships there (but failed to take control of Fort Pickens guarding Pensacola Bay, thereby limiting usefulness of the facility).[38]

The major coup for the Confederacy was occupancy of the abandoned Gosport navy yard at Norfolk, Virginia, on April 20-21, 1861. This was the nation's "premier naval base and the largest shipbuilding and repair facility in the South." It had a superb dry dock that could handle any ship in the U.S.A. Navy. In fact, "The whole navy yard held every facility for building and servicing a modern, steam-driven, wooden fleet." Gosport had been under the command of Commodore Charles McCauley, who panicked when told that Virginia militia was heading for the facility. On April 19, the commodore, fearful that Federal property would fall into enemy hands, ordered that the navy yard be burned and the cannon spiked, and that four ships, including the forty-gun steam frigate *Merrimack*, be scuttled. When Virginia militia occupied the vacant yard the next two days, it obtained "11 ships and 3,000 pieces of ordnance," including "300 modern Dahlgren smoothbore cannon" and 2,000 barrels of powder, 11,089 pounds of bread, 1,600 barrels of pork and beef, and other provisions. Furthermore, the Southern troops were able to extinguish many fires, most of the cannon were salvaged, and the hull of *Merrimack* was raised and subsequently converted into the ironclad CSS *Virginia*.[39] However, the South could never capitalize fully on this stroke of good fortune, because the Union reoccupied Gosport in May 1862 when the Confederacy chose to move back to protect Richmond in response to General McClellan's peninsular campaign.

The organization of the Confederate States of America Navy was quite different from that of the navy to the north. In a strong states' rights environment, the individual state navies provided the foundation for activities to follow. Seceding states had seized numerous small U.S.A. ships such as revenue cutters, lighthouse tenders, and coast survey ships before the war opened. The state navies also quickly began to build more suitable warships. When the Confederate Navy was authorized on February 20, 1861, and during the time when the C.S.A. Congress met in July and began passing implementing legislation, the states started to turn over all or parts of their navies to the central government. The Confederate Navy initially established command posts at Norfolk, Charleston, Savannah, Mobile, and New Orleans.

A unique characteristic of the Confederate Navy organization was that some ships served under the direct control of the C.S.A. Army while operating under the overall command of a naval officer. One such group was "the Mississippi River Defense Fleet, composed of 14 ships manned by the army and under the overall command of Capt. J. E. Montgomery, CSN ... A second army group, the Texas Marine Department, established in 1861, was charged with the defense of coastal waters and rivers, especially in the vicinity of Galveston."[40] In August 1861, Commander William W. Hunter, Confederate States Navy (CSN), was ordered by the secretary of war to command this department. In the end, these unique organizational arrangements did not work out so well. There were too many instances of petty jealousies and lack of trust and coordination between the individual components. There simply was too much division of authority to manage effectively. Not only was authority split between the Confederate and state governments; it also was split between the army and navy.

The Confederates quickly developed the nucleus of a navy by incorporating transferred state vessels into the organization. In March 1861, the provisional congress authorized construction or purchase of ten gunboats, propelled by steam, and displacing from 750 to 1,000 tons. By late the next year, the Navy Department had built or purchased 68 vessels while another 32 ships were under construction. Some of these were formidable vessels and were covered with railroad iron, but most were small craft ideal for work in harbors or rivers. As stated earlier, the Confederacy also resorted to privateering to make war on United States commerce. Under the authority of the C.S.A. government, about 20 privateers were fitted out, sought out U.S. shipping during the summer and fall of 1861, and took 60 or more prizes. However, this activity was curtailed when it became more difficult for the privateers to get their prizes into Confederate ports; European ports, to maintain their neutrality, refused use of their facilities. The Confederacy countered by ingeniously having large ships built in English shipyards (ostensibly for commerce) and then fitting them out on the high seas as warships. Through the skill and enterprise of Captain James D. Bulloch, four commerce-destroying ships were acquired for the C.S.A., and they played havoc with United States commerce. On occasion this required that Union ships be diverted from blockade duties to pursue the raiders. Through all of these state and Confederate efforts, something on the order of 500 large and small vessels ultimately took to the high seas and to bays, harbors, and the rivers of the South. These efforts to defend the coastline were often supplemented with strategically placed artillery fire from shoreline fortifications.[41]

The best ship in the world does not sail herself. A well-trained crew is an absolute requirement to make best use of the vessel, be it steam or sail. The Confederate States of America was fortunate that so many United States Navy officers chose to fight on the side of the rebels. According to Professor James R. Soley, 322 former U.S. Navy officers joined the Southern cause and 243 of these were line officers. Furthermore, by the end of the war, 94 graduates of the United States Naval Academy had served the Confederacy. Consequently, the C.S.A. began the war with a cadre of skilled and experienced naval officers who were able to provide leadership up and down the line. Initially, there were not sufficient ships available for them, and they were assigned to separate state organizations or various other duties, such as commanding a coastal gun battery. However, as the navy grew, they gradually were absorbed into the C.S.A. Navy.[42]

The C.S.A. had much more difficulty recruiting ordinary seamen because there was no seafaring tradition in the South as there was in the North, and the average Southerner had little interest in the sea. Many of the coastal ships were relatively small and did not require large crews, while the high sea raiders often were manned with foreign crews. These young recruits required training for their seafaring adventures. Since the South had no counterpart to the United States Naval Academy at Annapolis, Maryland, it created the "Confederate States Naval Academy." The "Academy" was established in 1863 and operated aboard the training ship *Patrick Henry* that was anchored at Drewry's Bluff, seven miles below Richmond, Virginia. This vessel was a seagoing steamer of brigantine rig and was armed with ten guns.

James M. Morgan received training aboard this vessel and he reports that his "school" also was "expected to sink itself in the channel between the obstructions in case the enemy's ironclads tried to force a passage by the land batteries." Morgan was one of about sixty young midshipmen on the *Patrick Henry* and he found the food "revolting." He says a meal generally was "a tiny lump of fat pork ... a piece of hardtack and a tin cup of hot water colored by chicory or grains of burned corn, groundup, and brevetted coffee." The school's superintendent was Lieutenant William H. Parker, who had been a professor at Annapolis; he turned out many well-trained young seamen.[43] By the end of the war, Confederate Navy personnel had consisted of a maximum of 5,213 officers and men, and 130 ships had been commissioned into that navy.[44]

The United States Navy had its problems providing crews for its ships as well. It had more men available, and many of them came from homes where a seafaring tradition existed. The Navy, however, had many more large vessels to operate that required bigger crews. The U.S. Navy was short of junior and senior officers because, as noted above, many of these men had joined the rebel cause. Some of those who joined the South were students at the U.S. Naval Academy at Annapolis. At the beginning of the war, there were approximately 250 midshipmen at the academy. One hundred six of these young men resigned between December 1860 and July 1861; of those remaining, the upper three classes were detached and ordered to active duty.[45] On August 1, 1861, there were 1,457 officers in the navy. Since this number was insufficient to meet the needs of an expanding fleet, 7,500 volunteer officers, chiefly from the merchant marine, were enrolled. The need for enlisted men likewise increased from pre-war strength of 7,600 to a total of 51,500 officers and men who manned about 690 vessels by war's end. However, in order to attract men to the navy, it was necessary to offer generous bounties.[46]

Since the armies took first priority, both the North and South struggled to recruit good men for their navies. Sometimes it would be necessary to divert soldiers to naval duty; often this did not work out well because the soldiers preferred land. In any event, the new recruit usually was sent to a training ship where he began to learn rudiments of navy life. This training lasted from several days to several weeks, depending upon needs of the moment. From that point, new recruits were assigned to active ships, where they continued their training "on-the-job."

United States sailors stationed on blockade duty often found themselves enduring long periods of monotony. The tedium was interspersed with infrequent periods of intense activity related to chasing as a blockade runner. The typical day for the sailor began with reveille at 5:00 a.m. followed by washing down the ship and eating breakfast at 8:00 a.m. Breakfast often consisted of coffee and salted beef. At 9:30 a.m., guns were inspected and cleaned, and this was followed by a period to relax and write letters. Noon was the fixed time for lunch, usually a piece of meat, vegetables, and coffee. After the noon meal, sailors would return to their stations, often would participate in drills and training, or would hone their skills associated with various onboard tasks. Blockade duty was so monotonous that the ingenuity of commanders was challenged to use this time creatively to keep sailors busy and boost their morale. At 4:00 p.m. a light evening meal was served; this was altered to conform to the watch sequence that usually was four hours on, four hours off. During the evening hours watches would be changed to meet the requirements of the situation, since nighttime was the period when blockade running was most likely to occur. At 5:30 p.m., the men were drummed to their quarters, and there was another inspection and cleaning of guns to prepare for the evening. Following was a period of relaxation for those who were not on watch,

and often there would be some form of entertainment or music. At around 8 or 9:00 p.m. (depending upon local sunset), the men would retire to their sleeping quarters.[47] This general routine was followed day in, day out, but frequently was altered due to weather conditions, orders to change stations, taking on coal and supplies, and, of course, pursuing (and hopefully capturing) blockade runners.

The abiding problem for men was sameness. Time passed slowly in spite of the daily activities of painting, scrubbing, drilling, caring for the guns, target practice, and other duties. Alcohol abuse became a problem because in both navies, sailors were permitted the traditional daily ration of grog—four ounces of whiskey mixed with water. In the Union navy, this daily grog was abolished by an act of Congress in September 1862. The practice continued in the rebel navy throughout the war. Union blockade personnel looked forward to shore liberty where there was pursuit of liquor, or women, or both. Sailors often would return to the ship drunk and with venereal disease. Frequently, fevers, scurvy, and diseases present in the region would debilitate them and render the ship less effective. Sailors also faced the hazard of shots fired from shore as they cruised on inland waterways or on large and small rivers with their confined, snake-like routes. All too often, steam boilers would explode or release steam when hit by gunfire, scalding the men. As far as blockade duty was concerned, "All the ship-to-ship fighting put together, totaled little more than one week of battle out of four years of war. For the Yankee and Rebel seamen it was indeed a war of watch and wait as they sat imprisoned on their ships."[48]

The one important potential reward, however, for the Yankee seaman assigned to blockade duty was financial in nature. In Lincoln's Blockade Proclamation, it was clear that if a vessel violated the blockade, she was to be captured and sent to a convenient port for prize court proceedings. In the United States, district courts were deemed to have jurisdiction and frequently the Southern District Court of New York was utilized as a prize court. Bales of cotton were eagerly sought after because they were valuable and transportable.

The weeks of tedium for the blockade runner could be broken by capture of a vessel carrying cotton, and the sixteen dollars per month salary paid the Yankee seaman could be well supplemented through such a capture. In fact, it was a dream of the Federal sailor to capture, unaided, a heavily laden blockade runner. That dream, in one instance, was fulfilled on July 31, 1862, when the USS *Magnolia*, under command of Lieutenant William Budd, spotted a steamer off

Opposite: CREW OF THE USS HUNCHBACK CIRCA 1864. This shows the typical uniforms and ages of Union navy crews. Young boys in the photograph were "powdermonkeys" who would bring bags of powder to gun crews. Many crewmen are wearing their "flathats" in the style of berets. Note the sailor reading the newspaper at the far left, to his left a person holding a small white dog, a sailor attired in civilian clothes smoking a pipe, men in the center peeling potatoes, and a black sailor playing a banjo. About a fifth of this ship's crew appear to be African Americans and the distinct grouping of black men to the right invites scrutiny. (Naval Historical Foundation.)

THE CONSCRIPT BILL!
HOW TO AVOID IT!!
U.S. NAVY.
1,000 MEN WANTED, FOR 12 MONTHS!

Seamen's Pay, — — — — — — $18.00 per month.
Ordinary Seamen's Pay, ... 14.00 " "
Landsmen's Pay, ... 12.00 " "
$1.50 extra per month to all, Grog Money.

$50,000,000 PRIZES!

Already captured, a large share of which is awarded to Ships Crews. The laws for the distributing of Prize money carefully protects the rights of all the captors.

PETTY OFFICERS,—PROMOTION.—Seamen have a chance for promotion to the offices of Master at Arms, Boatswain's Mates, Quarter Gunners, Captain of Tops, Forecastle, Holds, After-Guard, &c.
Landsmen may be advanced to Armorers, Armorers' Mates, Carpenter's Mates, Sailmakers' Mates, Painters, Coopers, &c.
PAY OF PETTY OFFICERS,—From $20.00 to $45.00 per month.
CHANCES FOR WARRANTS, BOUNTIES AND MEDALS OF HONOR.—All those who distinguish themselves in battle or by extraordinary heroism, may be promoted to forward Warrant Officers or Acting Masters' Mates,—and upon their promotion receive a guaranty of $100, with a medal of honor from their country.
All who wish may leave HALF PAY with their families, to commence from date of enlistment.
Minors must have a written consent, sworn to before a Justice of the Peace.

For further information apply to U. S. NAVAL RENDEZVOUS,

E. Y. BUTLER, U. S. N. Recruiting Officer,
No. 14 FRONT STREET, SALEM, MASS.

FROM WRIGHT & POTTER'S BOSTON PRINTING ESTABLISHMENT, No. 4 SPRING LANE, CORNER OF DEVONSHIRE STREET.

CIVIL WAR NAVY RECRUITING POSTER. The U.S. Congress passed the Enrollment Act of 1863 which proved to be most unpopular. This military draft was resented and the U.S. Navy capitalized upon this human reaction by giving the person enlisting into the Navy a legitimate way to avoid conscription. This poster is interesting because it stresses that $50 million had been distributed as prize money, inferring that such money could be awarded in the future to crews of ships. (Naval Historical Foundation.)

Charleston Harbor. *Magnolia* pursued the vessel for two hours before capturing it. The ship turned out to be the British steamer *Memphis*; it had departed Charleston the previous evening laden with 1,600 bales of cotton and 500 barrels of resin. *Memphis* was taken as a prize to New York. After adjudication, prize money was distributed: Lieutenant Budd "received $38,318.55 and each ordinary seaman received over $1,700."[49]

Another example will serve to illustrate how the prize system worked. On July 9–10, 1862, Union bark *Arthur* was stationed off the Aransas Pass just north of Corpus Christi. *Arthur*, in company with the yacht *Corypheus*, proceeded up Aransas Bay on that date and captured the schooner *Monte Cristo* that was loaded with 52 bales of cotton. Later, another schooner, *Reindeer*, was captured with a cargo of 45 bales of cotton. The bales were loaded on board *Arthur* on July 10 and that ship proceeded to the Aransas Pass, where it waited for fair weather to go outside the bar. This cotton had been seized as a prize and it was forwarded to New York along with appropriate papers and witnesses.[50] Records have not survived as to the amount of prize money awarded. Nevertheless, after the seizure was deemed to be legal by the prize court, the ship and cargo would be auctioned and this prize money, by Navy regulation, would be distributed as follows:

> 50% was kept by the government; 5% went to the commander of the regional blockading squadron; 1% was received by the local commodore; 44% was given to the crew of the capturing ship(s), divided into 20 equal shares disbursed to the: Captain 3 shares; Officers & Midshipmen 10 shares, divided amongst them; the Enlisted Men 7 shares, divided amongst them. Some men got rich on an afternoon's work ... As an example, the crew of the tugboat *Eolus* received $3000 apiece for the captures of *Hope* and *Lady Sterling* [in October 1864]; the captain received $13,164 for the *Hope* alone. High-ranking officers made a fortune in prize money without necessarily having ever confronted a blockade runner ... Admiral David Dixon Porter pocketed $91,528 for his two months on patrol. By war's end, the U.S. Government had distributed well over $10,000,000 in prize money.[51]

As might be imagined, with this kind of money available, capture of prizes and award of prize money sometimes became an end in and of itself. This can be illustrated by an incident that occurred during the 1864 Red River expedition in Louisiana led by Union General Nathaniel Banks. When Banks arrived in Alexandria on March 25, he was in shock. Admiral David Porter, who was commanding the accompanying supporting fleet on the Red River, was demonstrating his organizational ability. Instead of preparation for battle, the sailors and marines of Porter's fleet were hauling cotton from riverbanks and surrounding countryside, and loading their barges and boats. They were seizing cotton as a prize of war. Following adjudication of the claim, the cotton was auctioned and proceeds were distributed as follows: one-half of the value of the captured property went to naval personnel for distribution and five percent of this proportion went to Admiral Porter. The remaining one-half was paid into a fund for disabled seamen.[52]

The amount of money navy personnel might receive could be many times their monthly salary. This incentive naturally stimulated them to seize as much cotton as possible, perhaps resulting in neglect of regular shipboard duties. To the contrary, there was no such incentive for the army, because any cotton they seized was handed over to a treasury agent without any recompense to army personnel. As if this were not bad enough, navy personnel would brag about the amount of money they expected to receive, engendering bad feelings by the army toward the navy.[53]

Cotton and greed clearly was dominating military affairs. At an earlier date, Rear Admiral David G. Farragut, commanding the Western Gulf Blockading Squadron, had become concerned about how cotton captured in a different manner might enrich those who captured it. When steamers running the blockade were chased for hours and days, they would lighten their loads by throwing cotton bales overboard to gain speed so they might escape. These floating bales would be picked up from the sea by pursuing ships and treated as salvage. Declaring it salvage enabled Union navy personnel to sell it rather than going through prize court. Admiral Farragut was of the opinion that this so-called "waif" cotton could not be sold without intervention of the courts. To clarify the matter, on May 21, 1864, he issued General Orders No. 7, "Perceiving the prevalence of an erroneous opinion in this squadron that the captors of cotton ... commonly denominated 'Waif,' have a right to appropriate the same or the proceeds arising from the sale thereof without the intervention of the courts of law, I feel it my duty to put a stop to all such appropriations, and to direct that all cotton ... must be taken into port and delivered up to the United States courts for adjudication, as though it had been captured, in order that the judicial authorities may distribute it as prize or award salvage to the captors."[54]

Farragut sent a copy of General Orders No. 7 to Navy Secretary Gideon Welles. This indicates the importance he imparted to the matter. His concern may have been occasioned by the more blatant theft of seized prize cargo by the captain and crew of a vessel in the Western Gulf Blockading Squadron off the coast of Texas on August 27, 1863. The U.S. bark *W.G. Anderson* captured the schooner *America* about 50 miles north of the Rio Grande. *America* was stopped and she proved to be carrying a cargo of 55 bales of cotton from Caney Creek, Texas, to Matamoros, Mexico, having departed from Corpus Christi. The vessel was seized as a prize and taken in tow, during which time she capsized. Next day the commander of the Union bark, Lieutenant Frederic S. Hill, and his crew "saved a portion of the cargo [and] as my men worked up to their necks in water to save this portion of the cargo, I propose to allow them the benefit of it as 'drift cotton' which they saved." This drift cotton consisted of about 13 bags and it is inferred in the report to the secretary of the navy that the remaining cargo was lost. That was not the case; the crew dried some additional cotton on deck. After the prize ship had sunk, Lieutenant Hill failed to enter in the ship's log that they had confiscated 40 bales in addition to the 13 bags of cotton. The *W.G. Anderson* proceeded to South West Pass, Mississippi River, and on September 25, 1863, this cargo was placed on board the bark *Sol Wilder*, consigned to Blake Brothers &

Company of Boston, Massachusetts. This vessel landed at New York where the cotton was sold for the benefit of the commander and his crew. Acting Assistant Paymaster L. L. Scovel then forwarded checks to officers and crew for their share of proceeds.

Lieutenant Hill was charged with "Scandalous conduct tending to the destruction of good morals" and appeared before a naval general court-martial at Philadelphia on June 7, 1864. He was found guilty, but it was determined that Lieutenant Hill's action was "attributable to a misconception of his duty in the premises rather than to any desire or intention to evade the requirements of law or to act fraudulently in the transaction." He was fined $900 and received a reprimand.[55] The punishment that Lieutenant Hill received was relatively light and one must wonder if such behavior was sometimes overlooked. Similar thefts probably were underreported and the entire matter exposes the avarice of men. In any event, it appears there were many opportunities for sailors to supplement their wages.

Chapter 2

Blockade Growth

Upon notification to the world of a blockade of ports located within the Confederate States of America in April 1861, it was apparent to all that it was a "paper blockade" and could not be enforced because no ships were stationed in the vicinity of the blockaded ports. For there to be a legal blockade, there must be created a sense of danger for the vessel entering or leaving the port through the presence of ships capable of preventing the intrusion.

Foreign powers were skeptical that the United States of America could carry off this gargantuan task. However, British Foreign Secretary Lord John Russell conceded on May 21, 1861, that the blockade might be made effective since there were a limited number of Southern ports to be covered. By February 15, 1862, he judged the blockade of these ports was sufficient for it to be considered effective and meeting the standards of international law. Although the blockade commenced without any means of enforcement, it nevertheless came to be considered by Great Britain to be a de facto blockade. Under these circumstances, neutral shipping had every right to sail for the port and to be warned off. The United States was aware of the need to strengthen the barrier so those vessels violating the blockade might be captured. The Union moved quickly to dispatch the few ships it had available to the vicinity of some of the ports identified.[56]

As early as May 2, 1861, Navy Secretary Welles ordered the steamship *Niagra* to institute the blockade of Charleston. On May 12, *Niagra* took as a prize the ship *General Parkhill* of Charleston, which was bound from Liverpool, England, to her homeport. On May 13, it was reported that a blockading squadron consisting of the *Cumberland, Star, Quaker City, Yankee, Young America,* and *Harriet Lane*[57] had arrived off Fortress Monroe, Virginia, and that notification of blockade had been issued on April 30. On May 14, the *Minnesota,* blockading the waters off Hampton Roads, took as prizes four vessels that had departed Richmond, Virginia. They were the *Mary Willis, Delaware Farmer, Emily Ann,* and *Argo.* On May

28, *Minnesota* arrived off Charleston Harbor. The blockade was moving westward as well. U.S.S. *Montgomery* reported that she had arrived at the mouth of the Rio Grande on April 29 and was inspecting papers. The frigate *Sabine* reported that she had sent a notification of blockade to General Braxton Bragg at Pensacola, Florida, on May 13. On May 29, sloop *Brooklyn*, while stationed off Pass a l'outre, Mississippi, captured as a prize the barkentine *H. E. Spearing* bound for New Orleans with a cargo of coffee from Rio de Janeiro.[58]

All of these citations give ample evidence of the significant progress the Union was making in erecting a legal blockade. Of course, at this juncture, there were not sufficient vessels available to run a "leak-proof" blockade at all Southern ports. Furthermore, there were significant gaps from time to time where blockades had been established because steamships had to leave their stations temporarily for a variety of reasons; they were not always promptly replaced. The lack of vessels to assign to blockade duty meant that some ports were not yet covered and others were too thinly blockaded.

Nevertheless, the Union continued to extend its blockade into the Gulf of Mexico as well as on the East Coast. In Galveston, the tallest structure in the community was the Hendley Building located at 20th and Strand streets. Atop this building was a wooden cupola in which men had voluntarily stationed themselves so they might observe activity in Galveston Bay and the Gulf of Mexico. They maintained a log, and an entry dated July 2, 1861, noted that at 1:10 P.M. the Union steamer *South Carolina* initiated a blockade. The blockading vessel was under the command of Captain James Alden, a career naval officer with thirty years of service.[59] *South Carolina* was a new vessel, having been built in Boston in 1860, and commissioned on May 22, 1861. She was propelled by a single screw, powered by two engines, and was capable of making 10.5 knots. The vessel was armed with four 8-inch guns and one 32-pounder, and she immediately made her presence known. On July 4, she captured six schooners off Galveston: *Dart*, *Shark*, *Louisa*, *McCanfield*, *Venus*, and *Ann Ryan*. The next day Commander Alden captured the schooners *Falcon* and *Caroline*, and on July 6, the schooner *George G. Baker* became a prize. A steamer, *Sam Houston*, was taken on July 7; the schooner *Tom Hicks* was captured and destroyed on July 8; and schooner *General T. J. Chambers* was taken as a prize on July 12. Alden became concerned with Confederate river traffic between the Sabine River in Texas and Berwick Bay in Louisiana. On July 26 he ordered an expedition to intercept a Southern steamer that was due to sail the next day. Ingeniously, he armed three captured vessels—*Dart*, *Shark*, and *Sam Houston*—and operated them with *South Carolina* crew. However, on July 31, this group failed in its attempt to capture several Southern steamers lying in the Sabine River. Nevertheless, the Union steamer had initiated the Galveston blockade and had extended the barrier to Sabine Pass with the use of the three captured ships.[60]

Rodney Baxter, the acting master of *Dart*, was returning to the *South Carolina* on the morning of August 3 when he passed near the rebel South Battery and was fired upon. *Dart* returned the fire; these were the first shots of the war between a Union vessel and the Galveston batteries. Three miles away, *South Carolina* observed the incident, thinking it may have been an accident on the part of the defenders. Since there was no explanation forthcoming from the rebels, he determined it to be a deliberate hostile act that required retaliation. Shortly after 4:00 P.M., Commander Alden moved his vessel to within one mile of the battery to test the effectiveness of their guns; an artillery duel between the battery and the *South Carolina* ensued over the span of one-half hour. After this short demonstration, the blockading ship returned to her station. One Union round, however, had detonated near civilians observing the duel and killed a Portuguese man named Fisher. He was the first casualty of the war in Galveston and his death sparked an international incident.

Eight foreign consular officers signed a letter written to Captain Alden by the British consul, Arthur Lynn, protesting the bombardment of the city without giving noncombatant civilians the opportunity to flee. Lynn stated that Alden's action caused the death of the Portuguese man and was an act "of inhumanity unrecognized in modern warfare, and meriting the condemnation of Christian and civilized nations." Alden replied to Lynn with an explanation of his actions. He expressed his regret for the unintended death, and he remarked in closing that this was the "first time that I have ever heard that the women and children or unarmed citizens of one of our towns were under the protection of foreign consuls." He reported the entire matter to his superiors. Nothing further came of it insofar as international relations were concerned. William Mervine, commanding the Gulf Blockading Squadron, wrote to Commander Alden on August 21, 1861, "I approve of the course you took.... [T]he English consul ... rejoiced at an opportunity to obtain a little notoriety at your expense." The Navy Department wrote Alden on September 12, stating, "Your course ... meets with the approval of the Department."[61]

One of the last captures at Galveston made by *South Carolina*—and one of the more interesting—was that of the *Soledad Cos* on September 11, 1861. This schooner was flying the Mexican flag; the blockading vessel was suspicious because her name was freshly painted on the stern and purported to be from Tampico, but the name "Anna Taylor" was on the bow. When Captain Alden boarded *Soledad Cos*, he recognized the captain from a previous stop he had made of the vessel. The schooner had run the blockade to Tampico, then Veracruz, where it loaded its cargo and cleared for Matamoros. Upon inspection, he found of 20 tons of coffee in the hold; it was seized as prize, as the ship was not fit for sea.[62]

All of this activity reveals that Galveston had something more substantial than a "paper blockade," and Ronald (or "Rodney" as he was known in the Navy) Baxter wrote home about it. In his letter dated July 31, 1861, he said, "We have captured twelve vessels in all, and I think that number equal to more than one half of all prizes taken in the Gulf of Mexico. The *Shark* is a fine new schooner of about ninety tons, coppered, and was built in Portsmouth, N.H., last November at the cost of about $8000."[63] Obviously, the blockade was becoming stronger in the Gulf region as well as along the Atlantic coast.

Blockade running at Savannah by the *Bermuda* in the fall of 1861 (which is covered in the next chapter) did justify the charge of their being a "paper blockade" at that port. Sometimes, however, these stories of nonexistent blockades were unjustified and inaccurate, and they probably resulted from hyperbole or political motives. Shortly after the blockade was announced, the *New York Herald* called Gideon Welles a "moron," the *New York Tribune* said the blockade was a "laughing stock," and the *Philadelphia Enquirer* stated there was "no blockade at all."[64]

One recent scholar concludes, "Most Northern papers can be trusted on this subject because they had special correspondents at blockade running bases." That scholar goes on to justify his position by stating that "in December of 1861, the British warship *Desperate* came to test the blockade at Galveston by making its presence known with smoke. When nothing happened, its commander wrote, 'Having seen no United States man-of-war here, I concluded that the port was not effectively blockaded and it will be my duty to report the same to my superior officer.'"[65] That officer did report to his superior, but the story does not end there.

There was a blockading ship, U.S. frigate *Santee* under command of Captain Henry Eagle, on station at Galveston on the date in question. This vessel had been built by the Navy at Portsmouth, New Hampshire, in 1855 and was commissioned on June 9, 1861. She displaced 1,726 tons.[66] *Santee* had come on station off Galveston bar on September 17, 1861, relieving the USS *South Carolina*. Captain Eagle reported his "ship guards the entrance of the channel in Galveston Harbor, and the blockade of the port of Galveston has been effectual since our anchorage here on the 17th of September last." Further, Captain Eagle reported that on the date in question, "smoke was seen as if from a steamer's smokestack to the southward and westward." He added, " When he [the British commander] comes to the conclusion that the port of Galveston is not effectually blockaded.... [I]t becomes my duty to expose his ignorance in not knowing where the ship channel is."[67] Apparently, the blockading captain chose not to leave his station in the ship channel to check out the smoke on the horizon, presumably as directed in his orders.

Further serious action had taken place in Galveston Bay on the evening of November 7–8, 1861 (the month before the British had reported the bay was not under blockade). Men in two launches that had been dispatched by the *Santee* captured the schooner *Royal Yacht*. This vessel had been chartered for $1,350 per month by the Confederate States Army, Texas Marine Department on October 10, 1861, for naval patrol duty off Galveston. She was reputed to be the fastest schooner on the Texas coast. The Confederate ship was reported to be appearing nightly off the entrance of the harbor. Captain Eagle believed she was waiting a favorable opportunity to escape; he decided to act first and capture her. That was accomplished by his crew around 2:00 A.M. on November 8 when they boarded *Royal Yacht* and after a brief battle took a few small arms, thirteen prisoners, and her colors. The crew of *Santee* suffered one man killed and eight wounded. They then came under fire and burned *Royal Yacht* after spiking a light 32-pound gun. Later, crew from the CSS *Bayou City* extinguished the fire. The *Royal Yacht* action was of sufficient import to the C.S.A. that it was investigated at the direction of Commander William W. Hunter, who then submitted a report of the incident to Secretary of the C.S.A. Navy Stephen Mallory. Commander Hunter reported he read published statements of the capture that had been taken from Northern newspapers. In fact, the incident was reported in the *Houston Telegraph*, which screamed, "Somebody was asleep!" Citizens there were concerned that if a Confederate vessel just off Galveston's shore could be captured, Union troops, if they wished, could also seize the city.[68]

U.S. Frigate *Santee* also was engaged in blockade action on October 27, 1861, when she seized the brig *Delta* that was sailing under English colors. The *Delta* (formerly *William M. Rice*) was said to have sailed from Liverpool, England, on September 4, 1861, bound for Matamoros, Mexico, with a cargo of salt. She entered Galveston harbor, where *Santee* captured her and sent her papers to the clerk of the District Court, Southern District of New York.[69] Apparently, British Consul Arthur T. Lynn of Galveston was well aware of the incident, because he sent an inquiry as to the circumstances of her seizure.[70] Captain Eagle reported, "I consider the blockade of this port to be effectual, as we are so near the bar as to prevent any ingress or egress without our knowledge."[71]

All of these incidents would suggest that *Santee* and *South Carolina* indeed had posted an effective obstruction weeks before the British warship *Desperate* appeared off Galveston. The *South Carolina* was on station on July 2, 1861, and the *Santee* was on station on September 17, 1861. Further, it is inconceivable that the papers seized from the British ship *Delta*, and sent to New York City, were kept secret from England. The British consul in Galveston was aware of the seizure of *Delta*, since he sent an inquiry about her capture. In addition, the capture of the *Royal Yacht* had been reported in the Northern press and a C.S.A. Navy commander, who sent a report to the secretary of the navy, conducted an investigation of the incident. Consequently, it appears ludicrous for England to send the *Desperate* to Galveston to check the status of the blockade. Perhaps Great Britain had other motives for sending the *Desperate* on this journey? It is also conceivable, but not likely, that the *Desperate* had been at sea for an extended period and was not able to receive any communications from British authorities or newspaper reports.

This is but one example of a false claim of an ineffective barrier, but undoubtedly there were others. After reviewing these incidents, it appears that the U.S. blockade of Galveston in 1861 was more effective than claimed by some scholars and newspapers. However, there is little doubt there were substantial deficiencies in the barrier at that time. Until New Orleans fell in April 1862, there probably was a maximum of only five Federal ships thinly spread to cover the entire coast. Even with this sparse coverage, there was naval activity designed to test the strength and range of shore batteries (for example, at Velasco and Pass Cavallo), skirmishes between small boat crews and shore patrols along the entire coast (especially around Matagorda and Aransas Pass), and bombardment of port facilities at Lavaca. After New Orleans capitulated, there were more ships available for blockade duty. By 1865 twenty vessels patrolled the coast.[72] The number of ships stationed there highlights the importance of the Galveston blockade. The *Galveston Weekly News* reported that on September 14, 1864, there were 11 vessels on duty and on the next day there were nine ships maintaining the blockade.[73]

An account of blockade duty was given in an article originally appearing in the *New York Times* and reprinted in the *Galveston Weekly News* on January 11, 1865. Apparently, it was written by a seaman or officer stationed aboard the USS *Bienville* that was stationed off this important port city on November 6, 1864. The *Bienville* was an armed side-wheel steamer that was built in 1860 by Lawrence and Foulkes of Brooklyn, New York, and commissioned by the navy on October 23, 1861. She served with the West Gulf Blockading Squadron from 1863 to 1865. The author speaks of "the dreary monotony of blockading duty" and adds that "The same uninteresting view greets the vision morning, noon and night [and it consists of a] 'wide waste of waters,' relieved only by a narrow strip of low, sandy shore, sprinkled with a few white, deserted looking houses." As far as activity is concerned, "Our sole occupation is drilling with the big guns and small arms, and getting up anchor twice a day, morning and evening, to take our 'station'— each vessel having a day station and a night station.... Very few prizes have been captured by this fleet [but] quite a brisk trade is carried on." This is "managed with much tact and skill, as our vessels form a cordon round the channel through which they have to pass." The report concludes with the statement that the blockade running could be stopped "by the occupation of the city or forts."[74]

By February 1865, the war was nearly over and those sailors on blockade duty around the coasts of Southern states believed the barrier they had erected had become impregnable. They also found that blockade duty still consisted of weeks and months of boredom punctuated by short periods of intense activity and excitement when a Confederate ship tried to slip through the barrier. William F. Hutchinson was the surgeon aboard the sloop-of-war *Lackawanna* stationed at Galveston. She was the 237-foot flagship of the second division of the West Gulf Blockading Squadron; with two engines and a single screw, she could develop 1,300 horsepower and cruise at 11 knots. Although he attended to the medical needs of the crew of 205 men, their needs were minimal and the doctor had time on his hands. Dr. Hutchinson describes the scene as he "gazes listlessly across three miles of brown water ... at the long white sand-beach in front of the town, along which are continually strolling parties to watch the Yankee men-of-war." On the morning of February 20, 1865, he was lying quietly in his berth reading a book when there was a commotion above him. He dashed to the deck and saw a small side-wheel steamer fly past the *Lackawanna* for the open sea. The Union blockade ship immediately pursued her and Dr. Hutchinson could see that the ship had "piles of cotton bales on deck ... and torrents of black smoke pouring from her funnels" in her desperate effort to escape. The *Lackawanna* pursued the vessel all day long, but at nightfall the little ship had pulled farther ahead. The pursuer continued the course toward Havana and at dawn they found her still in sight, throwing bales of cotton overboard to lighten her load. About noon, the sloop-of-war began gaining on the steamer and hours later the Lackawanna pulled close enough that she could fire a shell in the direction of the small ship. The projectile exploded just a little short and rained iron fragments upon the vessel, whereupon she quickly surrendered. The surgeon states, "The ship was 'Isabel,' from Galveston for Havana, with 600 bales of cotton and no passengers." The vessel was taken as a prize and later condemned at Key West. Dr. Hutchinson reports, "My share was $750, which made a nice day's work and a promise of many a nice day's play."[75]

The U.S. Navy had other assigned duties that made it necessary, in many instances, to divert ships from the blockade and thereby diminish its effectiveness. One task was coordinating with the army in various campaigns where the navy participated in an active combat role bombarding emplacements and troops, or defending against enemy ships. Examples of this activity in the west included Fort Donelson in February 1862, Shiloh and New Orleans in April 1862, and the Vicksburg campaign in 1863. Further joint action with the army involved collaboration in carrying supplies and soldiers, and evacuating the wounded.

A second task was chasing and destroying rebel privateers and commerce raiders on the high seas. Often, the ships engaged in this activity came directly from the blockading unit that was guarding the port from which the rebel vessel had departed. For example, in the summer of 1861, Navy vessels were dispatched to deal with a Confederate commerce raider, the Sumter (previously the Habana). The C.S.A. Navy had readied this steamship at New Orleans and she slipped out to sea past the blockading ship Brooklyn on June 30, 1861. Sumter had a remarkable career. For the next seven months she operated against Northern merchantmen and captured 18 vessels. She was under the command of Lieutenant Raphael Semmes, later of Alabama fame. The Sumter at first operated off Cienfuegoes, Cuba. While in that area in mid–July 1861, the U.S. steam frigate Niagra, the gunboat Crusader, the sloop of war Vincennes, and five revenue cutters were dispatched to deal with the Sumter and other raiders in that area. In this instance, the flagship Niagra had been caused to leave her station at New Orleans. Consequently, that blockade was less effective.[76]

Another factor that made the blockade less effective was the state of repair of the ships. Because of sustained and often hard use, ships had to return to yards for repairs. Problems with boilers often were time-consuming and the breakdown of other equipment was common. Officers sometimes complained of shoddy work on relatively new vessels. Commander Sam L. Swartwout of Portsmouth complained, "I have but two carpenters on board, and they are constantly at work repairing defects about the ship which should have been attended to before she left the Portsmouth yard." Rear Admiral Farragut wrote to Navy Secretary Welles, "The Department would be astonished to see the condition in which vessels are sent out to me on this station." He then proceeded to enumerate various deficiencies that should have been taken care of in naval yards. The upshot of all this was that some vessels were not in "fighting trim" while others had to leave their stations for repairs and could not always be replaced immediately.[77]

While the Federal barrier in the gulf was a sieve early in the war, it became less penetrable in time and certainly was an inhibiting force in reducing the supply of equipment, arms, and food needed by the C.S.A. armies. The prime focus of the blockade and concomitant blockade runners was on the military side of the equation, rather than the civilian side. Therefore, effects of the obstruction upon civilians probably were severe, because food and manufactured goods coming through the blockade were prioritized for troops first, civilians second. Another problem was that blockade running was not an organized and efficient operation, particularly insofar as civilians were concerned. The blockade runner was a freelancer whose primary motive was profit rather than consideration of common human needs. Often he would bring in high profit luxury items such as liquor (that did not take up much space in the cargo area), rather than lower profit goods such as lumber (that required more cargo space).

The South faced staggering problems feeding its civilians because the military got first priority. Land lay relatively untended because of the absence of farmers, and the amount of farmland available was reduced due to occupation of farms by Federal forces. Before the war, many large plantations had grown just enough food to feed residents of the settlement, since most of the land was devoted to cash crops such as cotton and tobacco. Food shortages required that crops suitable for human consumption be grown instead of cash crops. Even where a food surplus existed, it could not be efficiently transported because of deteriorating roads, insufficient numbers of wagons and carts, and an inefficient railroad system. Railroad building was halted during the war and the critical military need of iron resulted in railroad engines and cars not being built and older ones not being properly maintained. In fact, in east Texas, railroad tracks were torn up and used in coastal fortifications. Southern civilians began to experience severe food shortages because of drought during the winter of 1862-1863. Inflation doubled the price of food every 12 months so that poor people could not afford some foods. A Confederate War Department clerk in Richmond wrote in March 1863, "The shadow of the gaunt form of famine is upon us and my wife and children are emaciated." A farm lady in North Carolina said, "A crowd of we Poor women went to Greenesborough yesterday for something to eat as we had not a mouthful of meet nor bread in my house what did they do but put us in gail in plase of giving us aney thing to eat.... I have 6 little children and my husband in the armey and what am I to do?"[78]

They rioted! Due to food scarcity, for which the blockade was partially responsible, people throughout the South participated in so-called bread riots during the spring of 1863. These occurred in a dozen or more cities when desperate women stole food from shops or supply depots. The Confederate capital was witness to the most serious uprising. President Jefferson Davis told the mob (after unsuccessfully pleading with them) that they had one minute left to disperse or the militia would fire upon them. This worked, nobody was shot, and the crowd scattered. Another significant bread riot occurred in Galveston the following spring when a mob, composed of members of the resident militia and their families, demanded government issued rations for their starving families. The group was broken up when a company of soldiers fired over their heads. Unfortunately, one man was accidentally killed when hit by a stray shot.[79]

Food was not the only shortage experienced by citizens of the Lone Star State due to the Union barricade. This barrier curtailed overseas imports as well as products from Northern manufacturers. One commodity that was in short supply was coffee. Texans developed substitutes by making this beverage from vegetables and grains such as potatoes, beans, peas, rye, and cornmeal. However, Eliza McHatton-Ripley, a refugee from Louisiana living in Texas, reported that the replacement beverages were "wretched imitations, though gulped down, when chilly and tired, for lack of anything better." Additionally, salt shortages led Texans to leach the dirt from floors of their smokehouses to recover saline deposits.[80] One account noted, "The price of salt increased from sixty-five cents per 200-pound sack in 1860 to seven or eight dollars a sack by autumn 1861."[81] Shortages of household goods were prevalent in Texas. For example, previously ubiquitous pins and needles became precious possessions. The loss of a needle was lamented, and due to the shortage of pins, "some were compelled to use mesquite thorns for pins."[82] Furthermore, many folks turned to homespun clothing since manufactured clothing was unavailable.

Paper was scarce. Sallie McNeill, a 24-year-old lady who lived on her grandfather's cotton plantation near Houston in 1864, wrote a diary of her life and experiences in Texas from 1858 to 1867. Although she was relatively prosperous, she too felt the impact of the obstruction. In her diary entry dated February 21, 1864, she records, "[This is] the last page of my neglected book. Hard times will no longer allow paper to scribble on." There are no more diary entries until November 10, 1865.[83]

In his Introduction to the book he edits (*Texas: The Dark Corner of the Confederacy*), B. P. Gallaway summarizes results of the blockade that produced shortages of essentials of life on the home front in 1864. He writes, "Many items such as paper, tea, coffee, and dinnerware were not available at any price. The scarcity of weapons, tools, horses, mules, articles of clothing, and most foods contributed further to the fears, wretchedness, and discomfort of Texas residents.... Medical supplies ... were impossible to obtain in most localities."[84]

An unanticipated benefit of the blockade was the consequent expansion of manufacturing in the affected state. Many new or revitalized industries quickly developed in Texas in response to unmet needs. In Austin, a cannon foundry and percussion cap factory were established. At the Texas State Penitentiary in Huntsville, a textile mill was established that produced three million yards of cotton and wool cloth for the military. Ordnance works were established at Tyler, Houston, and Galveston, and numerous other towns were involved in the manufacture of army goods such as tents, wagons, shoes, harnesses, and saddles.[85]

In the west, the blockade worked most effectively when it was a combined navy and army action. One good example of this was at Vicksburg in 1863, where the army established a barrier on the land and the navy blockaded the Mississippi River. Vicksburg was effectively shut off from the world and both soldiers and civilians were starved into submission. In war, civilians often suffer as much as the troops. Southern civilians and soldiers alike shared the misery of extreme want during the war.

Chapter 3

Blockade Running and Blockade Evasion

The Federal blockade of the Confederate States of America had been proclaimed in April 1861, and within three months, some Southern citizens were beginning to feel walled in. Mary Chesnut wrote in her diary on July 16, 1861, "Already they begin to cry out for more ammunition, and already the blockade is beginning to shut it all out." The next year, on March 12, 1862, she still was feeling the effects of the obstacle: "The blockade or stockade which hems us in—only the sky open to us." But two days later she exclaims, "Thank God for a ship. It has run the blockade with arms and ammunition."[86]

Most Southerners throughout the Civil War must have felt this roller coaster of emotion, from the valley of depression to the mountaintop of elation. The common man on the street probably had not anticipated effects the Union barrier would have on him personally, either psychologically, as expressed by Mrs. Chesnut, or from physical misery caused by the coming shortages of life's necessities. Most Southern people took for granted the fact that a majority of imported goods coming from overseas arrived first in New York City and then were distributed by rail and sea on a set schedule and by established routes throughout the South. In contrast, most foreign vessels they now saw coming into Charleston and other Southern ports arrived with ballast or military supplies, and departed with cotton. The Civil War and its accompanying blockade interrupted established practices; the South had to begin a wholesale reordering of its infrastructure. It needed to establish ports and a concomitant web of commercial arrangements with trading partners in Europe, and it had to develop a merchant marine, which up to this point did not exist. This huge undertaking was further complicated by imposition of the Federal barrier.

Initially, the South was unconcerned about the obstruction because it believed the North's task of blanketing a 3,500-mile coastline with a line of ships to be impossible. It was indeed hopeless, and Northern planners at first determined only to close down specific Southern ports. The North foresaw that the South's lifeline for receipt of materiel for the military and goods for civilians would be trade routes into great seaports of the South. Such ports needed to have a minimum depth over any bars at the harbor entrance of from twelve to twenty feet to accommodate deep draft oceangoing vessels. In addition, an adequate channel and anchorage, docking, and wharf facilities were required. The coastal cities also needed to be major banking and commercial centers that were connected to the interior with a sound railroad system. Last, port cities needed to be firmly in Southern hands.

Two of the finest ports in the South could not meet these last criteria: Richmond and Norfolk in Virginia shared an outlet to the Atlantic Ocean that passed through Hampton Roads, which was anchorage for the U.S. Navy's Home Squadron; two Federal installations, Fort Monroe and Fort Calhoun, were nearby. Only a few cities met the critical requirements: Wilmington, North Carolina; Charleston, South Carolina; Savannah, Georgia; Mobile, Alabama; and New Orleans, Louisiana. The United States targeted these coastal cities as primary pressure points for application of the blockade, and especially earmarked New Orleans as the city to defeat and occupy as soon as possible. New Orleans was so designated because there was early intent to possess the Mississippi River by controlling her mouth and her junction with the Ohio River at Cairo, Illinois. In addition, the city was desired as a forward U.S. naval base because of its extensive shipbuilding and repair facilities, as well as its potential as a supply depot.

It quickly became apparent to all that the two most important Southern ports for importing goods necessary to maintain Confederate armies would be Wilmington and Charleston. These ports were closest to locations of rebel armies and to geographic areas where important battles of the Civil War would be fought. They had the best railroad facilities in the South, enabling goods unloaded at the wharf to be rapidly transported to the interior. Consequently, a significant portion of the Union blockade effort was directed toward these two cities. Inevitably, prominent blockade running efforts by the South would concentrate on these two ports that presented distinct opportunities for this activity. Wilmington was located twenty-eight miles from the mouth of the Cape Fear River and there were two serviceable channels leading to the river from the ocean. These two estuaries were widely separated and could be used for either egress or ingress. These outlets were to become vital for blockade runners because the Union fleet had to be separated, and out of communication with one another, in order to cover both of them. Further, the blockade runners could come into the northernmost of the two inlets (called "New Inlet") and avail themselves of protection from guns of a strong rebel installation, Fort Fisher. Charleston was formed by the convergence of the Ashley and Cooper rivers, had a deep harbor, and could be entered by at least two of four channels. Gun batteries placed at strategic locations heavily defended that harbor entrance. Blockading ships and blockade running vessels were to meet often near these two great seaports.

The character of the ships being used for these contests was in the midst of change. The world was just emerging from the grand era of great sailing ships and was moving toward use of steamships. For transatlantic passage, sailing vessels were still favored at the onset of the Civil War. These ships could carry more cargo since they required no machinery associated with the steam-powered plant; they did not have to carry in the hold tons of coal rather than cargo. Steamships had the advantage over sailing vessels in the matter of speed, because in a given period, any steam-powered ship could overtake a sailing vessel on the open ocean. The Yankees quickly converted former sail-powered merchantmen to steam-powered vessels, armed them with a few guns, and then sent them on blockade duties to stop merchant sailing vessels. The South owned a few large sailing vessels at the beginning of the war, but some were sold to private interests or taken over by the Confederate navy and converted to warships. Larger sailing ships that the South had for commercial trade were easy prey for blockading steamships; smaller schooners that could avoid seizure by blockading vessels had lesser cargo capacity. In response to these challenges, the South turned to a type of steamer that was classified as a "coaster" or a coastal packet. Before the Civil War, these types of smaller ships had participated in commercial trade along southeastern coasts and the Gulf of Mexico. They would carry cargo, mail, and some passengers along the coast, perhaps out of Savannah or from Mobile. They were designed for shallow water coastal work. They were suitable as blockade runners because they were fast and had low freeboards and light drafts. They could duck into inlets and small bays and hide out from blockading vessels. Limited cargo space was their main deficiency.

The United States proceeded to put its barrier in place on April 30, 1861, when it isolated Norfolk. Once obstructed, Southern authorities would be formally notified of the action and a grace period of fifteen days would be granted to neutral shipping to leave port. Any ship approaching the naval barrier would be warned off and it would be seized if it were caught again. Other Southern ports were isolated over the next three months. Wilmington, inexplicably, was the last port to be blockaded and would become one of the most important havens in the Southern lifeline. The barrier was imposed at Wilmington on July 21 when *Daylight*, a small converted merchantman, came on station.[87]

As might be expected, the announcement of the obstruction being imposed on a Southern port was not passively received. Port commander Braxton Bragg told U.S. Navy Captain H.A. Adams that because of the blockade, Yankee vessels were not welcome in his harbor. He wrote, "Sir: Your communication of yesterday's date, announcing ... the blockade of this port, I accept as such.... You will please consider the harbor as closed against all boats and vessels of the United States."[88]

One of the first blockade runners on the East Coast was the *Bermuda*. Her story illustrates the need for infrastructures to be put in place to establish a commercial tie between England and the Confederacy. This was typical of the arrangements made for most other blockade runners. The first task facing the C.S.A. in April 1861 was providing armaments for its proposed 100,000-man army. This job fell to the Confederate Army's Ordnance Bureau, which was under the command of Major Josiah C. Gorgas. He turned out to be an excellent bureau chief and went about his work with enthusiasm and dedication. Major Gorgas recognized that there was insufficient manufacturing capacity in the South to provide necessary armaments; importing these goods would be required to meet current needs. This, of course, meant blockade running. However, before this could be done, there had to be in place some arrangement for purchasing weapons in England. Gorgas assigned this mission to Captain Caleb Huse. As the new C.S.A. purchasing agent, Huse needed money. This was to come from an established business having financial connections in England.

One such firm that had operated a successful steamship line and had extensive business connections in England was John Fraser and Company based in Charleston. This organization was an importing and exporting business and the son of the founder, John Augustus Fraser, and his chief clerk, George Alfred Trenholm, oversaw its operation. By the 1850s, Trenholm had become the company's head. At the outbreak of the Civil War, Trenholm was supervising the operations of John Fraser and Company in Charleston, as well as Fraser, Trenholm, and Company in Liverpool, England. Caleb Huse turned to the Trenholm firms to finance his initial trip to England and to gain funds for purchase of arms there. George Trenholm was glad to cooperate. He was a loyal supporter of the Confederacy and wished to demonstrate the inefficiency of the blockade so that other firms might be encouraged to aid the Southern cause. Of course, he also was aware of the immense potential profits for his firm.

Captain Huse sailed to Liverpool, arriving there on May 10, 1861. He immediately began searching for Enfield rifles, while cooperating with other Southern agents who likewise were seeking armaments. All of these agents were successful and the English warehouses began filling up with the goods of war purchased for the Southerners. Now that the financial scheme had secured the arms, the next step was getting them to the Confederacy. Again, the agents turned to the Trenholm operated firm. The company was preparing for a trip to Georgia with the newly purchased 1,003 ton gross iron-hulled steamship *Bermuda* that was 211 feet long and had a 30-foot beam. The Confederate agents were offered part of the cargo space for their goods at a "high" freight charge, which they accepted. Thus, part of the cargo space was devoted to armaments purchased by Huse and other agents, and a greater part was retained by Fraser, Trenholm, and Company to be sold to the C.S.A. at a large profit. Among other things, the ship's cargo consisted of 24,000 blankets, 50,000 shoes, 6,500 Enfield rifles, 200,000 cartridges, 4 heavy seacoast guns, 18 rifled field pieces, 180 barrels of gunpowder, and medical stores. On August 15, Charles Francis Adams, the U.S. Minister to Great Britain, informed interested parties of this vessel's imminent departure and *Bermuda*, with its valuable cargo, sailed on August 22. Captain Eugene Tessier was in charge. She arrived safely at the main entrance at Savannah, Georgia, on September 18, 1861. Apparently, the Union barrier was in the vicinity, but the *Bermuda* skipper said he saw no blockade ships. On October 29, 1861, *Bermuda* departed Savannah with 2,000 bales of cotton and arrived back in Liverpool in mid–November. Again, the ship's captain reported exiting the port as easily as he had entered. The round trip of the *Bermuda* not only provided a great supply of armaments to the Confederacy, but also provided immense wealth for several of the principals involved in the shipping venture. This trip alone validated to both sides the value of blockade running.[89]

This event caused a row on both sides of the Atlantic and in the North and South. Ship owners congratulated themselves on the profits made, the British had their suspicions confirmed that the blockade was ineffective, Southerners rejoiced in the success of the British steamship, the Confederate army was elated with the arms and equipment that were now available to them, the Union was mortified, Lincoln's opponents pointed out that nothing other than a "paper blockade" existed, and Navy Secretary Welles demanded to know the name of the vessel that was stationed on blockade when the *Bermuda* arrived. A combination of thin blockade coverage and good timing had allowed the *Bermuda* to enter Savannah so easily. The blockading ship *St. Lawrence* had to return to Hampton Roads around September 13 for provisions and water. She was replaced by the steamer *Savannah*, which had departed for her blockade station from Hampton Roads on September 16. She probably arrived near the port city Savannah about the same time as the *Bermuda*, but evidently was blown off station by a heavy gale. The British vessel was able to get out of Savannah for her return trip without difficulty presumably because of a lack of vessels to enforce the blockade. Because of *Bermuda*'s round trip, the Union reacted by strengthening the blockade, the Confederacy stepped up its overtures to Great Britain to come into the conflict on the side of the South, and Great Britain maintained its neutrality.[90]

However, the nature of penetrating this naval barrier was to change over time as the U.S. obstruction strengthened, making it more difficult for large ships to bring contraband directly to major coastal seaports. Larger shipping companies were reluctant to assume greater risks associated with running the blockade at major Southern seaports. They established a new pattern of movement. Instead of shipping directly to ports such as Charleston and Wilmington, English commercial shipping interests took their cargoes to Nassau and Bermuda and placed them in warehouses for C.S.A. accounts. From these intermediate ports, Southerners loaded warehoused goods into their smaller coastal ships and assumed the risk of evading the blockade.

One year after the *Bermuda* entered and left Savannah harbor without difficulty, another Trenholm vessel left Charleston, ran the blockade, and encountered problems. A light-draft steamship, the *Herald*, departed in October 1862 and turned back after being fired upon by an U.S. sloop-of-war. It was a cloudy, drizzly night on October 9 when the blockade runner tried again; in silence, and running without any lights, she departed Charleston harbor undetected bound for St. George, Bermuda, 600 miles away. James Morris Morgan was a 17-year-old midshipman aboard the *Herald* and he described the scene at St. George:

> We ran around the islands and entered the picturesque harbor of St. George shortly after daylight. There were eight or ten other blockade-runners lying in the harbor, and their captains and mates lived at the same little white-washed hotel where the commodore and I stopped, which gave us an opportunity of seeing something of their manner of life when on shore. Their business was risky and the penalty of being caught was severe; they were a reckless lot, and believed in eating, drinking, and being merry, for fear that they would die on the morrow and might miss something. Their orgies reminded me of the stories of the way the pirates in the West Indies spent their time when in their secret havens. The men who commanded many of these blockade-runners had probably never before in their lives received more than fifty to seventy-five dollars a month for their services; now they received ten thousand dollars in gold for a round trip, besides being allowed cargo space to take into the Confederacy, for their own account, goods which could be sold at a fabulous price, and also to bring out a limited number of bales of cotton worth a dollar a pound. In Bermuda these men seemed to suffer from a chronic thirst which could only be assuaged by champagne.[91]

A similar pattern was devised in the Gulf of Mexico. Vessels from England would bring their cargoes to Havana, Cuba; from there, the goods would be loaded into smaller coastal ships owned or leased by the Confederacy. This would increase the chance of successful blockade running into Galveston, the only major seaport in Texas. This was a trip of approximately 850 miles. Havana was a friendly port for the Confederacy because there was much support there for the Southern position on slavery. Many Cubans feared that should the North win the war, there would be negative repercussions among her own slave population. Further, Havana had a large, deep-water harbor that could accommodate seagoing vessels of any size. The C.S.A. took care to nourish this port by stockpiling equipment near the Havana wharves. All was not ideal, however, because the British government preferred that their ships frequent the British colonies of Bermuda and Nassau rather than have their business go to an old enemy in Spanish-controlled Havana. In addition, the Spanish-Cuban community did not have a well-established shipping industry in its background, as did Great Britain.

Blockade running vessels were adapted for successfully negotiating perils of the barrier. A steamer propelled by a paddlewheel on the side was the ship of choice. Side-wheelers were preferred because these light-draft ships frequently were working in shallow rivers, inlets, or coastal waters. Using a vessel powered by propellers required extra depth at the stern. Otherwise, the boat might go aground and damage the propulsion system. Favored construction was a long, slender iron hull with narrow beam and powerful engines capable of high speeds. These "Clyde Steamers" operated in the Clyde River in Scotland and were widely purchased and converted to blockade runners. The complex conversion process involved removing staterooms to enlarge cargo space in the "narrow beamer," and modifying smokestacks so they could be telescoped when unneeded to facilitate hiding the vessel in backwaters. In addition, masts and spars would be hinged so they could be lowered (sails could be used on steamers when in the open ocean to conserve coal), and hulls would be painted light gray or bluish green so they would blend in with their background. The boats might be stocked with anthracite coal that produced very little smoke; this enabled the vessel to avoid detection. Sometimes they would be stocked with two kinds of coal: "hard" coal (anthracite for smokeless operation), and "soft" coal that was cheaper but produced more smoke (and could be used for cruising on the open ocean). However, as the war continued, the blockade runners obtained anthracite coal with increasing difficulty due to restrictions on its sale by the Federal government.

A blockade runner named J. Wilkinson, who was a captain in the Confederate States Navy, described a vessel he observed in the harbor at Nassau. He said, "Here and there in the crowded harbor might be seen a long, low, rakish-looking lead-colored steamer with short masts, and a convex forecastle deck extending nearly as far aft as the waist, and placed there to enable the steamer to be forced through and not over a heavy head sea. These were the genuine blockade-runners, built for speed; and some of them survived all the desperate hazards of the war."[92]

When a ship was modified, experienced sailors, often of English or Irish heritage, manned it. The most sought after captains, however, were those Southerners who had been steamboat captains before the war, because it was felt they could be trusted to do their patriotic best for the cause. More importantly, they had intimate knowledge of inland waterways. Top dollar was paid to the captain for risks he was taking and for his experience. For example, for one voyage in and out of a blockaded port, a skipper was paid $5,000 in gold for the journey. Sometimes captains also were allowed to use a portion of cargo space for their private goods. At the completion of the voyage, they would sell this cargo at a great profit.[93]

There are many documented examples of successful blockade running and one popular point of departure was Nassau, located on New Providence Island in the Bahamas. One blockade runner described the scene in Nassau in the middle of the war as, "Cotton, cotton, everywhere! Blockade-runners discharging it into lighters, tier upon tier of it, piled high upon the wharves, and merchant vessels, chiefly under the British flag, loading with it."[94]

One of the most successful to run the blockade from Nassau to Wilmington, North Carolina, was Thomas E. Taylor, skipper of the *Banshee* (I). This vessel was constructed in Liverpool, England, and she was built specifically for blockade running. She was a steel hull on an iron frame, of about 500 tons gross, and long and narrow (214 feet long with a 20-foot beam). Her draft of eight feet was suitable for shoal water work. Her rated speed was 11 knots and she carried a crew of thirty-six hands.[95] Early in 1863, the *Banshee* was ready for sea and Taylor began learning the tricks of the trade. He found that a successful run was considered impossible except on moonless nights and that a proper tide was useful.

BLOCKADE RUNNER BANSHEE. Actually, there were two vessels named Banshee: *Banshee I* and *Banshee II*. This illustration is thought to be *Banshee I*. Both were built for the Anglo-Confederate Trading Company in England and Scotland, respectively. In March 1865, *Banshee II* ran the blockade from Havana to Galveston and back. (Guild Press of Indiana, Carmel, Indiana.)

To make the *Banshee* as invisible as possible, everything aloft was taken down and the ship was painted a dull white to blend into the sea. Once underway, Taylor would alter his course frequently, maintain a sharp watch, and seek out rain squalls, clouds, and fog to escape detection. If chased by a blockade vessel, he would try to outrun her by putting on all sail and firing the steam engine to the maximum. His favorite maneuver was to run before the wind so that the pursuer would have to do likewise. The ship following him usually was a gunboat that was shorter and tended to pitch in the rough water. This would cause the stern to come out of the water, exposing the propeller and slowing the pursuer. Of course the *Banshee*, like other blockade runners, never was armed, not only to save weight, but also to ensure that if captured the ship and cargo would be dealt with under provisions of the blockade proclamation and not charged as an armed pirate ship, which might subject the crew to the death penalty. Mr. Taylor was a bold, experienced, and expert captain who gained fame and fortune. The vessel was crewed almost entirely by men from England, Ireland and Scotland. In spite of the *Banshee* being captured on her ninth trip, Taylor reported that "she earned sufficient on the eight successful round trips which she made to pay her shareholders 700 percent on their investment."[96] *Banshee* (II) was then constructed in Scotland for the Anglo Confederate Trading Company and in March 1865 ran the blockade from Havana to Galveston and back.

Another successful blockade runner that worked in the Gulf of Mexico was *Rob Roy*, a sailing schooner with a centerboard that could be pulled up in shallow water. The *Rob Roy* measured 78 feet long and 22½ feet wide. She was under the command of Captain William Watson, a Scotsman.[97] In December 1863, Watson ran his ship, which was heavily loaded with over 25 tons of iron and other miscellaneous goods, from Havana to Galveston. Sailing ships were suitable for heavy cargoes because they did not have to carry coal for a steam engine. However, because of the weight of cargo, they often were awkward to sail. Watson reported that his ship did not ride easily at sea due to the dead weight of the iron. During this particular trip, Captain Watson exhibited the usual deception of a successful skipper by clearing Havana for Matamoros, sailing to the west in the afternoon, and then changing course toward Galveston during the night. Near the beginning and end of this voyage, he encountered gales that tested the mettle of skipper and boat. On the sixth day out, near the Texas coast, *Rob Roy* was followed by a gunboat; for a day or so Watson had tense times as he battled the sea in a gale while losing his pursuer, first in a rain squall and later under darkness of night. As he neared the Texas coast, the situation demanded an approach to Galveston by way of a narrow side channel in order to evade the blocking boats; his navigational skills in the dark of night and thick rain were tested to the utmost. Through skill and his prudent use of a calculated degree of recklessness, Captain Watson completed a profitable run through the Union blockade. Many other ships duplicated this achievement at Galveston.[98]

Watson and the *Rob Roy* made runs from Havana not only to Galveston, but also to another Texas port. In September 1863, he slipped into Velasco on the Brazos River with his boat flying the British flag. He was required to deliver his papers to British Consul Arthur T. Lynn in Galveston. Captain Watson left his schooner to make the trip; upon return, he found Confederate officials had impressed his boat. Watson asked Mr. Lynn to intervene in his behalf and on October 3, 1863, Lynn wrote to Confederate General Magruder, who was in command of the district. Consul Lynn made clear that the *Rob Roy*, while flying the British flag, had entered Velasco as a result of Magruder's proclamation of January 20, 1863, that stated this port was not actually blockaded, and that friendly neutral nations were invited to resume commerce. The British Consul added that it was deceptive for the Confederates to invite neutral shipping into Velasco, and then seize the *Rob Roy* for their own military purposes. On October 21, 1863, General Magruder replied to Arthur Lynn explaining, "The schooner *Rob Roy* was released as soon as she was ascertained to be a British vessel. She was seized as a military necessity, to aid in constructing defenses at the mouth of the Brazes [sic]." Further, it was indicated by General Magruder that the vessel's bulwarks may have been damaged "in preparing her for the service" and that the Confederates would pay for those damages to be repaired. Obviously, on journeys such as this, Watson's troubles were not over once he reached Confederate soil.[99]

Although William Watson was famous for his exploits with the *Rob Roy*, his last trip into Galveston was in March 1865 when he was hired as pilot of a 445-ton steamer named *Pelican* (but identified as *Phoenix* in his 1892 book, *Adventures of a Blockade Runner*). *Pelican*, an iron vessel with a single screw, had been constructed in Hull, England, in 1863. Watson was in Havana, having sold the *Rob Roy*, when the captain of the *Pelican*, who was unfamiliar with the Texas coastal waters, hired him to pilot his vessel into Galveston. Watson told an inquirer, "This makes my fourth trip in Texas, and my third into Galveston." The pilot left Havana harbor in the *Pelican* near sunset on March 1, 1865. As was his practice, he had cleared for Matamoros and steered toward that port until nightfall, when he shaped his course toward Galveston to deceive any ships observing him. The captain objected to Watson running without lights at night and voiced his concern about colliding with another ship. Watson explained that there were few vessels on the seas, "but with lights there would be danger of collision with a ball, which might be sent across our bows." They proceeded unlighted in the dark with a good lookout posted. Later the pilot talked to the chief engineer and explained it was necessary to limit the emission of black smoke since this was where blockading cruisers had the advantage over blockade runners. The cruisers had anthracite coal that emitted little smoke, while the "runners" (in 1865) had access only to inferior coal that produced heavy black smoke that helped the cruisers spot them. Watson further explained that a comparative disadvantage of "runners" was that their bottoms were cleaned less frequently, thus retarding their speed.

The journey of *Pelican* was uneventful until they were about 35 miles southeast of Galveston and were seen by a distant cruiser that followed them. Watson proceeded on a false course to the west-southwest blowing smoke until dark, expecting that the cruiser would follow that smoke trail. After nightfall, he altered his course directly for Galveston, minimized smoke emissions, and anticipated that the pursuer would continue in the direction indicated by the smoke trail. The captain then brought the *Pelican* in near the coast in shallow water toward the swash channel to the west of blockading ships. As they were approaching shallow water, he had the engineer fill the boilers with clean water before the muddy bottom was stirred up. As the ship reached the three-fathom mark, they slowed and "felt" their way in while navigating partially by the light atop the Hendley building that was illuminated to guide blockade runners into the harbor. They took soundings with the lead to the port side and found the channel with eight feet of water. As Watson had expected, the water shoaled down to seven feet and *Pelican* was grounded. Watson determined that they had come in at low tide and a flood tide was now running; he waited quietly in the dark for the vessel to float off the sand and presently it did so. They then sailed into the main channel and reached the guard boat in the midst of a violent thunderstorm. After daylight, boarding officers came on board and they cleared the boat for dockage. Watson noted that "Some five or six steamers were loading at the wharfs [sic], and arrivals and sailings were quite frequent." Further, he observed that early in the blockade of Galveston, only the *Santee* was on station and few took the risk of running past her. He added, "Now, a fleet of from twelve to fifteen heavily armed steamers lay off the port, and a number of fast cruisers patrolled the waters in the neighbourhood of the port, and cruised all over the Gulf of Mexico, overhauling and capturing vessels wherever they found them, yet in the face of all this, notwithstanding, the number of steamers and schooners that pass in and out was almost incredible."

Watson was one of a daring breed of gentlemen who repeatedly ran the blockade with a degree of *savoir-faire*. At convivial meetings of these men, this was a common toast: "The Confederates that produce the cotton; the Yankees that maintain the blockade and keep up the price of cotton; the Britishers that buy the cotton and pay the high price for it. Here is to all three, and a long continuance of the war, and success to blockade runners." After concluding his voyage, Watson signed on as master of the steamer *Jeannette* and proceeded to Tampico, Mexico. He remained there for the rest of the war after contracting smallpox.[100]

For a variety of reasons, the volume of activity in the gulf coast region never approached that of the East Coast. The fall of New Orleans in April 1862 was one reason. This was the most important port in the South other than Wilmington and Charleston, and it was the largest cotton port in the world. New Orleans had a large fleet of coastal steamers that could have been converted to blockade runners; instead, the C.S.A. and Louisiana chose to convert several of them into gunboats for defense of the coastline and area rivers. The Southern Steamship Company in New Orleans was in a position to originate a blockade running trade. A native of New Orleans ran the company, but he was a relative of New York financier Charles Morgan, founder of the organization. The Confederacy never felt the firm was trustworthy and loyal to the Southern cause. Consequently, the C.S.A. never used the company's ships for blockade running. Moreover, the fall of New Orleans led to the death of blockade running out of that port.[101]

There were steamers operated by profit-minded parties that did escape New Orleans before her fall. These boats began working out of Havana, where the enterprising Confederacy was stockpiling military equipment. They operated in late 1861 and early in 1862; some ran the blockade into New Orleans, while others shipped into Sabine City, Texas, through Sabine Pass. The fall of New Orleans disrupted blockade running, but Mobile, Alabama, the number two port in the gulf, quickly picked up that activity. In response, the Union strengthened the Mobile blockade in the last three months of 1862, and blockade running there was curtailed.

The *General Rusk* was available in Galveston and she was converted to a blockade runner. On June 5, 1862, she successfully ran the blockade with a load of cotton and made it to Havana. Cotton was, of course, a most valuable commodity. A 500-pound bale could be purchased in Texas for around five cents a pound and sold in Liverpool, England, for around sixty cents a pound. Careful use was made of precious cargo space to maximize the number of bales that were to be carried in order to guarantee the greatest possible profit. Typically, cotton bales were "packed so closely that a rat could hardly find room to hide among them. Then the hatches were put on, and a tier of bales put fore and aft, in every available spot on deck[,] then another somewhat thinner tier on top of that."[102] In Havana, *General Rusk* was loaded with munitions that were delivered to Indianola, Texas.

Blockade running remained active all along the Texas coast with shallow draft vessels visiting many of the smaller ports or even, in emergencies, discharging cargo on beaches. Waterways behind the barrier islands, which were located between the mainland and the Gulf of Mexico, were particularly suited to this kind of activity; smaller ships with lighter cargoes were adept at "bumping" over numerous sand bars. This type of blockade running was impossible for the Union to stop. The most blockading units could do was impede the flow by catching a few "runners," or occasionally destroy dock facilities at some ports by bombardment. Much of this activity, however, was transfer of cargo from one Texas port to another. Since the loads were minimal to decrease the draft of the boat, the volume of cargo actually made available is thought to have been small. Nevertheless, the volume of shipping involved in this activity probably has been underreported due to scarcity of data.

Galveston was an active blockade running port throughout the war. This activity increased after the C.S.A. victory at the Battle of Galveston in January 1863. It had a flourishing cotton trade before the war, and this infrastructure was in place thereafter. Nearby Houston was the cotton center of Texas. The staple was processed, bought, and sold in Houston, then usually shipped through Galveston. The blockade initially stifled this trade, but it became reinvigorated after the Union's failed attempt to seize Galveston and its inner harbor. At the same time, blockade running became more sophisticated, with better techniques and improved vessels. As Southern ports to the east were closed during the last two years of war, blockade running at Galveston expanded.

A number of successful Houston businessmen invested heavily in this activity and profited handsomely. One of these was Thomas W. House, the owner of T. W. House and Company. Initially the firm was involved with dry goods and groceries, but expanded to become the largest wholesaler in the state. Before the war, the mercantile establishment accepted cotton as payment for goods and cotton factoring was set up as a separate department. During the early part of the war, the company's cotton wagons made their way to Brownsville and returned with vital supplies. Later, House branched out to blockade running through Galveston and by 1864 he either owned or had an interest in a string of vessels running the blockade.[103]

Another prominent Texas merchant, John Swisher, owned the Austin firm J. M. Swisher and Company; it was involved in banking, merchandising and cotton factoring. During the war he lived in Matamoros and worked as a purchasing agent for the Confederacy. He owned five vessels running the blockade and in 1863, his total income exceeded his indebtedness by 105 percent. There is no evidence that his ships had any difficulty with the Federal blockade.[104]

Although the Galveston blockade was initiated in July 1861, vessels were usually stationed only at the main shipping channel. San Luis Pass, located at the south end of Galveston Island beyond West Bay and carrying eight feet of water, often was ignored. Small vessels frequently used San Luis Pass to run the blockade; no Federal vessels were stationed there until November 1861 when schooner *Sam Houston* patrolled it intermittently. The British consul in Galveston, Arthur Lynn, reported in late 1861 and early 1862 that vessels made successful runs of the blockade by using shore channels to the east and west of the main channel. Further, he reported that all channels west of Galveston were open. Rear Admiral Farragut was aware of the importance of San Luis Pass and on August 16, 1862, expressed regret that he did not have sufficient vessels to make the blockade efficient at that location. By spring 1864, however, records reveal that this pass was continuously blockaded and there were numerous captures of vessels running the blockade, particularly in April and May.[105]

Blockade running at Galveston diminished in late 1862 because of more Union vessels on station, and occupation of the city by Federal troops. Southern runners presumably moved to other Texas ports such as Velasco and Sabine Pass. An additional factor accounting for this was development of a blockade evasion route through Mexico. In 1864, blockade running increased; this is documented by increased captures of these ships by Union vessels in the spring. Most of these craft were small sailing vessels and this limited the amount of cargo being carried. As the year progressed, sailing vessels were supplemented by an increasing appearance of steamers. The majority of these vessels were privately financed, but four steamers were purchased for the Confederate government in Liverpool and were under the control of the Navy Department. One of them—*Owl*—was 230 feet long, had a beam of 26 feet, and could carry 800 bales of cotton. This steamship was reported to be in Galveston on April 28, 1865. She sailed for Havana on May 3 with 478 bales of cotton, arrived safely, and then departed Havana around May 21 for the return trip to Galveston.[106]

The peak period for Galveston blockade running was between November 1864 and May 1865. On April 28, 1865, one Union dispatch relayed the information that "there have been as many twenty-five different steamers engaged in running into Galveston, and nearly all have been successful. The business is decreasing, not because there is any danger from the blockading fleet, but from the scarcity of cotton at Galveston."[107] Historian Robert Warren Glover concludes that during this time-span, "At least thirty-seven vessels engaged in the Galveston trade.... These sixteen steamers, twenty schooners, and one sloop violated the blockade a total of fifty-two times." Two of the more successful steamers were *Lark* and *Wren* that had been built in England and departed Liverpool in November 1864. Each vessel could carry a maximum of 700 bales of cotton. These two steamers completed six round trips through the Galveston blockade.[108] Union Navy Secretary Welles acknowledged the obvious on May 15, 1865: "It appears that blockade running at Galveston is still carried on with much success. The following are the arrivals reported at Havana, all from Galveston, with cotton: *Lunar*, April 15; *Wren* and *Badger*, April 21; *Fox* and *Evelyn*, April 22; and *Denbigh*, May

1."[109] During the months of April and May 1865, there was a corresponding increase in Union vessels capturing Southern ships that were violating the barrier. Nevertheless, Acting Rear admiral H. K. Thatcher, Commanding the West Gulf Squadron, wrote to Navy Secretary Welles on April 11, 1865, saying he required "fast steamers of light draft" to serve the needs of his blockading fleet. He forwarded a communication from Captain B. F. Sands, Commanding the Second Division of the West Gulf Squadron, in which numerous complaints were made about the conditions of the blockading ships, including: deep drafts that prohibited proper action near bars; fouled bottoms on iron vessels that diminished their speed; and gunboats needing to be sent north for repair.[110]

The favored port for blockade running to Texas was Havana; it was a good deep-water location with adequate dock and warehouse facilities. Most important was its proximity to the Texas coast. Blockade runner J. Wilkinson gives us a good description of Havana during that period:

> There are many beautiful rides and drives in the environs, and the summer heats are tempered by the cool refreshing sea breeze which blows daily. That scourge of the tropics, yellow fever, is chiefly confined to the cities of Cuba, the country being salubrious.... It must be confessed that Havana itself possesses few attractions for the stranger and that its sanitary arrangements are execrable. In addition to the imperfect municipal regulations in this respect, all the sewage of the city empties itself into the harbor, in which there is no current to sweep the decomposing matter into the Gulf Stream outside.[111]

Sabine Pass also was a popular location for blockade runners. This pass is a seven-mile long estuary that connects the Gulf of Mexico to Sabine Lake, to the north. Sabine Pass has a long history as a small seaport and a haven for smugglers. Due to its isolated location and proximity to deep-water ports, it became a logical place for operations of smugglers and pirates from 1816 through 1821. Africans in bondage would arrive in Galveston in deep draft ships that had crossed the Atlantic with their human cargo. From Galveston, they would be transferred to shallow draft vessels because the bar at Sabine Pass generally would run only six feet of water. Once in Sabine Lake, slaves would be moved to sugar cane plantations in the Western Louisiana Bayou Teche region. By 1830, the first keelboats loaded with cotton came down rivers entering Sabine Lake where New Orleans cotton schooners waited to purchase their cargoes. A customhouse was established just above Sabine Pass in 1840 where ships were expected to pay tonnage fees for loading Texas cotton, but there was an abundance of smuggling to bypass this checkpoint and avoid paying fees.[112] This customhouse was located near the town of Sabine City that, before the Civil War, had been a prosperous and thriving community with a large hotel, sawmill, and weekly newspaper.

Although Sabine Pass was generally unappreciated by many as a significant area for blockade running, those on the scene were well aware of its importance. The C.S.A. chief engineer for East Texas in July 1862 wrote, "The Pass at Sabine is certainly a very important port, and in fact, the only port from where we receive our powder and other articles." Around this same time, the Federal blockade commander at the inlet reported, "The importance of Sabine Pass to the Rebels has been entirely underrated by us." At one point, several thousand bales of cotton had been stockpiled at nearby Niblett's bluff in anticipation of breaking the barrier.

Some residents of the area were boat owners who outfitted their vessels for blockade running. The earliest blockade runner in the region was the schooner *Clarinda* that departed Sabine Pass with a load of lumber on August 29, 1861, and returned to Sabine estuary with merchandise. Captain Henry Scherffius of Orange, Texas, owned *Clarinda*; he made 12 successful trips aboard his schooner carrying 150 bales of cotton on most voyages. Otto and Charles H. Ruff were brothers from Beaumont who also ran the blockade. They owned the schooner *Tampico*, which made at least four trips to Matamoros carrying cotton while registered under the English flag. With 112 bales of cotton on board, *Tampico* was captured off Sabine Pass by the Union gunboat *Cayuga* in March 1863. When Otto Ruff died in October 1862, his estate included $4,410 received from cotton sales resulting from the schooner's activities and $5,787 in gold owed by a Mexican cotton factor in Matamoros.[113]

In summer 1862, eight rebel vessels arrived at Sabine Pass with cargoes of gunpowder and munitions. Although a blockade theoretically was imposed during this period, one official reported, "There are vessels of the enemy off the bar occasionally during this time. There never was more than one vessel at a time. Sometimes ... there were intervals of from one to four weeks during which no vessel of the enemy appeared in sight." When barricading vessels were in sight, blockade runners often would work together by going out the pass in groups of two to ten on a high tide on a dark night, or in fog. Then they would turn east or west hugging the coast until it was safe to go in the ocean. The blockading ship was, of course, unable to pursue all this traffic. In September 1862, there were thirteen blockade runners loaded with 2,000 bales of cotton waiting on Sabine Lake for favorable conditions to run the barrier. Obviously, blockade running out of Sabine Pass was active and successful.[114]

Fearing that the Union blockade would strengthen, the Confederacy cast eyes upon the Mexican town of Matamoros, across the Rio Grande from Brownsville, Texas.[115] Brownsville came into existence after the United States built Fort Brown during the Mexican War. The town grew around that installation to supply the needs of troops stationed there. Francis Stillman, the head of a shipping enterprise, founded Brownsville. In 1860, Brownsville's population was 2,672 people, but it was prosperous and growing. Trade with the Northern states of Mexico fueled this expansion. On the other hand, the town across the river, Matamoros, was in economic distress because of a three-year civil war in Mexico. She had been established in 1821 but recently had declined from a population of 25,000 to 5,000 people at the opening of the American Civil War.[116]

For over a year, Confederate leaders had been in contact with Mexican officials with a desire to use Matamoros to evade the U.S. barrier in the western gulf.

Initially, trade agreements were reached, but they could not be fulfilled because of political instability and civil war in northern provinces of Mexico. The state of Tamaulipas was under siege because of a power struggle between two rival governors. Mexican President Benito Juarez took decisive action to end this rivalry in February 1862, ultimately producing trade routes. A Union blockade was placed near the mouth of the Rio Grande, but it was only partially effective because the Mexican War's Treaty of Guadalupe Hidalgo declared that river neutral. By terms of the treaty, the blockade could not be placed within a mile north or south of its mouth. With regard to traffic coming in or out of the Rio Grande, Flag Officer Farragut made it unmistakable that the blockading ships were "not to interfere with the commerce of friendly powers more than you can possibly avoid," but were expected to carefully investigate vessels suspected of carrying contraband for the Confederacy. Further, this investigation was to be "rigidly maintained." The investigative process was to include the following procedure: board ships in the area and determine if cargoes are intended for Matamoros; examine each ship's papers to see that they are in order; obtain a signed certificate from the captain that cargo will go to Matamoros and not pass through Texas; in some instances secure certificates as to the honesty of intentions from British and American consuls; and obtain similar certificates from outbound vessels guaranteeing cargo to be of Mexican origin and not from Confederate Texas.[117]

This order was enforced to the point that English and French shipping complained about the rigidity of the barrier. Throughout the western gulf, shipping bound for Matamoros was stopped and papers were examined. On March 17, 1862, Commander Sam L. Swartwout of USS *Portsmouth* ordered some of his crew to board and inspect the French steamer *Le Tage*. The French objected, and Swartwout referred the matter to Flag Officer Farragut. This satisfied the French.[118] On March 18, 1862, a British officer, Captain Edward Tatham of HBMS *Phaeton*, complained that these examinations were causing a "stagnation to the trade of neutrals with Matamoras [sic]."[119] This stagnation may or may not have been factually accurate, but the inspections probably were justified. There is extensive documentation of blockade running by British ships containing contraband cargo bound for the Confederacy through Matamoros. One example is a letter written by F. H. Morse of the U.S. Consulate in London on November 28, 1862, that was addressed to Secretary of State Seward. The letter encloses a British document that provides extensive and detailed information regarding how the British government was carrying on contraband trade with the Confederates. The enclosure shows "one way adopted by British merchants of sending out supplies by British steamers under the English flag to be sold in rebel ports at a stipulated value above costs and charges. It also shows the facilities they have and are preparing to carry on trade through Matamoras [sic] and Texas."[120]

These matters eventually were smoothed over, but Commander Swartwout was concerned enough about United States blockade policies in the area that he wrote to Admiral Farragut. The commander suggested that the barrier be erected so as to extend well to the north of the one-mile neutral limit around the Rio

Grande. Swartwout expressed his fear plainly: "This course would prevent the possibility of a breach with England and France, growing out of the rights of neutrals. The trade on the Rio Grande ... had better be abandoned rather than by attempting to interfere with two powerful nations, particularly at this time, when we have such a gigantic rebellion in our country to suppress." He added, "I am satisfied that it is impossible to prevent illicit trade on the Rio Grande unless we can take possession of Brownsville and the American side of the Rio Grande from there to its mouth."[121] These suggestions eventually were implemented, reducing friction with France and England, and leading ultimately to the Rio Grande expedition by General Banks late in 1863.

Maintaining the blockade near the mouth of the Rio Grande was especially difficult because of its remoteness. Union ships usually were on station for two or three months. At the beginning of the blockade, they often were in poor repair when arriving because of the rush to get them on station. Subsequently, the vessels had to return to Navy yards at Pensacola or New Orleans for repairs and refitting or to receive supplies, especially fresh water. The water at the Rio Grande was unsuitable for crews or boilers because of high mineral content. The health of crews likewise caused blockading ships to leave the area because scurvy and yellow fever were prevalent. For example, Lieutenant Henry French, commanding the USS *Albatross* off the Rio Grande had to leave his station on September 30, 1862, because of malaria and two fatal cases of yellow fever among his crew. *Albatross*'s departure left that region without a blockading vessel because one was not immediately available. Similarly, the *Montgomery* had to give up her patrol because of the need for provisioning and there was no vessel available to replace her.[122] This also resulted in the Rio Grande area not being blockaded. Rear Admiral Farragut was troubled about the western gulf blockade not having enough ships present and therefore becoming ineffective. On August 16, 1862, he wrote to another officer and said, "I regret to see that there is no vessel at Brazos River, San Luis Pass, or Matagorda Bay. I fear that there are not near enough vessels to make the blockade efficient, but you will have to go down to the Rio Grande and Brazos Santiago, where there has not been a vessel since the *Montgomery* left. In fact, I have not had the vessel or a commander to do the duty."[123]

On occasion, as dictated by the situation at hand, some consideration was given by Union officials to taking the extraordinary step of cooperating with the French in a joint blockade. The French had invaded Mexico and had extended a blockade of the Mexican coast to the south side of the Rio Grande in May 1863. At the same time, the United States had extended its blockade to the north side of the Rio Grande; some of the friction between America and France arose because of the close proximity (about one nautical mile of separation) between the blockades of the two nations. France's blockade was designed to prevent munitions and clothing from entering Mexico. It did not interfere with importing general merchandise into Mexico or exporting cotton. Thus, both France and the United States were trying to keep military supplies from entering Mexico if (in the case of France) the ultimate destination was Mexico, or (in the case of the United

States) the ultimate destination was Texas and the Confederacy. This arrangement was confusing to all and caused conflict and numerous misunderstandings. Rear Admiral Theodorous Bailey thought he saw a potential solution and he suggested to Navy Secretary Gideon Welles on March 19, 1863, "In case a military occupation of the Rio Grande can not be undertaken ... an arrangement with the French for a joint blockade of that river ... would produce the desired result." Because France had violated the Monroe Doctrine by being in Mexico, the suggestion was not acted upon, but it may have fortified a resolve to launch a land campaign along the Rio Grande as soon as possible.[124]

There were other factors that made Matamoros trade less desirable, the most serious of which had to do with the transportation system. Since a railroad extended westward only to Alleyton (near Houston), it was necessary to use other land transportation, usually ox carts. These carts could not move heavy goods such as artillery. Additionally, the area between the Rio Grande and Nueces River had always been subject to pillaging and murder by bandits, which further disrupted the system. Further, Mexico placed a high tariff on goods shipped out of Texas through Matamoros to sea. The tariff was high enough that it eroded profits; sometimes cotton merchants declined to sell their product for export because the profit margin was too thin. All of these factors inhibited Confederate plans for evading the Federal obstruction. Nevertheless, Southerners began resolving these problems with the view of opening the back door to the Confederacy.

In Texas and throughout the South, cotton was the chief staple exported to the world and it readily earned the sobriquet of "King Cotton" due to the immense wealth it generated as the main cash crop. This was a labor-intensive plant that made the institution of slavery vital to ensure economic viability. Both Britain and France were significant purchasers of exported cotton, with England being the biggest buyer. By the late 1850s "Annual British cotton imports from American averaged nearly two million bales and provided 75 to 80 percent of the cotton used in British mills."[125] In his inaugural address delivered in Montgomery, Alabama on February 18, 1861, Jefferson Davis, as provisional president of the Confederacy, used carefully couched language to let it be known that Southern cotton was vital to the well-being of the world. The president said that the South's chief interest was "export of a commodity required in every manufacturing country." He added that "The cultivation of our fields has progressed as heretofore, and even should we be involved in war there would be no considerable diminution in the production of the staples which have constituted our exports and in which the commercial world has an interest scarcely less than our own." President Davis concluded that this important trade of staples could be "interrupted by an exterior force [but this] course of conduct ... would be unjust toward us [and] detrimental to manufacturing and commercial interests abroad."[126] This official C.S.A. statement highlighted the importance of cotton both to the South and to Europe. Unofficially, "King Cotton" would become a tool for applying pressure to England and France to draw them to the aid of the Confederacy. The rebels hoped to motivate these nations toward positive overtures to the C.S.A. by withholding this vital staple from their textile mills. Thus an unofficial embargo was born.

When the war began, most of the previous year's crop had already been shipped, and if there was to be a cotton scarcity to provoke the proper European response, it would be necessary to create an unofficial and artificial restraint of trade. From summer 1861 through spring 1862, cotton planting was reduced and cotton bales were burned so that this staple would not reach Britain and other nations. During this period, "All the consuls in the south, including Arthur Lynn in Texas, reported massive destruction of cotton."[127] The Confederacy then sat back and waited for desired reactions from the international community. Those reactions, however, were not forthcoming. One reason was that England and France had a cotton surplus from the 1860 exports and a high inventory of finished goods. In addition, these countries adjusted to the changed circumstances by reducing their use of cotton in favor of other fabrics, and by increasing their imports of cotton from other countries. In fact, the cotton embargo was hurting the Confederacy as much as it was hurting Europe, because the South was becoming cash poor. Ultimately, the C.S.A. found it necessary to sell cotton abroad in order to finance the war effort. Most importantly, the cotton embargo was not pressuring any nation to recognize Confederate independence. For all these reasons, the Southern states reversed themselves and began producing and exporting cotton by late 1862.

Against this backdrop, Texas began considering ways of getting its immense cotton crop to market. The state found itself in a tight spot in late 1862. Its gulf ports were effectively obstructed, the transportation system was restricted by the fall of New Orleans, and the Matamoros cotton trade was stagnated. Cotton had been planted during the spring and summer of 1862 and Texas planters sought a way to get it to market. Merchants in Matamoros and the surrounding area were eager to broker Texas cotton by engaging in the import-export trade. These common interests led to circumventing the United States blockade.

The American blockade was not to be imposed on any neutral nation because the Lincoln administration felt the U.S. had insufficient resources to engage in another conflict in addition to the Civil War. Mexico was a neutral nation and by treaty, the Rio Grande was a neutral waterway. The United States was determined to honor this status of neutrality by imposing a blockade on Texas, but no closer than one mile north of the mouth of the Rio Grande. This restriction did not significantly weaken the barrier since the best ocean access from Brownsville was Brazos Santiago Pass, located between Brazos Island and Padre Island (and outside the neutral zone). Before the Civil War, there were wharves on the lagoon side of Brazos Island at the port of Brazos Santiago. Goods destined for Brownsville and Matamoros had to be off-loaded at the Brazos Santiago port because sandbars at the mouth of the Rio Grande did not carry enough water to enable ocean vessels to cross them and proceed upriver. From Brazos Santiago, the off-loaded goods were lightered across to Point Isabel, then hauled to Brownsville by oxcart and ferried across the Rio Grande to Matamoros.[128]

Brazos Santiago was in Texas territory and became legitimately blockaded when the 22-gun U.S. sloop *Portsmouth* took her station off Brazos Santiago Pass on February 24, 1862.[129] The Brownsville-Matamoros connection was about thirty miles inland and required difficult navigation to go seaward down the neutral Rio Grande and avoid the blockade. Creative thinkers in Texas and Mexico addressed this problem: was there a better way to evade the blockade instead of descending the Rio Grande? Already some seaports farther down the coast of Mexico were being used to bypass the blockade. The primary problem with using these ports was very long distances from the cotton supply. Urgently needed was a seaport near Brownsville, but located in Mexico, and consequently not subject to interference from Federal barriers.

Unfortunately, no such seaport existed. There was, however, a dusty little village named Bagdad located near the mouth of the Rio Grande in the state of Tamaulipas, Mexico. It was about to become a great seaport for the duration of the war. Bagdad was approximately thirty miles to the east of Matamoros. Because of its location in a neutral country, Bagdad was not subjected to the United States barrier.[130] However, its neutrality status would be challenged in early 1862.

On April 29, 1862, Lieutenant Charles Hunter, commanding the USS *Montgomery* (which had relieved the *Portsmouth*) confronted lighters flying the Mexican flag and unloading cargo off Bagdad onto neutral vessels. Lieutenant Hunter did so because he knew these lighters actually were owned by Confederates, had been placed under Mexican registry, and were flying the Mexican flag while transporting Texas cotton to ships off Bagdad. John "Rip" Ford had suggested this subterfuge in order to evade the blockade. When the *Montgomery* proposed to interfere with these neutral vessels, a British man-of-war, HBMS *Phaeton*, under the command of Captain Edward Tatham, intervened. Captain Tatham promised to turn his guns on *Montgomery* should she attempt to patrol south of the mouth of the Rio Grande. Lieutenant Hunter chose to avoid a confrontation and Captain Tatham had effectively extended a veil of protection to the Rio Grande trade and to Matamoros merchants.[131]

This was not the first occasion on which there was a major conflict between Great Britain and the United States regarding the neutrality issue at or near the mouth of the Rio Grande. An incident occurred on February 1, 1862, that could have erupted into warfare but did not due to the wisdom of commanders in charge of British and American fleets. It is understandable that such conflicts would occur between two great powers. The blockade was a massive undertaking in scope and complexity and extended the interpretations of international law into new spheres. The role was unfamiliar to the United States; for the first time in her history, she was the blockading nation rather than the recipient of such action. The situation was complicated by the proximity of three nations involved with the blockade. Place foreign merchant ships in the area, along with United States blockading vessels, and warships of Britain and France that are monitoring the situation, and what is produced? The outcome was a volatile mix that led to an imbroglio resulting from interaction between the U.S. sloop-of-war *Portsmouth* and the British steamer *Labuan*.

Portsmouth arrived at an anchorage off Boca Chica on February 1 and found ten vessels anchored there. Boca Chica is located where the mouth of the Rio Grande empties into the Gulf of Mexico. Captain Sam L. Swartwout, commanding the *Portsmouth*, found *Labuan* to be in the process of loading cotton. The British vessel had been at the anchorage for about a month taking on cotton and had on board 439 bales of the fiber, and 500 tons of coal. Captain Swartwout seized *Labuan* as a prize and sent her to Ship Island off New Orleans. The flag officer commanding the Gulf Blockading Squadron, William M. McKean, wrote a letter of censure on February 18, 1862, to Commander Swartwout for his lack of conformity to rules regulating prizes. Specifically, he was concerned that *Labuan* may have been captured while anchored in Mexican or neutral waters and therefore not a legal prize. The incident escalated with a formal objection from the British vice-consulate in Matamoros. Vice-Consul Louis Blacker contended that *Labuan* had been anchored off the mouth of the Rio Grande, which constitutes the port of Matamoros, and he suggested that the seizure was just short of piracy. Vice-Consul Blacker added that on February 5 he visited with Captain Swartwout on board the *Portsmouth* to learn why the *Labuan* had been seized. Blacker told the captain the vessel "lay in the neutral port of Matamoras [sic], the commander answered that he did not care, that he knew the cotton had come from Texas, that Matamaras [sic] was no port, that 'he would not be fooled,' but seize all cotton and every vessel carrying cotton and violating the blockade, and that he would even seize a vessel in Tampico, if cotton were found on board, and he knew it to be from Texas." Blacker protested that the matter was an outrage to the British flag. He continued by pointing out that up to February 1, neither the port of Brazos Santiago nor Brownsville was blockaded and that the Treaty of Guadalupe Hidalgo provided that neutral waters extend one nautical league north and south of the Rio Grande.

The next step was that the British warship HBMS *Phaeton* was dispatched from Veracruz by the commodore of the British squadron in the Gulf of Mexico, Hugh Dunlop, to verify facts of the case. Not to be outdone, the French steamer of war *Berthollet* also was dispatched to observe the situation at the mouth of the Rio Grande and ascertain to what degree neutral commerce had rights of entry and free trade with Mexico. *Phaeton* arrived near Boca Chica on February 16; *Berthollet* followed the next day. Commander Swartwout had "conversation of a friendly nature" with Captain Tatham of the *Phaeton*. Nevertheless, he warned Rear Admiral Farragut that anyone trying to do his job on the blockade ran a serious risk of irritating the French or British to the point that it "may bring our country in collision with these two neutral nations."

British Commodore Dunlop wrote a conciliatory letter to American Rear Admiral Farragut that said, "I trust you will unite with me in giving such orders to the captains and commanders of our respective squadrons as will as far as possible tend to suppress all vexatious and irritating questions by a strict adherence on both sides to international law." He also implied that the prize court would come to a just decision on the matter. Clearly, Great Britain wished to avoid warfare and the French would follow suit. In turn, U.S. Navy Secretary Gideon Welles issued an order on March 14, 1862: "You will instruct the commanding officers of vessels assigned to duty in that quarter [Boca Chica] to make no more captures of vessels off the Rio Grande, unless the vessels shall be on their way to a port of Texas, after having been properly warned of the existence of the blockade." War had been avoided with Europe and blockade rules had been clarified.[132]

Bagdad was destined to become the center of overland Texas trade and a base for flourishing international businesses. The village had been used since 1780 as a port of entry into Northern Mexico, but it consisted of only a few small huts. Before the Civil War, Bagdad's chief claim to fame was its beaches that had been used since the 1840s for swimming and sunning. It was to play an important role in the Civil War blockade and would become a full-fledged town of 15,000 citizens. The hamlet disappeared from the map after being struck by a hurricane in 1867.[133]

The main advantages of Bagdad were that it was on the ocean, but near Brownsville and the Rio Grande, and it had a good beach that could be used for temporary storage of goods. Its great disadvantage was the existence of an offshore sandbar that was an obstruction to reaching deep water. Lieutenant Colonel Arthur J. L. Fremantle, a member of Great Britain's Coldstream Guards army unit, came to America in the spring of 1863 to observe the Civil War. In order not to violate the blockade, he landed at Bagdad. By this time, the small town had grown to more than two thousand people. Fremantle kept a journal to record impressions of his trip and described Bagdad as he saw it. His ship anchored outside territorial waters on April 1, 1863, and the next day he crossed the sandbar. His representation of this obstacle suggests the difficulty it presented in loading steamers. Fremantle says, "the bar [had] 3½ feet of water, and smooth. It is often impassable for ten or twelve days together: the depth of water varying from 2 to 5 feet. It is very dangerous, from the heavy surf and under-current [and] boats are frequently capsized in crossing it." He adds, "Seventy vessels are constantly at anchor outside the bar; their cotton cargoes being brought to them, with very great delays, by two small steamers from Bagdad [that] draw only 3 feet of water and realize an enormous profit. Bagdad consists of a few miserable wooden shanties ... [and] for an immense distance endless bales of cotton are to be seen." The colonel gives more detail to the transport of cotton when he says that the Rio Grande is "tortuous and shallow; the distance by river to Matamoros is sixty-five miles, and it is navigated by steamers, which sometimes perform the trip in twelve hours, but more often take twenty-four, so constantly do they get aground."[134]

Other eyewitnesses, as reported by historian Tom Lea, independently confirm Fremantle's estimate of the number of ships anchored near Bagdad. These observers reported seeing 60 to 70 ships off the Bagdad bar in March 1863. By late 1864 and early 1865, this number grew to 200 or 300 ships and led Lea to describe this area as the "backdoor of the Confederacy."[135] In April 1863, Rear Admiral Theodorous Bailey, acting commander of the Eastern Gulf Blockading

Squadron, received reports that off Bagdad there were from 180 to 200 vessels of all nations waiting to discharge their cargoes and load cotton.[136]

Another visitor during this period was Admiral Raphael Semmes, commander of the Confederate raider *Alabama*. He found the seaport to be a busy town and he noted, "The beach was piled with cotton bales going out, and goods coming in. The stores were numerous and crowded with wares." The town itself had all the characteristics of frontier boomtowns.[137]

Potential rewards were abundant, but Texas shippers and merchants had their problems in maintaining an adequate flow of the desired staple. Although cotton crops were ample, the first problem was transporting that cotton to the Mexican border. The solution of this problem proved to be torturous in planning and execution. There was no railroad system of any sort, other than that north and east of Houston in the other end of the state. Initially, the usual mode of transport was the Mexican cart, constructed of timbers fastened together with wooden pegs and rawhide thongs. The wheels were seven feet in diameter, the bed was six by fifteen feet, and five or six pairs of oxen would pull the cart. Later, this cart was abandoned because it was so slow. It was replaced by a large freight wagon with running gear of solid iron, and ten or twelve mules drew it. Each wagon could carry sixteen cotton bales. Most bundles were packed in eleven yards of India bagging and bound with twelve to fifteen yards of Manila rope, although sisal was acceptable. On the wagon, a tarpaulin bearing the train number and the name of the owner covered the bales.[138]

Hundreds of these wagons and carts moved from southern Arkansas and northeast Texas, and rumbled slowly southwestward toward San Antonio and the Mexican border. From the east, Texas cotton was transported by railroad to Alleyton, just west of Houston, where the Buffalo Bayou, Brazos, and Colorado Railway ended. The terminus of this southernmost railroad in the state had been completed in 1860, and since it was on the cotton route, Alleyton became a boomtown.[139] Lieutenant Colonel Fremantle arrived in town on April 29, 1863, and said, "This little wooden village ... was crammed full of travellers [sic] and cotton speculators."[140] Cotton was then loaded on carts and made the long, slow journey to the Richard King Ranch, located 125 miles north of Brownsville. In fact, all of the various routes toward Brownsville converged on the King Ranch, and in effect, it became a cotton depot. The ranch consisted of more than 68,000 acres, providing generous space for cotton storage. Richard King had made a fortune in steamboat interests and land purchases, and his ranch was well known throughout the state. During the Civil War, he increased his fortune by entering into contracts with the C.S.A. to supply European buyers with cotton. In return, these foreign interests supplied the Confederacy with munitions, medical supplies, shoes, clothing, horses, and beef.[141] The long journey from the King Ranch toward Brownsville extended over semi-arid or desert country and it was described as "a broad thoroughfare along which continuously moved two vast, unending trains of wagons; the one outward bound with cotton, the other homeward bound with merchandise and army supplies."[142]

This manner of transporting cotton out of Texas, and military and civilian goods into the state, was hectic and inefficient. Because the transportation system could not keep pace with the requirements, much cotton sat idly in the interior awaiting ox carts or wagons. Attempts were made to deal with this by increasing the use of river transport on the Sabine River; a depot was built at a river port near Marshall. This was partially successful, but the small boats could not keep up with demand. Some problems were resolved by collecting the valuable staple at various county storage points. Collection stations located in eastern Texas would move the cotton to Houston to ship out of Galveston, while those near San Antonio and Goliad would transport the staple to Brownsville. However, cotton processors were faced with a problem associated with creating a bale of cotton. Although there were sufficient cotton presses, there were instances in which no bagging and rope were available to bale the cotton.[143]

After arriving at Brownsville, most of the cotton was transported across the Rio Grande to Matamoros, where it was delivered to the purchaser. The price of cotton at Matamoros varied according to supply and demand, as well as special factors such as bad weather affecting loading of ships at Bagdad, or the risk of fires in cotton warehouses. Cotton cost five to ten cents per pound to produce, but transportation costs and duties elevated the price. In August 1862, the going purchase price was 16 cents per pound; in November 1863, during Union occupation of Brownsville, it sold for 90 cents per pound.[144] At the end of 1863, this valuable fiber brought eighty-four cents in Liverpool; one year later the Liverpool quote reached one dollar and twenty-five cents. At the same time, the staple was quoted at one dollar and ninety cents in greenbacks in Boston.[145] At these prices, the potential was great for immense profit. One contractor invested $651,000 and grossed over $4.5 million "on non-contraband goods conveyed between two neutral ports. According to one source the lucrative war-trade produced at least ten millionaires in Matamoros and Brownsville."[146]

When the wagons or carts reached the Rio Grande, they were required to pay the Confederate export tax of one-eighth of a cent per pound of cotton, an exorbitant ferry toll, and the Mexican import duty, which varied according to which greedy warlord was in control of the area. Under Governor Santiago Vidaurri, the tariff ranged from one-half to two cents per pound, but General Cobos charged $20 per bale and General Juan Cortina sometimes charged one-fourth of a convoy's cargo. In 1863, Vidaurri was collecting about $175,000 in import duties monthly, which translated to 25,000 bales of cotton crossing the border. With the cotton in Mexico, merchants who bought it could hold it hoping for a price rise, or ship it from Monterrey or Matamoros and Bagdad. A Union general complained, "Matamoros is to the rebellion west of the Mississippi what the port of New York is to the United States. It is a great commercial center, feeding and clothing the rebellion, arming and equipping, furnishing the materials of war."[147]

Matamoros became submerged in a sea of cotton coming in from Texas and a flow of imported manufactured goods destined for Texas and the South. The cotton was loaded into light draft river steamers that took the 65-mile trip down the Rio Grande to Bagdad, or it was loaded on carts for the shorter (35-mile) land route to Bagdad. In Bagdad, the cotton usually was stored while waiting for small steamers to take it across the bar to offshore vessels that were prepared to load. There were significant delays because the bar could not be crossed when water was low. During the winter, ships could be loaded only about two days per month because of this factor. These delays were tolerated since Bagdad was not subject to an American blockade, and this was the best route to the Gulf of Mexico.[148]

Most vessels arriving with imports were from Britain or Europe, but some loaded with contraband cargoes were flying the United States flag. As one account noted, "During one four-month period in the middle of the war, some fifty-nine merchantmen, loaded with arms, military equipment, and quartermasters' stores, sailed from New York City to Bagdad."[149] Surprisingly, trade between New York City and Matamoros, which had been virtually nonexistent before war, became immense in spite of its illegality. "From August 1861 to March 1864, 152 vessels, with aggregate capacity of 35,000 tons, sailed to the Rio Grande." These cargoes consisted of military goods (pistols, carbines, uniforms, shoes, and blankets) and civilian goods (dry goods, provisions, spirits, wines, and silks).[150]

This illicit trade used two methods for shipping contraband between New York and Matamoros. The first was a "direct" system by which shipments were protected by fronts using straw men in Mexico and reliable brokers in New York. Under this system, cotton in Texas was sold to one of the import-export houses in Matamoros for the account of the planter or buyer in Texas, and shipped out of Mexico in the name of the Mexican merchant. The broker in New York would fill the order requested by the Mexican merchant that upon arrival in Mexico would be credited to an account of the Texas shipper.

If clearance could not be obtained for this direct system, or if deeper cover was needed to protect the exchange of goods and commodities, it was time to switch to an alternative, the "broken-voyage" system. With this system, vessels bound for either of the ports would ship goods to an intermediate point such as Saint Thomas or Havana. The ship papers would show this connecting port to be the destination for the cargo and it would be unloaded. The cargo would then be loaded on another ship whose papers would reveal only the second leg of the journey from the intermediate port to its ultimate destination. In this fashion, another layer of protection was added to avoid suspicion of trading with the enemy.[151]

One of the large Matamoros merchants involved in this activity was Charles Stillman, who was in partnership with Richard King and Mifflin Kenedy. During the 1850s, these men had operated a fleet of river steamers on the Rio Grande. King and Kenedy were both steamboat captains and Stillman provided much of the capital. In April 1863, the partnership of King, Kenedy, and Stillman of Brownsville became one of the chief impresarios of cotton in Texas through favorable contracts with the Confederacy. Their first contract was signed on April 28, 1862, and provided that the partnership would supply General H. P. Bee's border troops for six months. In turn, the C.S.A. government would deliver 500 bales of cotton to the firm for each of those six months. "The partners, it is estimated, made about 20% on the transaction or in specie about $60,000 each." By late 1862, the three men were shipping cotton regularly to du Fay & Co. of Manchester, England, and that fall they realized a profit of 131 percent on 636 bales of cotton.[152]

Stillman was executive director of the partnership and took care of most of the business transactions that were extralegal in nature. The firm did not consider laws against trade with the enemy to be an absolute. This perception was common among most cotton dealers, whether they lived in the C.S.A. or the U.S.A. The profit motive from cotton was a powerful stimulus, just as it was from oil and steel years later. Stillman developed methods to deal with legal restrictions. Occasionally ships would sail under British registry, and sometimes New York customs officials could be bribed to permit direct shipment from New York to Matamoros. At other times, direct shipment would be permitted upon posting a bond indicating that the shipped goods would not be delivered to Confederates.

Nevertheless, Stillman found it convenient and necessary to devise fronts to disguise his activities. A front consisted of three people: a New York broker, a Mexican citizen (a straw man), and a Texas Confederate. Stillman's New York broker was John M. Donahue, and later James Smith. Stillman developed a business relationship with the firm of Brackenridge and Bates of Texana, Texas, and this company was his prime cotton supplier.[153] The New York broker purchased goods ordered by Stillman and received the cotton shipped by him. In order to isolate himself and protect his interests, Stillman handled all his contacts and mail through his straw men, Jeremiah Galvan, Jose Morell, and Santiago Yturria in Matamoros and Monterrey. Goods from New York would be shipped in care of the straw men, delivered to Stillman's account at his Matamoros warehouse, and then quietly transferred to his Brownsville warehouse across the river.

Stillman and his partners operated a fleet of three ships and sometimes their direct shipment system was even nurtured by the Union blockade. Southern cotton was needed to manufacture Northern uniforms. On occasion, the shipper could obtain a permit and clearance for the cotton to go directly to New York City, and blockade instructions were carefully written to legalize this trade. There were fortunes to be made in this type of commerce. For example, on two shipments, Stillman's firm cleared a profit of $152,681.43 and $132,874.68. Stillman's associate, James Smith, boasted of making "a million dollars" for Stillman.[154]

The money to be made from cotton also impressed Colonel Fremantle. In a diary entry dated April 4, 1863, Fremantle wrote that he "called on Mr. Oetling, the Prussian Consul, who is one of the richest and most prosperous merchants in Matamoros." The next evening he had dinner with the Prussian consul. His diary states, "Mr. Oetling is supposed to have made a million of dollars for his firm, by bold cotton speculations, since the war."[155]

On April 24, 1862, the U.S. consul at Matamoros, Leonard Pierce, Jr., wrote, "I am afraid our Government undervalues the possession of this frontier. It is now the grand thoroughfare for their foreign mails, passengers, commissioners, cotton, or, indeed, anything that they wish. Of course all the cotton that is shipped from this port comes from Texas, and it is probable that most of the merchandise brought here finds its way into the interior of the Southern States, and were this line occupied by our armies it would be giving a heavy blow to the rebellion. I have addressed Mr. Seward on this subject."[156]

Commodore H. H. Bell of the West Gulf Blockading Squadron wrote to Secretary of the Navy Gideon Welles on August 19, 1863, and acknowledged the continued importance of the "Bagdad connection." He said, "The blockade of Texas is successfully maintained, except at the Rio Grande, where everything is in favor of the contraband traders, the shipping business at that point being chiefly in the hands of the inhabitants of the Mexican village at Bagdad, at the mouth of the river, who are mostly Texans and refugees from New Orleans, though the vessels are consigned to houses at Matamoras [sic]."[157]

The blockade of the Texas coast grew stronger as the Civil War progressed, but the flow of cotton through Matamoros and Bagdad was unimpeded throughout the last three years of the war. This evasion of the blockade through neutral territory was vital to the Confederacy and enabled it to trade cotton for untold tons of supplies with which to keep the military machine running. According to historian Ralph Wooster, "By the end of the war approximately 320,000 bales of cotton had been shipped across the Rio Grande."[158]

Chapter 4

Moves and Countermoves

By mid–1862 the war most people supposed would be over in ninety days had labored on for over a year. Both sides had experienced victories and defeats and had settled for a protracted and deadly engagement. The Union now looked for ways to strengthen the blockade, for targets of opportunity aimed at occupation of Texas land and for disruption of the flow of Texas cotton.

The Lone Star State was examining ways it might best defend itself against expected land invasions by Yankee soldiers, and diminishing the effects of the blockade. One important countermeasure was the formation in August 1861 of the Texas Marine Department, Confederate States Army, under the command of W. W. Hunter, CSN. He was given authority in September to use all available shallow draft vessels in the area to patrol Texas coastal waters and transport troops and supplies. His first act on September 26, 1861, was to charter the *Bayou City* from the Houston Navigation Company. Originally she had been a mail boat that ran between Galveston and Houston and her captain was Henry Lubbock, the brother of the Texas governor. Hunter continued to charter or acquire other similar vessels and he amassed at least 28 other ships. One of these was the *Henry Dodge* that had been seized on March 2, 1861, shortly after General David Twiggs had surrendered vast amounts of war materiel and troops. *Henry Dodge* was under the command of Captain W. F. Rogers of the U.S. Revenue Marine, who remained in that position as he willingly assisted the Confederate Army in defending the Texas coast. In December 1862, the cutter was transferred to the Army Quartermaster at Houston. In 1864 she passed into private hands, was renamed *Mary Sorley*, and operated as a blockade runner. On the evening of April 3-4, 1864, she ran the blockade in a gale out of Galveston bound for Havana and was laden with 257 bales of cotton. She was pursued by the blockading U.S. gunboat *Sciota* (a new Unadilla class screw gunboat that had been commissioned in December 1861) for two and one-half hours and was stopped at daylight 25 miles southwest of

Galveston. *Mary Sorley* was sent to New Orleans to be dealt with as a blockade prize.[159]

Another ship of the Texas Marine Department was the *Clifton*, and it also became a blockade runner. On March 24, 1864, she was carrying cotton and attempting to run the blockade from Sabine Pass when she grounded on a bar. The crew destroyed the vessel rather than allow it to be captured. The *General Rusk* (renamed *Blanche*), another department ship facing a similar fate, was bound for Havana in October 1862 and was pursued by the *Montgomery*. While attempting to escape, she ran aground at Marianao, Cuba, and was seized by a boat crew from the *Montgomery*. This seizure caused official protests from England, under whose flag *Blanche* was sailing, and from Spain, on whose neutral soil the vessel was captured. CSS *Harriet Lane* also was converted to blockade running as *Lavinia* and made one trip to Havana carrying cotton in April and May 1864. She remained there for the rest of the war. Most other vessels of the Texas Marine Department performed general transport of arms, stores, and personnel. Ships performing these duties included *A. S. Rathven, Era No. 3, Florilda, Grand Bay, Lucy Gwin, Mary Hill, Neptune,* and *Sunflower*.[160]

Fortifying the coastline to protect Texas against aggressions of the United States Navy was a high priority task. At the beginning of war, Texas found herself to be helpless in the face of anticipated Federal naval activity and invasion. The essence of coastal defense against a sea assault was to arm strategic locations with heavy artillery and to obstruct channels. There were few heavy cannons in Texas and none were mounted for coastal defense. No channels had been artificially obstructed. Texas officials moved quickly to rectify these deficiencies beginning in February 1861. At the direction of the Secession Convention, Colonel John S. Ford captured 32 smoothbore guns from Fort Brown on the Rio Grande and from Brazos Santiago. These became the first heavy cannons to be used for defense against the U.S. Navy and twelve of the guns were sent to Galveston to protect that important port. In March, additional cannons were captured at Fort Clark in west Texas. During that same month, the Secession Convention voted to build earthen fortifications at other strategic locations, including Sabine Pass, Aransas Pass, Matagorda Island, and Point Isabel. Consequently, planning and activity for erecting a coastal defense was well underway before the Civil War commenced in April 1861.[161]

On June 12, 1861, Captain of Engineers W. H. Stevens, CS Army, wrote a letter to Confederate President Davis outlining plans for defending the coast of Texas. He recommended the number of artillery pieces needed for protecting Galveston Island and the Sabine River, and suggested the number of companies of volunteers required for the two locations. Similarly, he proceeded with a discussion of the needs at the mouth of the Brazos River, at Pass Cavallo, and at Aransas Pass.[162] This letter became the outline for planning defensive fortifications. Much of the rest of the summer and early fall was devoted to recruiting men to serve coastal batteries and to secure heavy artillery from Confederate headquarters in Richmond, Virginia. Initial efforts were focused on protecting Galveston, the only major seaport in the state. Major Joseph J. Cook organized the first seven artillery companies in that area in early summer 1861; he was promoted to lieutenant colonel in December when he was placed in overall command of the growing artillery defense in and around Galveston. By the end of the year, thirteen heavy guns protected Galveston. Other artillery units were concentrated in the vicinity of Matagorda Bay and Corpus Christi, Caney Creek, and Sabine Pass. The first artillery at Pass Cavallo, which protected the entrance to Matagorda Bay, was in place by October 1861 when an earthen embankment protected four 24-pounders, two 12-pounders, and a 6-pounder.[163]

By late 1861, the blockading force west of Galveston came to recognize the importance of the town of Velasco as a favorite port for blockade runners. It was located on the Brazos River, four miles from the gulf, and the river drained a region rich in cotton. Schooners could navigate inland to serve the cotton centers of Brazoria and Columbia. Furthermore, the boat traffic between Matamoros and Velasco had increased in volume. This traffic could be readily observed at Pass Cavallo that had been fortified by Texas coast defense troops and artillery. The Union moved to correct this blockade deficiency. Union vessels began testing defenses in the Pass Cavallo area in early January 1862. On January 11, *Midnight* and *Rachel Seaman* shelled the emplacement of guns at Pass Cavallo near the lighthouse. Their mission was to force the rebels to expend their ammunition, but during the course of the 30-minute "practice," the Confederate gunners did not return fire. On the morning of January 18, the two vessels commenced firing upon the town of Velasco in Matagorda Bay. The defenders returned fire and the objective of encouraging the enemy to expend ammunition was achieved, apparently without injury to anyone. The Union vessels had gained valuable information as to the armament at these two locations and the shortcomings of their own weapons. In response to the demonstration, Major Dan D. Shea of the C.S.A. army chartered the pilot boat *Lecompt* to guard against a surprise attack on his exposed fortification, Camp Esperanza. The boat was "to act as a guard and patrol, to range through the different channels and up and down the peninsula."[164]

A few days later, Union blockader *Arthur* was in the same area. This vessel was patrolling off Matagorda Island about 17 miles north of Pass Cavallo on January 25 when she spotted a blockade runner, the schooner *J. J. McNeil*. The rebel vessel was fired upon and surrendered to *Arthur*. The schooner, which earlier had taken a load of cotton to Veracruz, was returning from there and proved to be carrying a cargo of coffee and tobacco to Indianola. She was seized as a prize. However, this type of activity on the inland passage continued throughout the war and was only temporarily interrupted by Banks's Rio Grande excursion from November 1863 to early the next year. The general pattern was that small lots would be shipped on schooners and sloops from Matagorda (located at the mouth of the Colorado River) to the Corpus Christi area on the south Texas coast. From there the cotton would be moved overland to Brownsville to avoid the Federal blockade.[165]

Major progress was made in erection of Texas defenses with the issuance of

General Paul O. Hebert's General Orders No. 34 on October 11, 1861. The directive ordered Captain Julius R. Kellersberg to construct works for batteries in Galveston Bay, and it specified gun distribution. Two months later, good progress was being made in erecting fortifications and removing channel markers.[166] Kellersberg was promoted to major the next spring, and appointed as chief engineer of east Texas. That summer he was directed to inspect Sabine Pass. In his report he noted the importance of the area, found the defense to be inadequate, and recommended improvements.[167] Major Kellersberg was ordered later to improve the defenses at Sabine Pass; on October 18, 1862 he reported he had completed the Sabine and Neches River defenses. Near Orange, Texas, he placed a 32-pounder howitzer, and about 8 miles below the town he erected a battery of two brass 32-pounder howitzers. He obstructed the channel in this area by sinking three flatboats (60 to 80 feet long and 20 to 30 feet deep) filled with shells. At the mouth of the Neches River he sank three more flatboats filled with shells and removed navigational markers. Seven miles up the river at Grigsby's Bluff, he placed two 24-pounder guns that "can blow anything out of the water that can cross the bar." Near Beaumont he proposed to mount two 12-pounder mountain howitzers. He concluded that the area is now "comparatively safe."[168] Major Kellersberg continued erecting defenses and obstructing rivers in east Texas with his engineering companies and a thousand slaves. He fortified the San Bernard River and the San Jacinto River; at the mouth of the Trinity River he built a fort and sank clamshell barges; on the Brazos River he built Forts Quintana and Velasco; and he built two forts near Harrisburg on Buffalo Bayou. All of this was done by November 1862. Significant progress had been made in developing a formidable defense against expected Federal incursions.[169]

In March 1863, the major was ordered to further improve the defenses at Sabine Pass and his principle task was to construct the new Fort Griffin that was "capable of withstanding a naval assault on the seaport city [Sabine City]." The resulting structure was solid since it was "covered with two feet of solid timber (logs), two layers of railroad iron, and four feet of earth on top." Major Kellersberg also saw that all guns were secured, mounted, and test fired. In addition, he computed elevation setting to establish distance to reach targets. This was a major undertaking and all the construction and armament was not completed until August 1863. Fort Griffin was ready to take on anything that might come its way.[170]

Meanwhile, in July 1862, elements of the West Gulf Blockading Squadron had been ordered to observe and interdict inland waterway traffic that had increased in volume because of successful blockade running from the Brownsville-Matamoros-Bagdad area, and from the Sabine Pass–Galveston locales. The United States ships imposing the barrier had been stationed at sea, and the Confederacy had been running shallow draft boats through the interior channels, lagoons, and bays. For example, from Brownsville to Matagorda, there was an inland waterway protected from the ocean and storms by a series of islands for a distance of nearly 200 miles. Small boat traffic was heavy throughout this stretch. Consequently, Federal naval officers directed their attention to a series of secondary ports serving this traffic. One area of principle interest was Matagorda Bay that served as an approach to the active minor ports of Saluria, Indianola, and Port Lavaca. A swarm of light draft vessels were found here, but the entrance to these towns was shallow and treacherous unless one was familiar with the channel.[171] Another area of concern was Corpus Christi, which had a good though shallow harbor, and underdeveloped dock and wharf facilities. It was located at the northern edge of Laguna de la Madre lagoon and significant light draft boat traffic from Brownsville would arrive at Corpus Christi. At both Matagorda Bay and Corpus Christi, cotton would be loaded for shipment out of Texas, and arriving military supplies and civilian goods would be unloaded for distribution to the interior.

On July 9-10, 1862, the U.S. bark *Arthur* was stationed off Aransas Pass just north of Corpus Christi, along with *Corypheus*, *Sachem*, and *General Butler*. On July 9, *Arthur*, in company with the yacht *Corypheus*, proceeded up Aransas Bay and captured the schooner *Monte Cristo* that was loaded with 52 bales of cotton. Later, *General Butler* captured another schooner, *Reindeer*, with a cargo of 45 bales of cotton. The bales from both boats were loaded on *Arthur* on July 10, and that ship proceeded to Aransas Pass where it waited for fair weather to go outside the bar. This cotton had been seized as a prize and it was forwarded to New York along with appropriate papers and witnesses. The next day, *Corypheus* captured the nine-ton sloop *Belle Italia* in Aransas Bay.[172]

A small Union fleet appeared at Corpus Christi Harbor on August 12, 1862, with the objectives of capturing or destroying C.S.A. vessels, testing coastal defenses, wrecking harbor facilities, and attempting to recover Federal property in that city. The fleet consisted of gunboat *Sachem*, yacht *Corypheus*, schooner *Reindeer*, and sloop *Belle Italia*. On that date, *Corypheus* pursued the Confederate ship *Breaker* and ran her aground in Aransas Bay. She was set ablaze by her crew, but the fire was extinguished. *Breaker* later was used as a tender along the Texas coast. That same day *Arthur* was at Corpus Christi and forced Confederates to burn the armed schooner *Elma* and sloop *Hannah* to prevent their capture. Lieutenant John W. Kittredge of *Corypheus* came ashore with a flag of truce on August 13, and informed Major Alfred M. Hobby (commanding rebel troops in Corpus Christi) and Judge Gilpin (chief justice of the county) that he wished to examine public buildings in town to ascertain their condition. Major Hobby informed him that there was no United States property in Corpus Christi. Lieutenant Kittredge was denied permission to land, whereupon he demanded that women and children evacuate the town within twenty-four hours since he intended to land with a force to carry out his orders. Major Hobby asked for forty-eight hours to evacuate civilians, and this request was granted. On the evening of the fifteenth, the Federal fleet assumed battle positions off Corpus Christi; at daylight on the sixteenth rebel batteries opened fire on the fleet. A gun battle between the two forces continued throughout the day with the Union fleet retiring at sunset. On April 18, the Union fleet opened fire on the C.S.A. battery and, failing to silence it, landed troops to flank the battery. The flank attack failed and the U.S. fleet withdrew to Aransas Pass.[173]

Lieutenant Kittredge and *Corypheus* were not yet done. He landed at Corpus Christi on September 12 under a flag of truce and asked permission to convey the family of E. J. Davis to New Orleans. Before the war, Edmund Jackson Davis had been the South Texas district judge. He remained loyal to the Union and was referred to by Major Hobby as "a renegade traitor of Texas." Davis had escaped to New Orleans, where he formed the First Texas Cavalry (Union) that later would be engaged in the Rio Grande expedition.

The Union lieutenant's request was not immediately acted upon. Kittredge then proceeded about fifteen miles away to the salt works on Laguna de la Madre. While patrolling there on September 14, the Union group noticed activity on land and Kittredge, along with seven of his men, boarded a small boat and went ashore at Flour Bluffs to investigate. A Confederate force under the command of Captain John Ireland surrounded the lieutenant and his men, and they surrendered. All the men eventually were paroled and returned to the North.[174]

Rear Admiral David G. Farragut now directed his attention to Sabine Pass and Galveston. Sabine Pass was of interest because it was lightly defended and was the departure point for many blockade runners. He ordered Captain Frederick Crocker to lead an expedition to Sabine Pass. Crocker arrived in that area on the morning of September 23, 1862, commanding the steamer *Kensington*, along with the schooner *Rachel Seaman*, Quincy A. Hooper, acting master. They found at anchor there the mortar schooner *Henry Janes*, Lewis W. Pennington, acting master. The next day Captain Crocker organized the vessels for the expedition and prepared by trying to kedge the boats over shallow water into the pass. He was unsuccessful in getting *Kensington* into navigable water and transferred part of his force to the other two vessels. At dawn on September 25, 1862, *Rachel Seaman* and *Henry Janes* glided into Sabine Pass after having kedged over the bar that obstructed the entrance into the pass. Both ships were ordered to reduce Fort Sabine below Sabine City or drive those manning the fort away from their guns.

At 9:00 A.M., the fort and the two-vessel fleet exchanged fire, but the range of two and one-half miles was too great for effective bombardment by the boats. Both Union ships kedged their way across the waters to come within their effective range. By 5:30 P.M. they had come within one and one-half miles and they opened fire, creating havoc for the garrison of thirty Confederate soldiers The ships hammered the fort and were outside the range of rebel rounds that fell short of the fleet. Finally, the Federal vessels ended the barrage at 6:15 P.M. and retired for the night. During the evening, the defenders assessed their situation and determined they had no way to defend themselves against the naval action. They abandoned the fort, spiked their artillery, and destroyed property they could not carry away. While the Confederates were contemplating their action, the attacking force decided to attempt a capture of the fort by land. At 11:30 P.M., a launch and a cutter, each armed with a howitzer and a crew of five men, started inshore. However, the boats were unable to get to the fort because of oyster bars and they ended their efforts at daylight. Shortly thereafter, *Rachel Seaman* and *Henry Janes* returned to the fort, found it abandoned, and then burned the barrack and gun carriages.

They found the town of Sabine City to be abandoned due to a yellow fever epidemic having decimated its population.

Yellow fever was a dreaded disease that had significant impact on other military operations on the Texas coast. By the start of the Civil War, the scourge was known throughout the nation. Through the first half of the century, it was a fearful summer visitor all along the Middle and South Atlantic coasts as well as coasts bordering the Gulf of Mexico. In 1853 terror was experienced as never before in Mobile, Alabama, and New Orleans, Louisiana. The curse of yellow fever fell on these cities with ferocity. In New Orleans, 29,000 people were attacked by this illness and 8,101 of them died. Mobile, with a population of 18,000 souls, lost 1,119 citizens. It is no wonder this fever created fear, panic and flight.

Infected people became jaundiced, displayed a yellowish pigmentation of their skin, and carried a high fever. The yellow skin and high fever prompted the name of the disease. It also has been called the "black vomit" because one of the terminal symptoms is the violent vomiting of black fluid resulting from chronic bleeding into the stomach. The medical community of that day did not know what caused yellow fever, but assumed that good preventive treatment included improving sanitary conditions and fumigation of infected areas. Since the belief was that the fever was contagious, those affected would be isolated and ships with afflicted sailors would be quarantined so as not to spread the disease ashore. Army and navy units often were required to go about their duties while facing the terror of the black vomit. However, on occasion, the military operation simply would be modified, as it was at Sabine City.[175]

On the evening of September 27, three boats from *Henry Janes* were launched at 9:00 P.M. with a mission to destroy a vital railroad bridge twelve miles north at Taylor's Bayou. This force arrived at the Eastern Texas Railroad bridge at around 1:00 A.M., set it afire, and returned to their vessel at 6:00 A.M. However, it was learned later that a guard had extinguished the fire, the damage was slight, and the bridge had been immediately repaired. On October 14, another expedition was dispatched to attempt destruction of the large railroad bridge. This raid was successful and the bridge was reduced to ruins. This action substantially concluded the Sabine Pass excursion.[176]

Meanwhile, the Western Gulf Blockading Squadron set its sights upon the port of Galveston and determined to continue the tactics of moving offshore blockading ships inshore to occupy the harbor. In May 1862, there had been a tentative probe and naval demonstration when the U.S. Frigate *Santee*, under command of Captain Henry Eagle, sailed into the harbor and demanded the surrender of Galveston. Major General Paul O. Hebert, in charge of the C.S.A. Department of Texas, directed Galveston defenses. He declined to surrender the city and Captain Eagle did not have sufficient troops with which to capture the town.[177] A more determined effort to occupy the harbor and maritime city was forthcoming.

On September 19, 1862, Rear Admiral David G. Farragut issued orders to Commander William B. Renshaw, who was aboard his flagship *Westfield* and commanded a mortar flotilla. They read, "You will proceed down the coast of Texas with the other vessels, keeping a good lookout for vessels running the blockade, and whenever you think you can enter the sounds on the coast and destroy the temporary defenses, you will do so and gain the command of the inland navigation. Galveston appears to be the port most likely for you to be able to enter, if the forts are not too formidable. I do not wish you to interfere with the officers now operating inside, unless you deem it absolutely necessary for the good of the country, in which case you will use your discretion as commanding or senior officer."[178]

At 6:00 A.M. on October 4, 1862, Commander Jonathan M. Wainwright entered Galveston Bay under orders to obtain the surrender of Galveston by peaceful means or by force. Wainwright approached the city in the *Harriet Lane* sailing under a flag of truce. It was his intention to notify the rebel commander that if Galveston did not surrender within one hour, the United States Navy would attack. *Harriet Lane* dropped her anchor within the bay and signaled for a boat from shore. None arrived promptly and it seemed to Wainwright that the Texans were purposely delaying. Commodore William B. Renshaw, commanding the gunboat flotilla, decided to join *Harriet Lane* near her anchorage and he sent forward *Westfield*, *Clifton*, and *Owasco*. As they came into the bay, a rebel battery on Fort Point opened fire; the fleet answered with heavy fire, whereupon the garrison fled the position. *Westfield* anchored and hoisted a flag of truce; a major and captain of the rebel army arrived presently and said they had been sent by the commanding officer on shore, Colonel Joseph J. Cook. Renshaw told the rebels he demanded unconditional surrender of the city within one hour. This demand was rejected; Confederates requested they be given four days in which to evacuate women and children from Galveston, after which the city would be surrendered. Renshaw agreed, with the "explicit understanding that they were not to increase the defenses of the city, and that everything was to remain as it was at the time." The Confederates returned later and accepted these conditions, with the addition that neither side would improve their positions or move any closer to the city.

These terms were agreed to, but nothing was reduced to writing. In his later report, C.S.A. Colonel Cook says he understood the agreement was "that during that time [the four day period] we should not construct any new or strengthen any old defenses with the city." Cook's understanding of the agreement permitted him to remove the guns at South Battery, plus two 24-pounders, and take them to safety at Virginia Point. Renshaw learned of the withdrawal of this artillery and concluded that he had not been sufficiently clear that these guns were to remain where they were. He demanded of the rebels that the guns be returned to their original positions. The Southerners demurred, indicating they thought they had acted in good faith and regretted that they may have misunderstood Renshaw's verbal instructions. Renshaw decided to leave it that way, and not seize the guns by force, because there was a yellow fever epidemic in the city that he did not want spread to his men. Galveston was then surrendered to the United States and the victory was celebrated with a symbolic one-half hour rising of the American flag at the customhouse.[179] Commodore Renshaw eventually withdrew from the bay because he had too few men to occupy Galveston. An unofficial gentleman's agreement had been reached that neither side would try to occupy the city so as to avoid subjecting the remaining citizens to gunfire, and exposing troops to yellow fever. However, neither side expected that this would be a permanent arrangement.

By the middle of 1862, the United States had confirmed it was hopeless to try to completely seal off the Confederacy by simply patrolling coastal waters. The Union changed its strategy. The new blockade was revised to include an additional element, that of mounting amphibious operations involving both the army and navy. The intent was that the navy would seize essential inlets and ports and the army would garrison these seized locations with infantry and artillery. The positions would then serve as forward bases of operations for the navy. This strategy had worked on the East Coast and was to become navy doctrine in the years to come.[180]

On October 15, 1862, Rear Admiral David G. Farragut, commanding the Western Gulf Squadron, wrote to Gideon Welles, secretary of the navy, "I am happy to inform you that Galveston, Corpus Christi, and Sabine City and the adjacent waters are now in our possession." He added that he needed soldiers to hold the places and needed vessels of light draft to work inside in shallow waters, as well as a few heavy vessels for outside work. He emphasized that the blockade was decidedly more effective with vessels working inside the harbor rather than obstructing the entrance from the outside.[181]

The last phase of this Union naval action took place when Renshaw left Galveston to capture Port Lavaca in Matagorda Bay. It was another haven for blockade runners. He moved with two vessels, *Westfield* and *Clifton*, arriving off the town at 1:00 P.M. on October 31, 1862. These two vessels were well suited for shallow water work and bombardment. Previously, they had functioned as Staten Island ferryboats that were designed to carry heavy loads and could operate in coastal waters. Renshaw informed the defenders of his intent to bombard, gave the town ninety minutes to evacuate civilians, and then commenced a gun duel with two rebel batteries. During this exchange of gunfire, the barrel of the heaviest gun on the *Westfield* burst. Thereafter the fight was inconclusive. At nightfall, the two ships retired out of range of the Confederate batteries but returned the next morning. The town did not surrender, but Renshaw's force departed after firing 252 rounds at the Confederates. No one was killed but the town was described as being a wreck. Major Daniel D. Shea, in command of the garrison there, reported, "The enemy succeeded in doing considerable damage to the town ... tearing up the streets and riddling the houses and otherwise damaging the place."[182] Further, Lieutenant George E. Conklin, the post adjutant at Lavaca, stated that "the ladies of the place, among whom Mrs. Chesley and Mrs. Dunn and the two beautiful and accomplished daughters of the former bore a conspicuous part, acted the part of true Southern heroines, supplying our tired soldiers with coffee, bread, and meat even during the thickest of the fight."[183]

From this activity over the last six months of 1862, the Union learned what they were doing right and what they were doing wrong. The Federal establishment determined it had sufficient ships with which to accomplish objectives, but putting men on prize ships diminished the number of sailors available to man the blockading vessels. Additionally, the thinning of the rank and file of crew members meant there were fewer men available for shore parties, and there was no infantry. The navy found it difficult to maintain any gain it had made; it was certain that more closely coordinated army and navy action was required.

The Confederacy had learned some lessons as well. They discovered they were vulnerable to hit and run attacks by the mobile U.S. naval force. Unhappily, the C.S.A. became aware that they had no navy worthy of the name. It seemed obvious that the Confederacy, in order to improve its defenses, needed to have an adequate supply of gunboats to maximize efforts of its troops on shore.

Near the close of 1862, the United States Navy enjoyed considerable success through a number of victories that resulted in a more effective blockade in eastern Texas. It had closed much of Matagorda Bay, and Indianola and Port Lavaca had become relatively impotent. This was true in Corpus Christi Bay as well, and the town there was reduced in importance. A more effective barrier had been established at Sabine Pass and the important port of Galveston had surrendered to the Union without a fight. Since the winter season was approaching and the yellow fever epidemic had ended, Federal troops were on their way to garrison Galveston and hold her securely so that she might serve as a Union enclave and forward supply base for future naval operations.

At the same time, the Confederacy was acting to counter the intentions of the Union. The C.S.A. found little to celebrate, but that fall Confederate headquarters assigned a new commander to Texas. He was Major General John B. Magruder, a veteran of the Mexican War and a commander of C.S.A. forces during the Peninsular Campaign earlier that year in Virginia. He took command of the District of Texas on October 10, 1862, and held this position until the end of the Civil War (his responsibilities later were enlarged to include New Mexico and Arizona). Magruder immediately gave hope to Texans as he began to assess the situation and develop a strategy for reversing U.S. progress in the area. He was determined to regain control of the harbors in coastal Texas; his first objective was Galveston harbor. Specifically, he set in motion a plan to gain control of the city of Galveston with its port facilities intact. After this was accomplished, he hoped to make Sabine Pass accessible to the Southerners.[184]

General Magruder quickly realized that this strategy could not be implemented without gunboats. There were none, but there were small river steamers available, and they would require armor and weapons to earn the title of "gunboat." Magruder was familiar with the concept of "ironclad" and "tinclad" in the east, but these riverboats were too light for such heavy armor. He was aware, however, that the concept of using cotton as a type of armor was not unknown in these waters, because it had been utilized in the capture of the *Star of the West* by Colonel Van Dorn onboard the *General Rusk* on April 17-18, 1861.[185] General

Magruder determined that he would armor his gunboats with 500-pound bales of cotton stacked on the decks. These compressed bales could stop the flight of a minnie ball or a rifled bullet in most instances, which would protect a portion of the vessel and personnel aboard. To properly become a gunboat, it obviously needed guns, or some kind of armament, and Magruder decided that army field pieces or obsolete naval guns would suffice.

He ordered that these "cottonclads" be constructed at shipyards in Houston and Beaumont, and he bought suitable vessels for conversion to gunboats. One of those purchased was the *Bayou City*, which had served as a merchant steamer in Galveston Bay before the war. This steamer was converted to her new role as a gunboat by removing her pilot house and placing cotton bales "on their narrow sides three high, backed by another row lying flat, providing breastworks and firing platforms for sharpshooters.... The bow [had] a refurbished 32-pounder, converted into a rifle." Another purchased steamer was *Neptune* and it was armed with two 24-pounder howitzers. Two other ships served as tenders and the fleet was placed under the command of Major Leon Smith of the C.S.A. army. Smith had skippered mail steamships in the Pacific Ocean and Gulf of Mexico earlier in his career; Magruder had known him from his army days while serving in the west.[186]

Since the vessels were rigged for sharpshooters, some expert marksmen were needed and they were found in the Sibley Brigade. These veterans had marched under the command of Brigadier General Henry H. Sibley across Texas and New Mexico, where they had fought two battles in their quest to extend the Confederacy to the Pacific Ocean. As a result of that mission's failure, the brigade had returned to San Antonio demoralized, and with a cloud hanging over its head. A sense of failure was about to be diminished. Colonel Tom Green of the Fifth Texas Cavalry and Colonel Arthur Bagby of the Seventh Texas Cavalry had volunteered their units to serve as sharpshooters on vessels that were to participate in the recapture of Galveston. Perhaps this was an act of bravado, an effort to repair damaged reputations, or an attempt to improve the morale of the men, or all three. In any event, Magruder agreed with the plan that was presented to him by the two colonels. Later, Colonel Green addressed the two regiments of the brigade and said, "I want 300 volunteers who are willing to die for Texas, and who are ready to die now. Volunteers will step two paces to the front."[187] Volunteers eagerly stepped forward and on the last day of the year they marched from their camps east of Houston.

Meanwhile, Federal Companies D, G, and I, of the Forty-second Massachusetts Infantry Regiment, under the command of Colonel Isaac S. Burrell, left New Orleans on December 21, 1862, on the steamer *Saxon*. Remaining companies of the regiment were to follow. Colonel Burrell and his 260 men had been ordered to Galveston by Major General Nathaniel P. Banks with the instruction that they protect the citizens of that city who remained loyal to the Union, and recruit soldiers for military service with the United States.[188] The three companies arrived at Galveston on December 24. On the advice of the fleet commander, Commodore Renshaw, Colonel Burrell landed his force on Kuhn's Wharf at the edge

UNITED STATES STEAMER HARRIET LANE. *Harriet Lane* was captured at the Battle of Galveston Bay. A paddle wheeler was often used in shallow water because it carried less draft than a ship driven by a screw. (Guild Press of Indiana, Carmel, Indiana.)

of the city on Christmas day. He immediately reconnoitered and found a Confederate battery of three guns near the city at Eagle Grove and a large gun situated in the middle of the bridge connecting the island with the mainland. On the other end of the bridge, at Virginia Point, he found a strong battery mounted with heavy guns. Colonel Burrell estimated the force facing him as consisting of 2,000 men.[189] The U.S. fleet in the harbor consisted of Commodore Renshaw's flagship *Westfield*, mounting eight heavy guns; *Harriet Lane* commanded by Captain Wainwright, carrying four heavy guns plus two 24-pounder howitzers; *Owasco*, mounting eight heavy guns; *Clifton*, with four heavy guns; *Sachem* with four heavy guns; plus two armed transports, two large barks, and an armed schooner.[190]

After he learned that Yankee troops were arriving at Galveston, General Magruder readied land defenses at the same time his cottonclads were being prepared. He reported that he had at his disposal "six siege pieces, the heaviest weighing 5,400 pounds[,] a railroad ram, armed with an 8-inch Dahlgren and mounted on a railway flat ... and fourteen field pieces, some of them rifled and some smoothbore."[191] Magruder had decided to attack as soon as possible to prevent a troop buildup and to destroy U.S. infantry as soon as they landed.

Around noon on December 31, 1862, the volunteers from the Sibley Brigade,

UNITED STATES STEAMER WESTFIELD. During the Battle of Galveston Bay, *Westfield* exploded, killing her skipper and several crewmen. (Guild Press of Indiana, Carmel, Indiana.)

armed with Enfield rifles and shotguns, took their places aboard two cottonclads, *Bayou City* and *Neptune*. They began their journey toward their staging point on the bay, arriving there around 1:00 A.M. on New Year's Day. The soldiers were not too impressed with their gunboats and one said of his steamboat, "we found it a joke." Once aboard, they learned that their "armor" would not protect them from the Union navy's large-bore solid shot, shell and grapeshot. The men became serious, somber, and nervous.[192]

On land, General Magruder placed his artillery along a line of two and one-half miles within the city limits. At moonset around 4:00 A.M. he opened fire, while a storming party attacked the warehouse where the Forty-second Massachusetts Infantry was arranged in a defensive position. The artillery fire by Magruder's men primarily was directed upon the fleet, and the U.S. ships immediately responded. *Westfield* ran up the channel to come to the assistance of ships firing on the rebel artillery, but she grounded herself on Pelican Island, where she lay useless throughout the battle. The firing on both sides continued until daylight. At this time, the two rebel gunboats, *Bayou City* and *Neptune*, engaged *Harriet Lane*, and attempted to ram her on both sides. In the process, *Neptune* was sunk, but *Bayou City* cleared the decks of *Harriet Lane* with her destructive small gun fire, and powered her bow into the Union vessel. The infantry on *Bayou City*

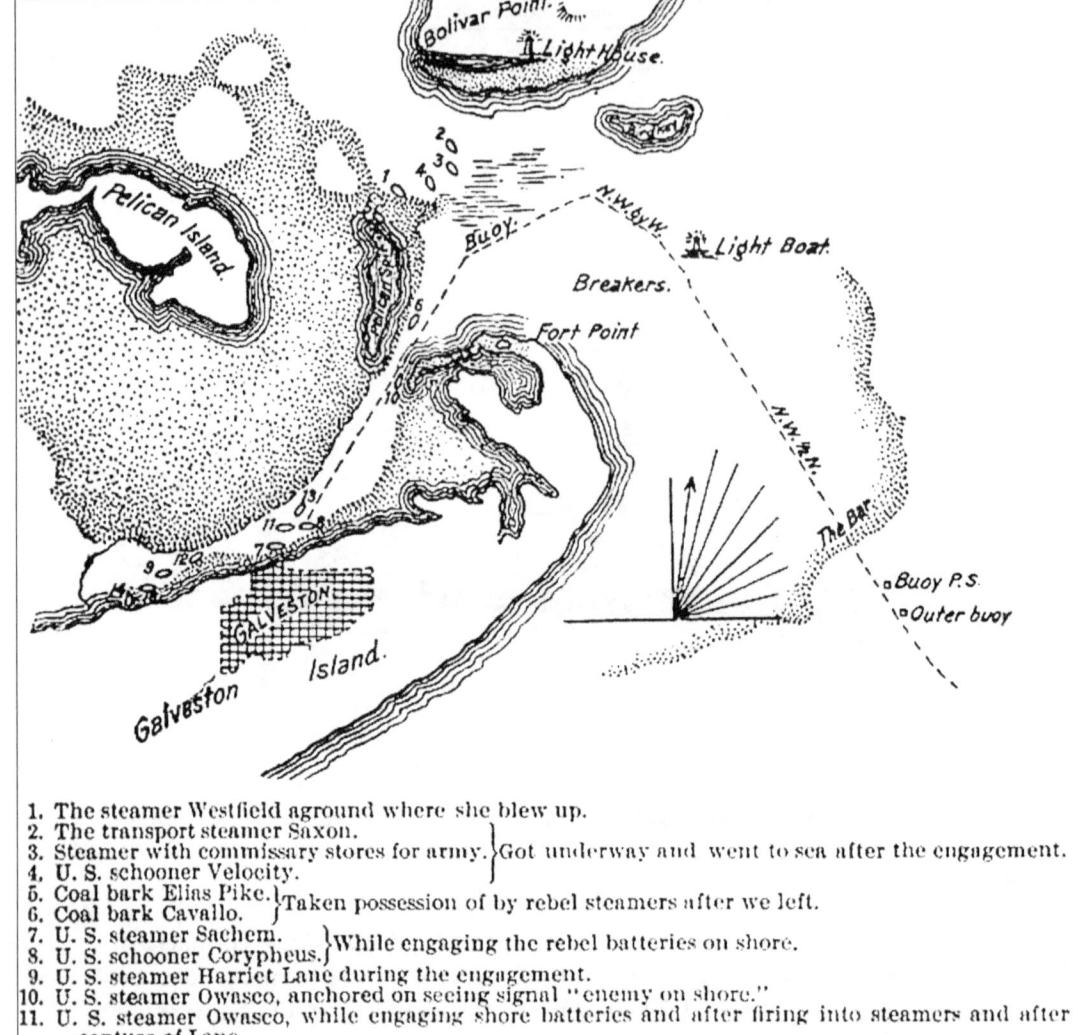

DIAGRAM OF BATTLE OF GALVESTON BAY, JANUARY 1, 1863. This sketch describes the position and action of ships engaged in the Battle of Galveston Bay. Union navy and army forces were badly beaten. (Guild Press of Indiana, Carmel, Indiana.)

boarded the ship after a short battle and Commodore Leon Smith demanded her surrender. The Captain, Jonathan M. Wainwright, along with his executive officer, Lieutenant Commander Edward Lea, were both mortally wounded and *Harriet Lane* was surrendered by surviving officers. Major Smith then sent a boat to the *Clifton* demanding that the fleet surrender. Lieutenant Commander Richard L. Law received this message and asked for a waiting period of three hours so he might consult with fleet Commodore Renshaw on board the *Westfield*. The request was granted and he discussed the situation with Renshaw.

Commodore Renshaw was adamant that the fleet should not surrender. He directed Law to get all vessels out of the bay as soon as possible, adding that he would blow up the stranded *Westfield* so it would not fall into enemy hands, and board one of the transports. On his return from *Westfield*, Law rowed close to *Corypheus* and instructed Acting Master A. T. Spear to "wait until the flags of truce are hauled down; then make sail and escape." The three-hour period was drawing to a close and suspicious Confederate officers got into an open boat under a flag of truce to close negotiations. It was around 10:00 A.M. and *Westfield* suddenly exploded as the result of a charge placed by order of Renshaw. Unfortunately, the explosion was premature and went off before Renshaw, two officers, and two crew members were clear of the vessel. They were killed in the explosion. In the confusion, the remaining ships in the fleet that could flee to the gulf did so. The Confederates had no vessels capable of pursuing them. In the meantime, the company of U.S. soldiers at Kuhn's Wharf surrendered; the Battle of Galveston Bay was concluded.[193]

The Confederate States of America had recaptured Galveston in one of their most successful military actions of the Civil War. The C.S.A. forces captured a steamship (*Harriet Lane*), two supply ships (*Cavallo* and *Elias Pike*), and one schooner (*Lecompte*); another steamer (*Westfield*) was sunk. In addition, the rebels captured fifteen artillery pieces and a large quantity of stores, coal, and other materiel, as well as three companies (240 men) of Union infantry. C.S.A. losses were light. *Neptune* was sunk but most of her officers and crew were saved. Confederates reported a loss of 26 killed and 117 wounded.[194] Casualties on the Union side were somewhat heavier. About twenty of the men in the captured Forty-second Massachusetts Infantry Regiment had been wounded and the United States Navy had over 150 casualties.[195]

The next day the Federal steamer *Cambria* arrived outside Galveston Island with two companies of the First Texas Cavalry, horses of the Second Vermont Battery, and refugees from New Orleans. Since there was no sign of a pilot, they came to anchor as nightfall arrived. The next morning they waited for a pilot boat until noon, and then sent in a boat to announce their arrival. That boat never returned. On January 4, a pilot boat arrived to bring in *Cambria* but the U.S. vessel recognized a ruse. A rebel was posing as a Union pilot but finally admitted the town had fallen to the Confederates. The men who had taken the boat in earlier were prisoners. *Cambria* returned with haste to New Orleans.

This final episode of the Battle of Galveston underscores the importance of the C.S.A. victory. The United States had hoped to establish a foothold in Texas, recruit Union loyalists into military service, and mount an invasion into the interior, or failing that, at least secure a forward supply base for naval incursions farther down the coast. Not only was this effort thwarted, but also it would result in Galveston remaining as the only seaport still in Confederate hands at war's end.

Two years later, General Nathaniel P. Banks reflected on the Union defeat at this maritime center. On April 6, 1865, he wrote Secretary of War Stanton and lamented the loss of Galveston "as the most unfortunate affair that occurred in the department during my command. Galveston, as a military position, was second in importance only to New Orleans or Mobile." He added that if the U.S.A. had been victorious at Galveston, "It would have held a large force of rebel troops in the vicinity of Houston, enabled us to penetrate the territory of Texas at any time ... and rendered unnecessary the expedition of 1864 [the Red River Campaign] for the re-establishment of the flag in Texas."[196]

All of this was a tremendous morale booster for the Confederacy; it demonstrated that a daring commander and a little fleet of cottonclads could defeat the invincible United States Navy. Texas men fighting in the east could look toward their Lone Star State with some assurance that she would stand strong and be there upon their return. The *Houston Telegraph* wrote that the recapture of Galveston was "the most brilliant affair of the war." Meanwhile, Rear Admiral David Farragut fumed that the battle "was the most melancholy affair ever recorded in the history of our gallant navy."[197] Events that would soon occur would not improve his mood.

On January 3, 1863, Farragut reacted to the changed situation at Galveston by ordering the 2,000-ton screw steamer *Brooklyn*, under the command of Commodore H. H. Bell, to leave her blockade station at Mobile and proceed to Galveston. Her orders were to retake Galveston and *Harriet Lane* if possible, and shell rebel troops. She was to be joined by six gunboats from the Mobile squadron. *Brooklyn* reported that she arrived off Galveston at daylight on January 7 and noticed a work party erecting earthworks for artillery positions. *Brooklyn* then shelled this point and with other arriving ships maintained the blockade.

The Confederate raider CSS *Alabama*, under the command of Captain Raphael Semmes, had been built in a private shipyard in Great Britain for the Confederacy and was launched on May 15, 1862. Commander Semmes had captured a vessel on December 7, 1862, near the coast of South America. While there he read newspaper reports that Union General Banks was preparing an expedition for the invasion of Texas with an intermediate stop at Galveston. Semmes deduced that Banks's transports would reach Galveston around January 10, 1863, and he departed South America's coast on January 5 bound for Galveston. Captain Semmes hoped to find a lightly defended fleet of U.S. transports within that harbor. He expected to fire upon them and destroy the fleet. *Alabama* arrived near Galveston about 3:00 P.M. on January 11, 1863, but Semmes changed his plans when he found only Union warships firing on Galveston with no transports in the harbor. He had no intention of engaging a fleet of Federal warships. Unfortunately, the Confederate raider was detected first by a lookout on *Brooklyn*. The *Alabama* was about to find herself in the unusual position of being the pursued, rather than the pursuer.

Around 3:30 P.M. on January 11, Commodore Bell sent a signal to Captain Homer C. Blake, commanding the *Hatteras*, to investigate the appearance of an

UNITED STATES STEAMER BROOKLYN. On January 7, 1863, this steamer arrived on station at Galveston to maintain the blockade. On January 11, she dispatched USS *Hatteras* to investigate smoke on the horizon. The ship making the smoke was the famous Confederate raider CSS *Alabama*. (Guild Press of Indiana, Carmel, Indiana.)

unidentified bark-rigged vessel well off to sea, assuming it to be a blockade runner. The Federal warship moved seaward and the mystery ship fled into the night toward the southeast. *Hatteras* gained on the stranger; by 7:00 P.M. it was dark and they met. *Hatteras* turned her broadside to the vessel in order to be able to fire four guns if necessary, and Blake hailed the ship asking, "What steamer is that?" The reply was, "Her Britannic Majesty's ship *Vixen*." (First Lieutenant John McKintosh Kell was executive officer of *Alabama* and he writes that they initially identified themselves as *Petrel*.)

Captain Blake replied that he would send a boat to examine their papers, whereupon the other ship turned her broadside toward *Hatteras*, saying, "We are the Confederate steamer *Alabama*" and immediately fired a broadside. Because of her greater speed underway, she was able to outmaneuver *Hatteras*, which was a converted merchantman. At close range, musket and pistol shots were exchanged. *Alabama* struck *Hatteras* with a number of shells, two of which produced separate fires below deck. Another shell exploded in the engine room and disabled *Hatteras*, while shells entered the vessel at her waterline. The ship rapidly began sinking; the crew was evacuated, and taken on board *Alabama*. Ten minutes later

CSS Alabama sinks USS Hatteras. This 19th century print depicts USS *Hatteras* (on the right) sinking after receiving broadsides from CSS *Alabama* off the coast of Galveston, Texas, on January 11, 1863. (Naval Historical Foundation.)

Hatteras sank, having gone down bow first 28 miles off Galveston. Powerful armament, good marksmanship, and superior machinery for propelling *Alabama* were largely responsible for her quick and decisive victory.[198]

On January 15, Rear Admiral Farragut communicated with Navy Secretary Welles about the fate of *Hatteras*, saying, "It becomes my painful duty to report still another disaster off Galveston."[199] Of course, he was referring to the loss of Galveston closely followed by the sinking of the warship *Hatteras*. He wrote of these matters on April 22, 1863, to his counterpart commanding the eastern blockading squadron in the Gulf of Mexico and said, "You say truly, my friend, that one disaster begets another; the capture of the *Harriet Lane* and the abandonment of Galveston was not only the most unfortunate thing that has ever happened to the Navy, but the most shameful and pusillanimous."[200]

Another discomforting event confronted the U.S. Navy. In sending *Brooklyn*

OFFICERS OF CONFEDERATE RAIDER ALABAMA. This August 1863 photograph shows Captain Raphael Semmes, *Alabama*'s commanding officer, standing by his ship's 110-pounder rifled gun. His executive officer, First Lieutenant John M. Kell, is in the background near the ship's wheel. (Naval Historical Foundation.)

and her six consorts from Mobile to Galveston, the Mobile blockade was weakened. Farragut's squadron had gotten thin enough so that a C.S.A. ship in Mobile Bay decided this might be an opportune time to get through that formidable barrier. This Confederate ship was *Florida*. She had steamed into Mobile four months earlier because of a yellow fever epidemic on board and had been bottled up ever since. Commander John Maffitt decided to run out at night under the cover of a northwest gale. *Florida* ran the blockade on the evening of January 15-16 and commenced a cruise that would result in the capture of twenty Union merchant ships within the next seven months.[201] The U.S. now had two Confederate raiders—*Florida* and *Alabama*—to contend with in the gulf. Chasing them deprived the Union of blockading ships needed elsewhere.

The United States Navy was confused and thrown off balance by these recent events, and was to be further embarrassed four days later. Following the recapture of Galveston by the C.S.A., General Magruder moved to destroy blockading ships off Sabine City to the east. He sent Company F of the First Texas Heavy Artillery, commanded by Captain Frederick Odlum, and Company B, led by Captain K. D. Keith, to Orange east of Beaumont where two steamboats were being outfitted with cannon, cotton bales, and heavy oak timbers. These soon-to-be cottonclads were the *Josiah H. Bell*, a large (412-ton) steamboat that was equipped with a single 6-inch Columbiad rifled cannon, and the *Uncle Ben*, a smaller (135-ton) steamboat equipped with two 12-pounders on the bow. Captain Keith's company was to fire these latter two cannon, while gunners from Captain Odlum's company were to discharge the weapon on *Josiah H. Bell*. Sharpshooters manned the cotton bale walls and the two vessels left on January 20, 1863, to seek out blockading ships off Sabine Pass. The blockade vessels *Morning Light* (a clipper ship) and *Velocity* (a small 87-ton schooner) sighted the two columns of smoke and hoisted sail to attempt escape. After a 30-mile sea chase, the Federal ships came within range at two miles' distance, and *Josiah H. Bell* fired with her rifled cannon upon *Morning Light*. This cannon fire damaged the main mast rigging of *Morning Light*, making it difficult to maneuver in a way so as to enable her guns to bear upon the Southern vessels. When the two steamships closed to rifle range, sharpshooters cleared the decks of both Union vessels, and thirteen men were hit on *Morning Light*. With both attacking vessels knocking holes into her hull, *Morning Light* surrendered and *Velocity* surrendered soon thereafter. C.S.A. vessels had seized 109 U.S. sailors and two Union ships.[202]

The rebels were jubilant, lagging spirits were lifted, and morale was boosted through capturing these two United States vessels, recapturing Galveston, and the exploits of the *Alabama* and the *Florida*. The harbors of Galveston and Sabine City were free of blockading ships. All this would help sustain Texan morale during the following lull in action in this part of the United States, and throughout the upcoming double Federal victories at Vicksburg and Gettysburg. After the Vicksburg triumph in July 1863, the Union had armaments, troops, and ships available in the west for another assault upon Texas.

Meanwhile, 35,000 French troops occupied Mexico in 1863. President Lincoln was anxious to establish a United States presence in Texas to signal the French that their troops in Mexico represented a disregard of the Monroe Doctrine. There was, however, disagreement between the president and some of his military leaders. While Lincoln wanted troops in Texas, General Grant and other military figures felt the war could be fought to better advantage by taking Mobile and applying the "anaconda squeeze" to the heart of the Confederacy. The president asserted himself in correspondence to General Grant dated August 9, 1863, when he said, "I see by a dispatch of yours that you incline quite strongly toward an expedition against Mobile. This would appear tempting to me also, were it not that, in view of recent events in Mexico, I am greatly impressed with the importance of re-establishing the national authority in Western Texas as soon as possible. I am not making an order, however; that I leave, for the present at least, to the General in Chief."[203]

President Lincoln had made himself quite clear and so had General-in-Chief Henry Halleck on August 6, 1863, when he had written a letter to Major General Nathaniel Banks in New Orleans indicating, "There are important reasons why our flag should be restored in some point of Texas with the least possible delay. Do this by land at Galveston, at Indianola, or at any other point you may deem preferable. If by sea, Admiral Farragut will co-operate. There are reasons why the movement should be as prompt as possible."[204] General Banks correctly perceived this to be a firm and direct order and he moved with alacrity. He had a grand strategy in mind that involved Sabine Pass and Sabine City because of the eastern Texas railroad that ran from near Sabine City to Beaumont, and the Texas and New Orleans railroad that ran from Beaumont to Houston. The general plan was that after seizing these two railroad lines, the Yankee army would be able to push into Houston, capture Galveston with an attack from the rear, and fan out to strategic locations in the Lone Star State. If successful, eastern Texas would be conquered and the rest of the state would be sealed off from the Confederacy.[205]

Banks decided he would send a joint navy-army expedition to Sabine Pass, establish a foothold on the west side of the pass, and send his army to Houston. From there, the army could proceed southward toward Galveston, occupy the peninsula joining it with the mainland, and isolate that port. That city would be blockaded from the sea, under siege by the army from the mainland, and would be starved into submission. Perhaps then he would be able to move up the Sabine River toward Shreveport, Louisiana, and seize the cotton in east Texas and western Louisiana. Furthermore, he would fly the flag along the way as a signal to the French.

Banks issued orders to Major General William B. Franklin on August 31, 1863, that he was to immediately assemble designated troops to load on transports awaiting him in New Orleans. The order specified that gunboats were to precede the transports and cover the landing of troops "for the immediate occupation of some important point in the State of Texas where the Government of the United States can permanently maintain its flag." Further, he was to "proceed to Sabine Pass, Tex., and if you find that the navy has succeeded in making the landing feasible, you will disembark your whole force" and attempt to seize the railroad at some point between Houston and Beaumont.[206]

General Franklin commenced preparations for the attack by meeting with his naval counterparts, Commodore Henry H. Bell, commanding the West Gulf Blockading Squadron, and Frederick Crocker, captain of the USS *Clifton*, who had conceived the outline of the operation in July 1863. The plan that was developed called for vessels to arrive off Sabine Pass the evening of September 6. Its success was partially dependent upon the element of surprise, but Southerners became aware of the vast assembly of ships and their destination in advance of that date due to confusion and miscalculation.[207]

General Franklin left New Orleans on September 4 with approximately 5,000 infantry troops and five batteries of artillery; on September 6, the force was joined by gunboats, enlarging the group to twenty-seven vessels. The fleet commander,

Lieutenant Frederick Crocker, had all ships prepared for attack upon Sabine Pass by the evening of September 7. Near sunrise the next morning, four gunboats (*Granite City, Sachem, Arizona,* and *Clifton*) crossed the bar and for an hour and a half shelled the fort from a distance of three miles. Since the defenders returned no fire, Lieutenant Crocker was uncertain if the fort was occupied.[208]

Failure of the defenders in the fort to respond to this shelling was by design. Fort Griffin, as it was designated, had been newly constructed during the spring and summer and it had six guns consisting of two 32-pounder smoothbores, two 24-pounder smoothbores, and two 32-pounder howitzers. Forty-seven soldiers of the First Texas Heavy Artillery (commonly known as the Davis Guards and under the command of Lieutenant Richard W. Dowling) manned the defenses in this fortification.[209] Moreover, these men were well trained by Dowling and he had used the month of August to hone their skills. He had planted marker posts in oyster bars 1,200 yards in front of the fort to mark the maximum range of his guns, and then held gunnery practice on a nearby sunken hulk of a schooner. During the course of the artillery barrage that morning, Dowling and his men crouched in nearby "bomb proofs." Next to the primed and loaded guns, they had stacked cannon balls and ample powder sewed in flannel.[210]

Around 3:00 P.M., Federal gunboats firing their weapons approached the fort. Dowling withheld his fire until the vessels came within range as indicated by his markers. Sabine Pass was divided into two channels by the presence of an oyster bar in the middle. The channel to the east was designated as Louisiana channel, while the channel to the west was designated as Texas channel. The *Sachem* led the advance up Louisiana channel followed by the *Arizona*. Dowling waited until the *Sachem* had passed the designated markers, then he directed the fire of his six guns upon her. A cannon ball soon pierced her boiler, which exploded and scalded many of the men. The disabled *Sachem* ran aground. Meanwhile the *Clifton*, followed by the *Granite City*, was proceeding up the Texas channel and all the guns of the fort were then trained upon the *Clifton*. She experienced similar horrors. *Clifton* lost her steering and was grounded on an oyster bed. Her boiler likewise was hit, releasing billowing clouds of steam under pressure. The C.S.A. batteries pounded *Sachem* and *Clifton* until they struck their colors and surrendered.

This left Dowling in something of a dilemma. There were only 47 Confederates available to accept and guard 350 prisoners, and he feared being overpowered and captured by his prisoners. Fortunately, General Magruder had directed Southern reinforcements toward the scene hours earlier when he became aware of the presence of the U.S. fleet. Upon their arrival, Dowling's dilemma was resolved.[211]

The *Arizona* and the *Granite City* fled the scene and in their haste grounded on a mud flat, from which they were pulled off. During the ensuing confusion and panic, the transports *Continental* and *Suffolk* collided and the transport *Crescent* grounded herself. The first two transports suffered only minor damage, but *Crescent* could get off the bar only by throwing 20,000 rations into the Gulf of

Mexico. General Franklin decided the defense at Sabine Pass was formidable. Since he had lost half of his gunboats in the fray, he determined he could not land the troops. Having gained nothing, the battered fleet returned to New Orleans in a state of shock.

In a remarkable battle, Lieutenant Dowling and his small group had not received a scratch, but the men were exhausted from loading and firing more than 100 cannon balls during the 40-minute engagement. Two of their six guns had been destroyed in the process. Dowling had captured the two gunboats, 13 heavy cannons, and 350 prisoners. The Union had lost these prisoners plus 100 men killed or wounded, the two gunboats, and 20,000 rations. The remaining Federal fleet lost more than that during the return voyage when it encountered a fierce gale. The storm damaged the transport *Laurel Hill* and she lost her smokestacks in the heavy seas. In order to avoid sinking, the vessel had to be made lighter and this was accomplished by throwing cargo overboard. Sadly, 200 mules made up the cargo they chose to jettison into the ocean. The army mules died in the service of the United States of America. It was an inglorious end for the Union.[212]

People of Texas were overjoyed and showered Dowling and his men with their gratitude, as did the C.S.A. government. President Davis had a special medal struck for each of the defenders. Lieutenant Dowling said his men had behaved as heroes. In forty minutes or so, the men had captured two Union gunboats, killed or wounded 100 of the enemy and captured 350 more. The defenders had turned back an invasion armada of 5,000 troops, five batteries of artillery, and 27 vessels. The Dowling force suffered no casualties. General Magruder "lauded the artillerymen as 'the greatest heroes that history recorded.'" The Confederate congress passed a resolution signed by President Davis that described the battle as "one of the most brilliant and heroic achievements in the history of this war." Years later, Jefferson Davis said that this battle had "no parallel in the annals of ancient or modern warfare." Others noted that the heroines of Sabine Pass were local residents Kate Dorman and Sarah Vosburg, who, during the battle, had delivered coffee, doughnuts, and a gallon of whiskey to the weary and grimy soldiers![213]

The real benefit of this episode to the South was that it prevented the United States from occupying Eastern Texas, Sabine Pass was kept open for blockade running, and supplies coming in through it would aid the Confederacy in the upcoming Red River campaign. It was a much needed morale builder for the South, which had to endure the recent fall of Vicksburg and the defeat at Gettysburg. Although Texans were not aware of this at the time, the year 1863 would stand as the high water mark of the war effort by the Confederacy in an around Texas. A remarkable string of Confederate victories had commenced on New Year's Day 1863 in Galveston Bay and had concluded on September 8 in Sabine Pass with the one-sided victory by a rebel artillery battery against a combined navy and army Union force. In between, the sinking of the *Hatteras* by the *Alabama* and the escape of the *Florida* through the blockade left two dangerous Confederate raiders roaming the gulf. In January, the Confederates had broken the obstruction at Sabine

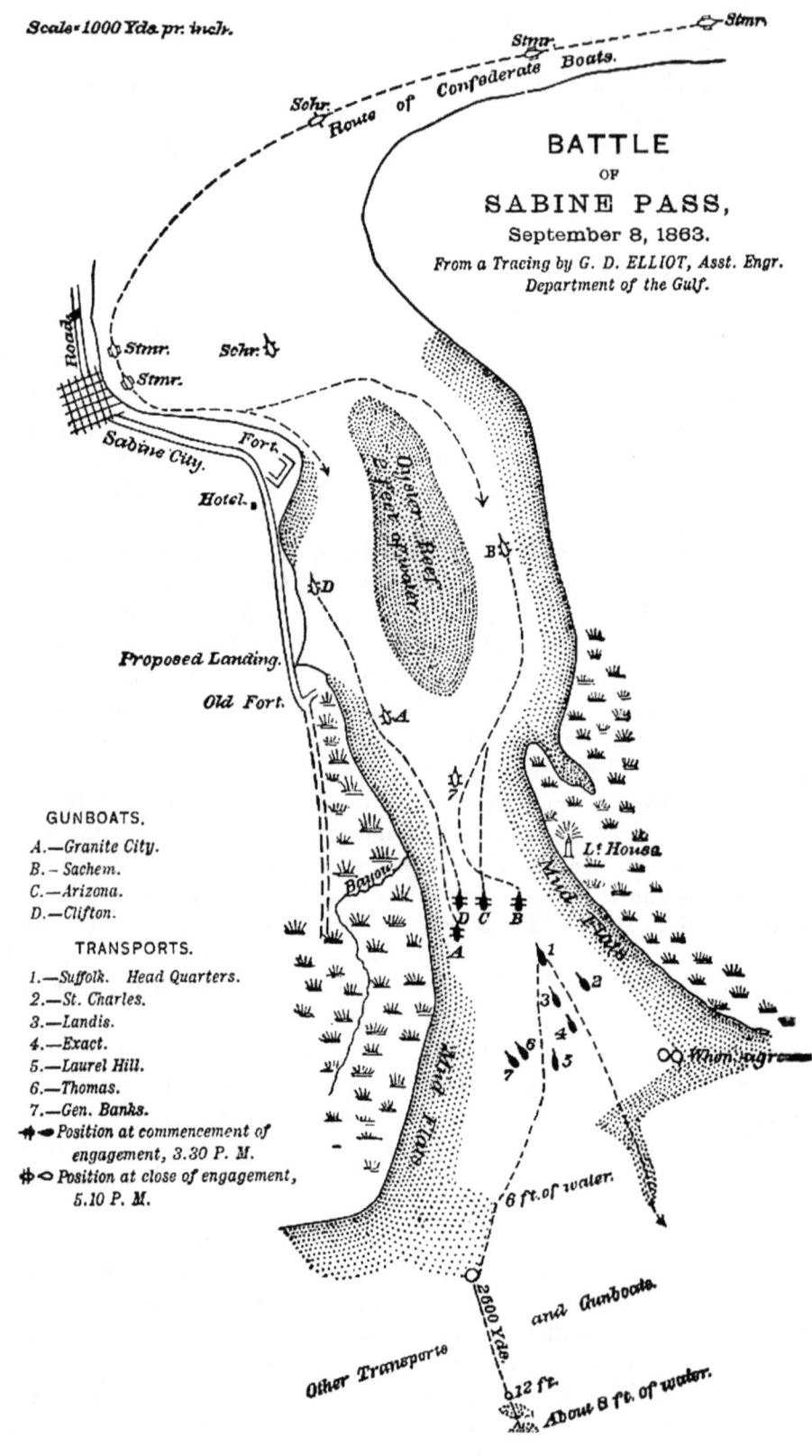

Pass and had captured two blockading ships. The September 8 episode was something like icing on the cake.

People of the United States were less joyous over this debacle. Their defeat was a loss of face, and the U.S. Navy came away believing the fort at Sabine Pass was impregnable. In General Banks's report to General Halleck, he deflects blame for the disaster away from himself and toward the navy. In his communication, Banks first softens the blow: "It is with regret that I am obliged to report that the effort to effect a landing at Sabine Pass was without success." Then he goes on to say, "The immediate cause of the failure was the misapprehension of the naval authorities of the real strength of the enemy's position, and the insufficient naval force with which the attempt was made." General Banks fails to mention the small size of the force defending against the armada. In addition, he chooses not to reveal that the C.S.A. fort had only six cannon facing the 26 guns of the four Union gunboats.[214] He complains about the heavy draft of the U.S. vessels and adds, "The attack would have been successful as it was had the boats been adapted to the waters in which they engaged." Regarding the Battle of Sabine Pass, Fred Harvey Harrington, General Banks's biographer, states, "Sound in outline, this campaign was thrown away by bad planning, the lack of army-navy cooperation, and a series of incredible mistakes." Andrew Forest Muir echoes this sentiment and unequivocally states, "The plans were impeccable and fitted the facts. Had they been executed with a reasonable degree of efficiency, there can be no question that most of Texas would have been returned to the bosom of the United States in September, 1863."

In any event, a future Red River campaign is clearly on Banks's mind in his report when he says, "It is impossible to move up the Red River at this season ... on account of the low stage of water. I have constantly borne in mind your suggestion as to a movement from Alexandria or Shreveport [to Texas] but the low stage of the water makes it impracticable at this season."[215] The Red River campaign was Halleck's favorite plan for invading Texas and when this campaign was launched the next year, Banks's concern about low water would come back to haunt him.

One result of this 1863 activity in coastal Texas, and on her offshore waters, was something that had not been anticipated by either side when the year opened. That was the diplomatic activity related to the blockade that would be stirred up by these rebel victories. After the Confederate successes at Galveston and Sabine Pass in January 1863, C.S.A. Secretary of State Judah P. Benjamin sent formal correspondence to the British consul at Galveston (and other consuls) that stated, "The blockade of the Port of Galveston [was] at an end." Benjamin went on to say this information was being forwarded "for the guidance of such of the merchants of your nations as may desire to trade with either of the open ports of

Opposite: DIAGRAM OF BATTLE OF SABINE PASS, SEPTEMBER 8, 1863. **This sketch of the Battle of Sabine Pass depicts the action that led to a stunning Union defeat. (Guild Press of Indiana, Carmel, Indiana.)**

Galveston and Sabine Pass."[216] General Magruder followed up with his own series of proclamations dated January 5, 20, and 21, 1863, all of which said that a blockade did not exist, and therefore the ports of Galveston, Velasco, Lavaca, and Sabine Pass were open to trade. The proclamations indicated that the blockading fleet had been withdrawn, and they invited "friendly neutral nations to resume commercial intercourse with this port."

Commodore H. H. Bell of the *Brooklyn* then issued his own proclamation, dated January 20, 1863, in which he warns that "The port of Galveston, and also Sabine Pass, as well as the whole coast of Texas, are under an actual blockade by a sufficient force of United States vessels [to maintain it]."[217] Federal Secretary of State Seward supported Commodore Bell's proclamation by indicating that although the blockade might have been interrupted, it was immediately resumed.[218]

Chapter 5

A Snarl: Cotton, Politics, and Foreign Involvement

Cotton in the South frequently has been called "King Cotton," and generally, this has referred to the economic and social impact of this agricultural product. Cotton meant much more than that. This commodity became an important plank in the foreign policy platform of the Confederate States of America. Much of that policy early in the war was guided by a belief that cotton was supreme and that European nations would quickly come to the aid of the Confederacy in order to sustain their supplies of that valuable staple. Senator James H. Hammond summed it up best on the floor of the U.S. Senate on March 4, 1858, when he said, "You dare not make war upon cotton! No power on earth dares make war upon it. Cotton is king."[219] Texas Senator Louis T. Wigfall addressed the same body on December 6, 1860, and expanded that perception about the plant when he proclaimed, "I say that cotton is king, and that he waves his scepter not only over these thirty-three States, but over the island of Great Britain and over continental Europe, and that there is no crowned head upon that island, or upon the Continent, that does not bend the knee in fealty and acknowledge allegiance to that monarch."[220]

What has been less understood is that this fiber largely dictated military strategy and much of the military tactics in coastal Texas, and on her offshore waters during the Civil War. In the Gulf of Mexico region, the blockade was designed to stop the flow of cotton out of the area and interdict a return flow of merchandise and military supplies. Texas land war was devoted to supporting the blockade, since it was found that combined land and naval action was essential for the most effective blockade. As has been seen, the Union had been unsuccessful in more rigidly enforcing the blockade in east Texas. In 1863 Southern forces had blunted an amphibious operation at Sabine Pass and had reclaimed

Galveston harbor. In west Texas, the Union had attempted to stop the flow of cotton out of the Confederacy, but the Lone Star State countered by establishing arrangements whereby cotton could be transported to Mexico. From there, it was exported from the Mexican port of Bagdad without interference from the U.S. Navy that would not dare blockade a neutral port. The cotton trade was thriving in the Brownsville-Matamoros-Bagdad triangle and the Mexicans and Confederates were pleased with the profitable arrangements for both sides. Interestingly, the greatest threat to this symbiotic venture was France; it was this menace that drew the United States to this theater of operations. The Union's Rio Grande Campaign would be launched to discourage French movement toward Texas and to tighten the blockade along the line of the Rio Grande.

France had long been interested in Texas. Its flag had flown there because of early explorations by that nation in the late seventeenth and early eighteenth centuries. Trading posts and small settlements were established, but it was not until the formation of the Republic of Texas that French interest in the Lone Star State peaked. In 1839, the French government sent A. Dubois de Saligny, who was an administrative assistant at the French legation in Washington D.C., to Texas to explore the possibilities of recognizing the Republic of Texas as an independent state or nation. France did subsequently recognize the new republic and Dubois, or A. de Saligny, was appointed chargé d'affaires on September 25, 1839. Following his appointment, he established a legation in Austin, Texas, and signed a treaty of amity, navigation, and commerce. Saligny's initial mission was to propose legislation to the republic that would result in French colonization in Texas.[221] Because of his efforts, two Frenchmen introduced the Franco-Texian Bill into the Texas Congress on January 12, 1841. The bill was "An Act to Incorporate the Franco Texian Commercial and Colonization Company," and it called for the company to introduce 8,000 families into the republic and maintain twenty forts to protect these settlers for twenty years. The bill ultimately failed, but French efforts to colonize Texas continued and the most successful of these efforts was the colony founded by Henri Castro in September 1844.[222] He had obtained a land grant that promised him more than a million acres of land if he would introduce at least 600 families or single men within three years. Settlers came to the Medina River, just west of San Antonio, and the town of Castroville was founded. Henri Castro brought more immigrants from France, established other less successful colonies between 1843 and 1846, and in all 2,000 immigrants arrived in Texas under his auspices. By the start of the Civil War, there were over 10,000 Texas citizens whose nationality was French.[223] French attention to Texas would continue throughout the Civil War.

Mexico in 1861 was trying to recover from a half century of civil war, combat with foreign powers, and internal conflicts arising from power struggles between liberals and conservatives. These wars and political instability had nearly bankrupted the republic. The country was disorganized and in debt when the Liberal Party candidate, Benito Juarez, was elected president. One of the first acts of President Juarez and the Mexican Congress in July 1861 was to suspend interest payments on foreign indebtedness for two years. Major countries to which Mexico was in debt (for $62 million) were Great Britain, France, and Spain; they did not take kindly to this debt moratorium. European bondholders had been promised overdue payments from funds obtained by Mexico through the Gadsden Purchase.[224] These compensations were not made and bondholders sought immediate satisfaction so they might reap their expected financial windfall. Napoleon's representative to Mexico was Dubois de Saligny (the same man who had served as the French agent to the Republic of Texas) and he urged a retaliatory strike against the Mexican ports of Tampico and Veracruz until reparation was paid. Napoleon was assured that any military resistance from Mexicans would be minimal.[225]

The three European powers had a common self-interest of private enrichment; they met to determine an appropriate response to the Mexican snub. On October 31, 1861, at the London Convention, they signed an agreement to occupy ports and military points in Mexico until that country paid her debts. Apparently, the original understanding was that these nations would occupy the customhouse (and collect duties) at the Port of Veracruz, where it was expected that income generated by that busy port would pay off obligations. They also had concurred that they would not interfere in Mexico's internal affairs. Initially, Spain landed an army of 6,000 men at Veracruz in December 1861; France (with a brigade), and Great Britain (with seven hundred marines) followed in January 1862.[226]

It quickly became clear, however, that the French emperor, Napoleon III, had more ambitious notions than just recovering a loan. Professor Steven P. Topik of the Department of History, University of California, Irvine, points out that "the debt was largely an excuse. ... [T]he more central motive ... was a drive for colonial conquest.... France had been undergoing unprecedented economic growth. Its factories were seeking foreign markets and raw materials, and its capitalists were becoming interested in overseas investments."[227] Because of its mineral wealth and lands available for cotton cultivation, France sought Mexico. The French flag was already flying in Africa, Asia, and the Middle East and a floundering Mexico may have appeared to the emperor to be a suitable target for colonial conquest. Napoleon III probably had in mind establishing a presence in Mexico in order to regain the glory of his famous uncle and to block the expansion and power of the United States. In any event, as England and Spain grasped Napoleon's ambitions and intentions, they began withdrawing their troops. By March 1862, all the English troops had been withdrawn except for a few marines that garrisoned Veracruz. The Spanish force had been reduced by one or more battalions.[228]

On September 7, 1863, C.S.A. Secretary of State J. P. Benjamin sent to John Slidell, his agent in Paris, France, an extract of a letter written by a professor from the University of Virginia who claimed he had a one-hour interview with the French emperor in 1860. During the interview, Napoleon outlined his grandiose ambitions. The professor stated that Napoleon III had in mind receiving compensation from Mexico "for the lost colonies in the West Indies." In addition, he saw it necessary to establish a foothold "on the Florida coast for the purpose of protecting her commerce in the Gulf." The professor additionally concluded that Napoleon III "revolved in his own mind the possibility of recovering a foothold in Louisiana."[229] This is a remarkable document because the author purports to be directly reporting Napoleon's plans for the New World. These may be splendid plans that are not based on reality. Instead, they may be only a dream issuing from lust for power. The problem with the document itself is attempting to assess its probative value. We are told it is an extract so we do not know what else was said, and how this extract fits into the whole letter. A further complication is we are not told who is the author of the communication, and therefore cannot assess the writer's accuracy and veracity. However, the missive cannot be dismissed, because it falls in place with similar events that are discussed below.

In 1862, an agent by the name of Benjamin Theron was stationed in Galveston, Texas, where he was both the French consul and vice-consul for Spain. In August, he wrote a letter to Governor Francis Lubbock raising the question as to whether Texas would be better served by reestablishing itself as a republic rather than being a member of the Confederate States of America. Governor Lubbock replied that the Lone Star State preferred being in the C.S.A. instead of returning to an independent status and he forwarded Theron's letter to President Jefferson Davis with a warning that the French were developing a suspicious plot. Later, a French consular official in Richmond voiced the same issue and C.S.A. Secretary of State Judah Benjamin became convinced that the French were conspiring to separate Texas from the Confederacy.[230]

On January 29, 1863, A. Dudley Mann of Brussels, Belgium, reported to Secretary Benjamin that "his Imperial Majesty aims steadily at the restoration of Mexico as it was prior to the independence of Texas."[231] This, of course, would revoke Texas's status as part of the United States of America and the Confederate States of America. Similarly, Secretary of the Navy Gideon Welles stated on July 31, 1863, "Louis Napoleon is making an effort to get Texas." On September 21, 1863, a Vienna, Austria, newspaper wrote, "The French government is supposed to have arranged with the American Southern States for the cession of Texas...."[232] The Vienna newspaper quote is a good example of how rumors can be spread and the air was saturated with such rumors in 1863. Nevertheless, all of these opinions and rumors may outline the general intentions of France.

One recent scholar concurs with the idea advanced by Secretary Welles— that Napoleon had in mind seizing "Texas in the name of Mexican territorial 'restoration' or French-Mexican expansionism." He sets forth another theory as well: that French- controlled Mexico could establish trade agreements with the Confederacy that would counteract the Union's strategic plan of depriving her of much or her resources, prolonging the war as a consequence.[233] Another scholar believes that Louis Napoleon hoped for "a strong and friendly Confederate States of America [that] would create a buffer between what remained of the United States and his new Mexican possessions. Secession appeared so consequential to Europe because it again exposed the western world to European partition."[234]

Historian David P. Crook says there is no doubt that Napoleon's motive for invading Mexico was to establish "a Catholic, Latin-cultured empire rivaling the creations of the Anglo-Saxons to the north." Crook also confirms that the French ruler had plans that are even more grandiose: he may have had in mind "that a French-controlled Mexico would be expanded to include Texas, and possibly the old colony of Louisiana."[235] In view of the material advanced above, the most plausible motivation that might be attributed to the French invasion of Mexico is that of territorial conquest.

Napoleon apparently felt Mexico would be a relatively easy conquest because she was weakened by years of internal conflict and he expected to find support from the defeated Conservative Party. In addition, he may have had visions of supporting rebel armies in their battles so that after a Confederate conquest of the Union, portions of the former United States might be awarded to the French for their aid. Confederate President Davis gave the French invasion of Mexico a slightly different twist. His viewpoint was that the invasion would cause the United States to challenge that intervention because it conflicted with the Monroe Doctrine. Therefore, the French would seek an alliance with the South and this would assure the independence and success of the Confederacy. Neither side seemed to consider the possibility that the Lincoln administration would steer a very careful course toward neutrality and follow the maxim of "one war at a time."[236]

To carry out these activities, Napoleon began strengthening the French army in Mexico to the point that 6,500 well-trained men were accumulated. The Spanish army and British marines had withdrawn from Mexico after it became clear that Napoleon III had more on his mind than money. The general of the French Forces, Charles Ferdinand Latrille de Lorencez, was confident and boldly proclaimed, "We are so superior to the Mexicans in race, organizaion [sic], morality, and elevated sentiments that as the head of six thousand soldiers I am already master of Mexico." Early in 1862, the French army composed of 5,000 men moved toward Puebla, 65 miles southeast of Mexico City, and attacked Puebla on May 5. Two thousand Mestizo and Zapotec Indians under the leadership of Ignacio Zaragoza defended the town. Their arms were poor, they were outnumbered by more than two to one, and they defeated a superior European army.[237] Over one thousand French soldiers died. The French emperor was concerned that an inferior force had defeated his army. This fact caused him to cast a wary eye at the strength of the United States army. He resented the Monroe Doctrine and was aware his presence in Mexico was a challenge to that creed. He was concerned that if the Union won the war, his action might evoke an American response. Napoleon reacted to the rebuff at Puebla by sending another 30,000 troops to Mexico. In June 1863, the French conquered that country by taking Mexico City.

Napoleon III then turned to Ferdinand Maximilian Joseph. Maximilian was Archduke of Austria and he was offered the position of emperor of Mexico, which he accepted in 1864.[238] One of his early activities as emperor was to strengthen his hold on the states to the north that bordered the Rio Grande, and he began to move his men toward Matamoros. There was uncertainty on both sides of the border as to the degree to which the French might disrupt cotton trade that had been established between Mexicans and Confederates, especially since soldiers were moving that way. In referring to this lucrative cotton trade between the Confederacy and Mexico, historian Ronnie C. Tyler unequivocally states, "The most serious threat to the profitable international commerce was the French invasion of Mexico."[239]

At the time of movement of the French army toward the states of Coahuila and Tamaulipas, Texas and the Confederacy had been working with these local governments and other points in Mexico for several years. They had been developing necessary marketing arrangements to get cotton out of Mexico, and to get war materiel and consumer goods back to Texas. Confederate President Davis sent a number of agents to the border states of Mexico; his first selection, on May 17, 1861, was John T. Pickett, who was named "as agent of the Confederate States near the Government of the Republic of Mexico."[240] Pickett was selected for this task because he had served at Veracruz as the U.S. consul there and had developed a relationship with President Benito Juarez. He was said to be forceful and shrewd, but of quick temper and sharp tongue as well. His instructions were to pursue the matter of border security for trafficking in cotton and war goods and to establish friendly relations. However, Pickett turned out to be tactless and lacking discretion. For example, he was asked if he was seeking Mexican recognition and he replied, "To the contrary, my business is to recognize Mexico—provided I can find a government that will stand long enough."[241] Not only did his mouth get him into trouble–so did his fists. When a Yankee attacked the credibility of the rebel government, Pickett became involved in a fistfight and was arrested as a common criminal. He was jailed and then expelled from Mexico for his combative behavior. He returned to Richmond to find that President Davis and his cabinet were outraged and angry about his conduct. Frank Lawrence Owsley makes the final diagnosis when he states that "Pickett was no diplomat."[242]

After its initial stumble in diplomacy in Mexico, the C.S.A. government turned next to Juan A. Quintero.[243] On May 22, 1861, the new agent was given instructions to make contact with Santiago Vidaurri, the governor of the states of Nuevo Leon, Coahuila, and later Tamaulipas. Vidaurri was a strong ruler of these northern border states and a nominal supporter of President Juarez. Quintero intended to reach an agreement with Vidaurri about border security, foster Vidaurri's friendship with the Confederacy, and determine the extent of natural resources in those states. On his part, Vidaurri expected that a closer relationship with the Confederates would help him resist Juarez's attempt to centralize authority and minimize Vidaurri's autonomy in the northern states of Mexico. Both the Confederacy and Vidaurri recognized the importance of the geographic location of Mexico. It could provide a means for evading the Federal blockade. Vidaurri stood to profit from Mexican products that could be sold to the C.S.A. at exorbitant prices, and from high tariffs that could be imposed on imported goods. He promised Quintero that he could secure the Mexican side of the border against the raids of marauding bandits. Further, he assured the diplomat that

Yankee troops would never be allowed to go through northern states that he controlled in order to reinforce their garrisons in Arizona.

These talks were most gratifying and resulted in a strong bond between Quintero and Vidaurri. Quintero wrote the Confederate State Department that "I have been entirely successful in my mission.... We have gained an ally."[244] One result of these talks was the establishment of a network of commercial relationships in northern Mexico. A number of large firms emerged in the northern border states of Mexico for furnishing supplies to the Confederacy in exchange for cotton. For example, "A. Urbahan of San Antonio, operating with Milmo and Company of Monterrey, contracted to deliver a million pounds of flour in exchange for 850,000 pounds of cotton." Milmo and Company was the largest of many such firms. "Patricio Milmo, head of this company, was Governor Vidaurri's son-in-law, and it appears that Vidaurri had his own financial stake in the company." Vidaurri wrote a personal letter to President Davis in which he said he could "supply as much ammunition as the Confederacy would be able to use."[245]

Quintero was not the only agent in Mexico who was enjoying a degree of success. In April 1861, the United States had dispatched Thomas Corwin to Mexico as its minister to the Juarez government. He was a very effective diplomat whose first mission was to counteract the efforts of Pickett. Further, Corwin was instructed "to convince the Mexican government that the safety and existence of Mexico depended upon the restoration of the Union, for the success of the Confederacy would be followed by the conquest of Mexico."[246]

Corwin discussed with Secretary of State Seward the possibility of loaning Mexico money to pay the interest on her indebtedness to European nations. She had suspended payment of her debt in July, and Corwin thought the intervention threatened by European nations in Mexico could be prevented if the United States paid the interest on the obligation. He feared that suspension of debt payments would give France and her allies an excuse for acquiring Mexican territory, but thought that paying the interest would secure Mexican independence. What Corwin had in mind was having a lien placed on Mexican land to guard against default on the American loan. This loan would amount to $11 million over five years. Corwin was aware he was outbidding Pickett, who, at the same time, was offering to purchase Mexican recognition with $1 million "judiciously applied."

Seward wanted to know reactions of England and France to the notion of the United States guaranteeing interest payments on Mexican debt. He wondered if this action would deter those powers from intervening in Mexico; he was not going to waste U.S. money if they were determined to intrude. In September 1861, Seward directed the United States minister in France, William L. Dayton, to interview the French foreign minister, Edouard Thouvenel; Dayton reported that France intended to interpose in Mexico because "France wanted the principal and not the interest."[247] England and Spain were of the same mind and in November made a joint agreement to intervene in Mexico. Consequently, the United States dropped the idea of a loan for payment of interest on the debt.

In spring 1862, Vidaurri gained control of the state of Tamaulipas that had within its borders the ports of Matamoros and Tampico. This opened trade through Matamoros to other Mexican ports and that was of interest since the water to the north of the mouth of the Rio Grande was being blockaded by the United States. Eventually, the village of Bagdad, on the south bank of the Rio Grande and not subject to the United States blockade, became the port of choice for shipping goods in and out of Mexico. By the end of 1862, commercial trade was in full swing and Bagdad had emerged from a small, dusty town to a busy port. Vidaurri continued to be extremely cooperative.

During 1862, a number of merchants in Matamoros and Monterrey became eager to trade for Texas cotton. Quintero proceeded to negotiate a number of important trade agreements with well-established businesses that had extensive contacts in Mexico and with the international community. The trade in this staple quickly began to pay off for Texas and the Confederacy and the Mexican merchants prospered as well. The glitter of cotton not only drew specie to finance the war effort. It additionally attracted about anything desired: war supplies (sulfur, lead, saltpeter, and small arms), foodstuffs (flour, coffee, sugar), and manufactured good (cigars, shoes, blankets, rope and twine).

There was concern, however, that the French could disrupt the cotton pipeline across the Rio Grande to Matamoros and on to Bagdad. The French occupation of Mexico City in June 1863 hastened the northern flight of President Juarez just ahead of the invading army led by General Achille Francois Bazaine. Governor Vidaurri had never been an ally of President Juarez; he was distressed that the president's movement northward ultimately could weaken the governor's autonomy in the northern provinces. Furthermore, Vidaurri realized that if the French occupied Matamoros, he most likely would lose his control of cotton trade in the state of Tamaulipas.[248] Finally, in February 1864, Governor Vidaurri received an offer from General Bazaine to join in the French intervention, and a command from President Juarez that he participate in the resistance to the French. Vidaurri chose the course of least resistance and fled to Texas, leaving the Mexican president and the French general to settle the dispute between them. Elements of the French army soon occupied Matamoros, but with sound groundwork laid, Confederates were able to establish good relationships with the French. There followed a new boom in uninterrupted commerce because everybody stood to gain from this commercial intercourse.

Northern states of Mexico continued to cooperate in their intermediary merchant roles, greatly profiting as exporters of cotton and importers of manufactured goods. The French and C.S.A. needed one another. The Confederate States of America continued to court France as a potential ally. The French continued to maintain an interest in colonizing Texas or establishing a trade colony there; this required Texas's cooperation and its independence from the United States of America because the U.S.A. would never permit this degree of foreign involvement in one of its states. In short, neither France, nor Mexico, nor Texas, nor the Confederacy could profit from a serious disruption in trade.

M. M. Kimmey was vice-consul in the U.S. Consulate at Monterrey and on

October 29, 1862, he shared his observations with Secretary of State Seward. Kimmey stated that for the past year there had been a flow of goods and armament between Texas and Mexico, "but within the past three or four months the trade has grown to be of great magnitude, and it is increasing every day." He added, "Enormous quantities of cotton, belonging to the Confederate Government and in charge of agents, are constantly arriving here [and] in return for the cotton[,] goods suitable for the Army are sent back, and from the great amounts it would seem that enough goods go from and through this place to supply the whole rebel army. An order came here a few days ago for 600,000 blankets suitable for soldiers." The vice-consul observed that "Large trains are daily leaving ... loaded with blankets, shoes, leather, cloth cotton goods of all kinds, coffee, rice, sugar, powder, saltpeter, sulfur, medicines, and, in fact, almost everything needed to supply the wants of the rebels."[249] Seward forwarded this communication to Secretary of War Stanton on December 16, 1862, saying the information "strongly illustrates the importance of occupying the line of the Rio Grande and cutting off the large supplies which the rebels are receiving from that quarter."[250]

Secretary of the Navy Gideon Welles likewise recognized the threat represented by the Matamoros trade. In an April 22, 1863, entry in his diary, he wrote, "An immense trade has sprung up on the Rio Grande.... Ostensibly the trade is with the little city of Matamoras [sic], but it is notoriously a Rebel traffic." He suggests that the government must "adopt some preventive measure; if not, the blockade will be evaded and rendered ineffectual."[251] Welles voiced his concern once again on June 18, when he wrote Seward that "the condition of affairs on the Rio Grande and at Matamoras [sic] was unsatisfactory.... Our blockade is rendered in a great degree ineffective because we cannot shut off traffic ... with the Rebels via the Rio Grande."[252]

Looming on the horizon was an external threat to this profitable trade now that the Union was recognizing its expansiveness. This threat was that the United States might interfere through insertion of troops at Brownsville. However, internal problems revolving around the pricing structure of cotton were of immediate concern for the Texans.

The cornerstone of foreign policy of the Confederate States of America at the outbreak of war was placement of an embargo on production and export of cotton. It was anticipated that because of lack of availability of this commodity, large textile industries in Great Britain and France would face bankruptcy. In turn, those enterprises would pressure their governments to restore flow of the fiber. The price of removing the embargo and restoring the flow of cotton would be recognition of the sovereignty of the C.S.A. by these European powers. For a number of reasons, this policy failed. France and Britain did not recognize the C.S.A. as an independent nation.

By the second year of the war, the C.S.A. acknowledged the failure of this foreign policy plank. The Confederacy realized it could not continue with a cotton embargo; selling this staple was mandatory in order to finance their war machine. Consequently, the embargo was lifted, the staple was planted, and the fiber began flowing to market in the second half of 1862. By year's end, cotton trading again became the most profitable enterprise for the South, but men became greedy. The Confederacy was finding it harder to compete against private speculators and was being squeezed out of the market. Obviously, this disruptive situation could not continue for long; the resulting confusion, disorganization, mismanagement, and bungling needed to be resolved for the good of the Confederacy. The C.S.A. was in a calamitous situation and clearly something had to be done about it, and quickly. Many leaders in Texas believed the only solution to this problem was for the C.S.A. government itself to regulate cotton trade.[253]

The Confederate States of America had the man to deal with this difficulty and his name was Lieutenant General Edmund Kirby Smith. General Smith had served in the Mexican War and had been active in major campaigns in the Eastern Theater at First Bull Run and the Battle of Perryville. In January 1863, he went to Richmond to aid in reorganization of the army. The next month he was transferred to the Trans-Mississippi Department that had been created on May 26, 1862, to encompass Texas, Indian territory, Arkansas, Missouri, and west Louisiana. He was transferred on February 9, 1863, to take command in west Louisiana and Texas, and on March 7, 1863, he assumed command of the entire Trans-Mississippi Department that included all rebel forces west of the Mississippi River. While the C.S.A. did control the western portion of Louisiana, it did not control any territory in Missouri. However, Missouri had a strong pro–Southern contingent that formed a Confederate state government that enacted an ordinance of secession. It was admitted as the twelfth state in the Confederate States of America on November 28, 1861, but following secession, the new Confederate state government was driven out of Missouri and thereafter existed as a government in exile. After the fall of Vicksburg in July, the Trans-Mississippi area was cut off from the rest of the Confederacy and in effect became a separate command. Because of General Smith's strong control over the area, it came to be known as "Kirby-Smithdom."[254]

In mid–July 1863, President Davis wrote a letter to the general acknowledging that the Trans-Mississippi Department had been cut off from the Confederacy. He suggested that the department is "in a new relation" with the C.S.A. The president added, "You now have not merely a military, but also a political problem involved in your command." Davis suggested that General Smith meet with the four Trans-Mississippi governors to deal with issues arising from this "new relation."[255] Secretary of War Seddon also wrote Smith about the same time, and in the letter (which has been lost), he apparently referred to Smith's becoming involved in the administration of civil affairs as well as military affairs.[256] Secretary Seddon is somewhat vague in his August 3, 1863, communication to General Smith. He states, "It is impossible to give you from here special instruction as to the measures to be adopted [to defend the Trans-Mississippi states]. They must be left, in large measure, to your superior knowledge of the circumstances of your command and to a wise discretion." He goes on to support communication with the governors of these states.[257]

On July 13, 1863, Kirby Smith had called for a meeting of governors and Supreme Court justices from the four states to convene in Marshall, Texas, on August 15, 1863. On July 25 he issued a general order directing that all future orders to the personnel in the Department of the Trans-Mississippi would be issued by him and not by President Davis. Further, on his own authority, General Smith announced in general orders on August 3 that a cotton bureau was being created within the department to supervise "the purchase, collection, or other disposition of Government cotton."[258] On August 15, the "Marshall Conference," with governors and Supreme Court judges of Texas, Louisiana, Arkansas, and Missouri, convened.

This "Marshall Conference" actually was the second of three such meetings. Marshall was selected as the meeting site because of its geographic location in northeast Texas near Arkansas and adjacent to Shreveport, Louisiana. The town was the seat of Harrison County, one of the most populous counties in the state. Marshall had a population of about 3,000 people and numerous governmental and military offices were located there. Confederate officials and the governor from Missouri had relocated to Marshall after a Union government was installed in that state.[259] Texas governor Francis R. Lubbock had called the first Marshall Conference in July 1862 at the suggestion of President Jefferson Davis. At this time Union forces were threatening to gain control of the Mississippi River and some of the Trans-Mississippi states were fearful the Richmond government might abandon them. Lubbock met with Missouri governor Claiborne F. Jackson to prepare recommendations for President Davis should the Union be successful in driving a wedge between eastern and western segments of the Confederacy. This activity served to placate the western states. The third Marshall Conference was to be called by Kirby Smith in May 1865 to develop a plan for surrender of Trans-Mississippi forces.[260]

The second Marshall Conference opened on August 15 with Kirby Smith presenting the agenda. The conference was organized with Governor Lubbock of Texas appointed to chair the proceedings, and then three committees were named. Committee No. 1 was chaired by Governor Thomas Reynolds of Missouri and primarily dealt with armament and being separated from other states of the Confederacy. Regarding this separation, the Committee report said, "The safety of our people requires that he [General Smith] assume at once and exercise the discretion, power, and prerogatives of the President of the Confederate States." This report supported General Smith's desire for broad authority to govern.

Williamson S. Oldham of Texas chaired Committee No. 2, which dealt with currency and cotton. The committee report declared, "The cotton of this department is the only safe and reliable means for carrying on efficient military operations for the defense of the country west of the Mississippi. The authority of the general in command [Smith] to use the cotton as a means of purchasing and accumulating military supplies cannot be doubted, under the provisions of the act of

Congress usually denominated the 'impressment Act.' Taking possession of the entire amount of cotton, with such exceptions and modification as the commanding general may deem necessary to meet particular wants or necessities of the people, would take the cotton trade out of the hands of speculators now engaged in it." This report supported the creation of the Cotton Bureau (which Smith had already announced) and set the framework for impressing this fiber.

Judge E. T. Merrick of Louisiana chaired Committee No. 3, charged with defining Kirby Smith's civil authority. This group, in referring to Secretary of War Seddon's letter of July 14, 1863 (apparently the "lost letter" referred to above), indicated, "The respective States composing the department have organized governments and it could not have been the intention of the Secretary of War to advise the commanding general to exercise civil authority which belongs to the States, they still having officers present ready to perform their respective duties and functions." This was one of the few rebukes encountered by Kirby Smith and is presented from a states' rights perspective that conveniently ignored the fact that the Missouri delegation represented a government in exile.

A special subcommittee was appointed and was chaired by Pendleton Murrah, who succeeded Francis R. Lubbock as governor of Texas in August 1863. This subcommittee considered the question of the "appointment of commissioner to confer with French and Mexican authorities in Mexico." The committee suggested that the department may wish to send an agent or commissioner to Mexico to confer with French and Mexican authorities as to their "disposition toward our Government ... and what we may expect from then in favor or opposition." The report adds that "if the French Government is honorably disposed toward our country ... important results may be anticipated from securing her good-will." This subcommittee report sanctions Kirby Smith's venture into foreign relations activities with France in Mexico, but what it does not say is important as well. It makes no mention of General Smith dealing directly or indirectly with Emperor Napoleon III in France.

All committee reports were unanimously agreed to, with the exception of one portion dealing with issuance of coupon bonds to pay for impressed cotton. Proceedings of the Marshall Conference, which adjourned on August 18, were transmitted to President Davis in Richmond on September 11, 1863.[261] Thus, the "Kirby-Smithdom" was solidified.

Through the Marshall Conference report of Williamson Oldham's Committee No. 2, General Kirby Smith had been sanctioned to address the cotton problem. The report had suggested that it was desirable for the Trans-Mississippi Department to establish a cotton bureau and seize all available cotton, with certain exceptions, through impressment.

On September 13, Kirby Smith said, "the Cotton business has long occupied my attention, it is the most tangled snarl that has ever come before me."[262] Cotton tangled everything it touched. It generated greed in men, ruled the economy and social structure of the South, and helped develop the shipping and textiles industries in the North. Military organizations were financed by cotton profits.

The power of this staple shaped foreign policy and military strategy. In short, cotton was such a force that it received homage from its "subjects" who referred to it as "King."

Part of this "tangled snarl" that Smith vigorously attempted to unravel was the greed of men involved in exporting the precious commodity. Private speculators dominated the trade of this fiber and made enormous profits. Kirby Smith tried to contend with this knotted controversy by establishing the Cotton Bureau in Shreveport with a branch in Houston known as the Texas Cotton Office. The plan of the branch was to use bonds to purchase one-half of a planter's cotton crops; in turn, the other half would not be impressed. No grower or merchant, however, could export the portion that was not seized without a license, and to get a license the individual had to agree to return a certain percentage of the value of the fiber to the department for purchasing military stores. The plan did not work well because prices paid under this arrangement were so low that private speculators outbid Cotton Bureau buyers. The Trans-Mississippi Department then turned to impressment of all cotton (with some exceptions) and that was unpopular with everyone. The private speculator loathed it because it cut him out of huge profits to be made from this commodity. The ordinary citizen disliked it because of the low price he got for his cotton and the abuses that were inherent in the system. All of this caused the state legislature to take corrective action.

In December 1863, this assembly moved to nullify the army plan. It devised a scheme that threatened to deprive C.S.A. purchasing and impressment officers of the bulk of Texas cotton. These were the main components of Governor Murrah's State Plan: the Texas State Military Board bought cotton at fair market prices and that purchase remained in the name of the state; the state in turn transported the fiber to the Rio Grande (since the commodity was in the name of the state, it was not subject to impressment by the Confederate Cotton Bureau); once the cotton was in Mexico, one-half of it was released to the original owner for disposal in any way he saw fit and the other half was retained by the state for the purchase of military supplies. Financially, this arrangement was decidedly more advantageous to planters and merchants, and was favored by them over the Cotton Bureau plan.

Governor Murrah then announced that the military board needed 60,000 bales to pay for arms and equipment, at which time Confederate competitors awoke to the fact that the State Plan had cornered the market by excluding 120,000 bales from impressment, which amounted to most of the cotton in Texas. By March 1864, the state had purchased 100,000 cotton bales. Due to this practice, the Department of the Trans-Mississippi was running low on this staple and could not meet its contractual obligations. Smith ordered the Cotton Bureau to buy or impress one-half of all cotton in the department. Governor Murrah contended that General Smith's actions violated state sovereignty. Because of the low price offered, planters withheld their crop since they hoped to sell privately at a higher price. This practice provoked wholesale confiscation of cotton throughout "Kirby-Smithdom."[263] Planters reacted by refusing to produce the crop.

Kirby Smith responded. He cajoled and he threatened. He told the governor that with an inability to impress the commodity in Texas, he was unable to defend the state from any Federal incursion. He requested that Murrah modify the plan and stressed how important the staple was to the department. Murrah demurred, but in July 1864, Smith and Murrah met for talks on the problem. Smith probably argued in a persuasive manner about the state's plan making it impossible for the Trans-Mississippi Department to defend itself. Further, there had been recent Southern reversals in western Louisiana and southwest Arkansas and some Texas newspapers had begun to turn against Murrah's State Plan. The governor capitulated to General Smith's demands on July 19 and abandoned the State Plan.

Smith's Cotton Bureau impressment program was back in business, but the populace continued an outcry against such harsh activity. Although Texas generally supported the rule of Kirby Smith, there was grumbling about his rigorous enforcement of conscription laws, about his widespread use of impressment of cotton and other agricultural crops, about war's impact on the economy, and about wholesale consignment of Texas boys to the east to fight and die.[264] This disaffection had been reflected in the August 1863 elections when six veteran C.S.A. representatives were voted out of office. Much of this sentiment, however, was not unique to Texas since the Confederacy was on her way to losing the war.

Impressment was particularly irksome. An act signed by President Davis on March 26, 1863, provided that property subject to being impressed (or taken without consent of the owner) would be only that needed for immediate consumption of men in the field. The local commander in the field was to make a decision as to whether the exigency of the moment required that something be impressed, and that "something" usually was cotton that could be sold to meet the armament and supply needs of the army.

Impressment was unpopular because of the scarcity of goods for domestic consumption, low prices paid for impressed goods, theft in the form of banditry, illegal seizure of cotton and other goods, and issuance of counterfeit payment certificates or no issue of certificates at all. The populace could not defend itself against this robbery and reacted by seeing to it that there was nothing to rob. Farmers and planters simply planted less of the staple and grain, or none at all, leaving their fields fallow. The grain crop declined by one-third. Both armies and civilians faced prospects of famine, but farmers continued the boycott. The next session of the legislature enacted laws to minimize the worst abuses of the impressment system, but there was little substantial change. The Cotton Bureau continued to operate during the last year of the war and impressment continued to flourish.[265]

A further dilemma around cotton was encountered when the Confederacy and the Trans-Mississippi Department found it was cash poor, but had surpluses of this commodity on hand that could be converted to cash. The Confederacy consequently engaged in illicit sales of the staple. This is not as nefarious as it sounds, however, since the United States did likewise when it bought Southern cotton. One side was cash poor and the other was cotton poor. The overall ascendancy of King Cotton fostered illicit trade among the United States, the Confederate States of America, and neutral nations.

New England's textile mills desperately needed the fiber, and the South needed manufactured goods that cotton could buy. It takes two to trade, and these two parties were eager to do so. In the middle were those who were ready to profit from this commercial intercourse. The lower Mississippi valley drew the most daring entrepreneurs, the most corrupt officials, and the most adept smugglers. There was money to be made where there was cotton, and the Confederacy could not stop illegal activities on the entire coastline, bayous, and river systems.

In July 1861, the United States Congress had severed commercial relations with the seceded states, but the president and the secretary of treasury were given authority to issue licenses for such trade with the South as might be in the interest of the U.S. When New Orleans was captured, a flood of speculators who had been issued licenses appeared, and planters were invited to bring their cotton to the Crescent City. To prevent any trade with the enemy, Confederate Governor Thomas O. Moore of Louisiana ordered this practice to be stopped and General Butler was unsuccessful in opening trade in the commodity. Three-quarters of the spindles in New England were idle and representatives of mills and state leaders urged Lincoln to take corrective action. The president responded by replacing Butler with Nathaniel Banks, a consummate politician from New England. Banks found corruption in New Orleans and he did his best to bring order out greedy chaos. He issued regulations to control and expedite the flow of cotton.

Confederates in the Trans-Mississippi had been buying the staple on behalf of the C.S.A. to discourage private commercial transactions, but bales were just accumulating. In late 1863, 105,000 bales of cotton belonging to the C.S.A. Treasury Department were stored in west Louisiana. It seemed absurd to allow such product neglect when the Confederacy needed money to finance the war effort and buy manufactured goods. By August 1863, Kirby Smith had established a system of negotiating exchange of the commodity for Northern manufactured goods and he formalized the procedure through the Cotton Bureau.[266]

General Smith was shipping the fiber from Shreveport or Alexandria, and Northern buyers (licensed by Lincoln) bought cotton in those locations. All sides pretended everything was on the up-and-up. Northerners convinced themselves they were buying from private individuals (not the Confederate government). Southerners deluded themselves into thinking their cotton was going to a neutral country (Great Britain) in return for goods. Banks did inhibit the sales of arms and the C.S.A. was glad to accept gold, sterling, or even U.S. currency. By the summer of 1864, the Trans-Mississippi Department had earned at least $30,000,000 worth of supplies and credit through cotton sales.

Two years earlier, C.S.A. Brigadier General Hamilton P. Bee, in command of the lower Rio Grande district, with headquarters at Brownsville, Texas, had been in contact with an intriguing character that he may have known in prewar days. In December 1862, he obtained permission from Major General John Magruder in Houston to send one A. Superviele on an important diplomatic mission to Mexico to hold discussions with French naval officers. Superviele was something of a shadowy figure that suddenly emerged into the diplomatic limelight for a few months—then just as quickly vanished. Little is known about this clever emissary, but professor Ella Lonn identifies A. Superviele as "a Frenchman by birth, as his name suggests, but for sixteen years preceding the war a resident of Texas."[267] Hamilton Bee was a resident of Texas during this same period. He fought in the Mexican War and served in the state legislature following his military service; Bee may have known Superviele through either of these activities. In any event, General Bee dispatched his emissary on January 1, 1863. His agent first went to Havana, Cuba, arriving there on February 3, where he met with the consul general of France. Superviele told the diplomat that he could help the French get mules for their inland expedition of Mexico, could furnish provisions as needed by them, and could supply cotton for their mills in France. The consul general said he would transmit this information to France. Superviele mentioned that while in Havana it became common knowledge that he was a Confederate agent, but in spite of this, he had a cordial relationship with a "Yankee spy."

On February 28, he arrived in Veracruz, Mexico; that same day Superviele met with the admiral of the French fleet on board his ship, *Dryad*, at Bahia de Sacrificios. He established friendly relations with the admiral and attempted to secure his commitment to carry out an expedition to occupy Matamoros in order that France and the C.S.A. might engage in a mutually advantageous commercial relationship. The admiral conveyed his sympathy with this notion, but indicated he did not have troops available to occupy the city. He added that the French army's cooperation would be required to accomplish this.

Over the next month, Superviele met with several diplomats and high-ranking members of the French army and navy. One of the more important contacts he made on the military side was with Adrian Woll, a Frenchman who came to Mexico with French troops at Veracruz in January 1862. Woll was named commandant general of the state of Veracruz and at Napoleon's request he developed a plan for organizing armed forces in Mexico. The purpose of Superviele's contact with Woll in March 1863 was to encourage the French government to seize Matamoros. General Woll, however, did not have authority to take troops that, at that time, were under command of General Elie Forey, who was unable to divert any troops; they were needed for inland operations at Puebla and later Mexico City. [268]

The French in Havana had instructed Superviele that his diplomatic contact in Mexico should be A. Dubois de Saligny, with whom he met in Puebla on April 17, 1863. At this meeting, the Confederate agent explained the purpose of his mission and Saligny declared his sympathies to be with the Confederacy. This was the same French diplomat who earlier had been active with the new Republic of Texas and signed his dispatches as "A. de Saligny." After the annexation of Texas by the U.S.A., Saligny represented France in several capacities; in 1860 Emperor

Napoleon III appointed him plenipotentiary to Mexico. From that post, Saligny sent dispatches to Napoleon urging French intervention in Mexico. These dispatches quickened the emperor's decision to send a French military expedition to Mexico in 1862 resulting in Maximilian being placed on the throne.[269]

Superviele next met with Saligny on May 3, 1863, at which time he presented to the French diplomat a most remarkable offer. Superviele told him that the C.S.A. looked upon France as a natural ally. Therefore, the Confederacy would sell France 300,000 bales of cotton to a vendor of its choice to ensure that French textile mills had an adequate supply of raw material for their spindles. He said he understood the French were having difficulty acquiring mules for their troops; he then offered to make it possible for the French to buy, in Mexico, any quantity of mules they required at a reasonable price. In addition, by crossing the animals to the left (Texas) bank of the Rio Grande, they could be driven down to the river mouth under C.S.A. protection. Beeves (beef cattle) could be driven in a similar fashion, and obtained at a price lower than in Havana. To get livestock on board ships, he would arrange for the Rio Grande bar to be crossed with three lighters supplied by the Confederacy, but flying Mexican colors. Furthermore, the French could use these lighters to land troops that would occupy Matamoros; the C.S.A. would lend them artillery and ammunition to support the landing.

When asked for his response to this generous offer, Mr. De Saligny answered that he was a "man already convinced of the importance of the undertaking, but that probably we [the C.S.A.] wanted something in return?" Superviele replied, "He was offering to France a golden bridge without expecting any compensation, excepting the non-interference of the river trade." The C.S.A. agent suggested that perhaps recognition of the Confederate States of America by France might follow in due course. Mr. De Saligny replied that the French government was very interested in the offer. He added, however, that men for an expedition to Matamoros were not presently available, because of the current battle in Puebla, and the probability the French would next march to Mexico City. Later, General Woll committed himself to taking command of the expedition and he said he understood the importance of seizing Matamoros. Before Superviele left, he extracted an understanding that the French would move on Matamoros as soon as additional troops arrived from France. Moreover, it was said that Napoleon understood the importance of taking Matamoros.[270]

When Superviele left Saligny on June 4, he had the Frenchman's assurances that "Matamoras [sic] will be taken possession of as soon as possible." The C.S.A. agent departed Bahia de Sacrificios on board the French steam frigate *Panama* on June 22 and arrived opposite the mouth of the Rio Grande on June 24, 1863. He sent messages to Brownsville announcing his arrival but there was no response. Finally, on July 3, he boarded a lighter flying the Mexican flag that had been carrying cotton across the bar to waiting ships, and stated his wish to be landed in Texas because he was a citizen of that state. The lighter's captain replied that the Mexicans forbade him to land anybody on the Texas side and he would have to get a permit to cross the river from the port warden. When Superviele landed in

Mexico, he was arrested as a "person of suspicious character" because he had arrived in Mexico from a French warship; they believed him to be a French spy. He was detained and then released on July 4 after explaining the situation to the satisfaction of all. On July 31, Superviele submitted the report of his mission to General Bee, who forwarded it on August 24 to General Magruder indicating that required additional troops from France for occupying Matamoros were expected hourly. He added that a French vessel had already taken soundings at the mouth of the Rio Grande and had selected a landing place.[271]

This most interesting journey by A. Superviele appears to have been productive. Although the agent had not been successful in bringing in France as an ally on the Rio Grande border, he did gain assurances that the French would occupy Matamoros in the future. Additionally, he effectively developed friendly relationships with that nation. Both the Confederacy and Union had listening posts throughout the Caribbean region and at their respective consulates. It seems quite likely that the U.S. had a general idea of Superviele's activities, without necessarily knowing specifics. Superviele made no secret that he was soliciting French aid in taking Matamoros, and early in his journey he had been clearly identified in Havana as a Southern agent. It is quite possible that the United States partially shaped its southwest Texas strategy in response to Superviele's actions. Certainly, the C.S.A. was concerned that the Yankees might mount an expedition into southwest Texas. General Kirby Smith manifested this concern on September 4, 1863, when he wrote General Magruder and said it would be necessary to have the cooperation of the French "to prevent the landing of the enemy at Lavaca and Rio Grande."[272]

A report of particular importance arising from the Marshall Conference was issued in August 1863 by Pendleton Murrah's special subcommittee, which dealt with the French in Mexico. It suggested that the Trans-Mississippi Department might send an agent to the French to gain their good will, and to determine how they might help the Confederates. Kirby Smith immediately opened the foreign relations door that had been left ajar by the Murrah subcommittee report. That report gave Smith the authority to communicate with the French in Mexico on behalf of the Trans-Mississippi Department, not the Confederate States of America. Kirby Smith expanded his foreign relations role to included direct contact with France. It appears that direct contacts by C.S.A. representatives with French officials in Mexico were not unusual. However, indirect communications with the French emperor by the Trans-Mississippi Department (not the C.S.A.) was a novel approach, even if it was through the auspices of an intermediary, John Slidell.

General Smith must have been impressed with Superviele's reported successes with the French officials during his February–June 1863 trip to Havana and Mexico, because he sent Superviele on a second mission. Concerned about the state of affairs in the Confederacy after the fall of Vicksburg, E. Kirby Smith wrote a pessimistic letter on September 2, 1863, to John Slidell, Confederate States commissioner in France. In his letter to Slidell, General Smith requested that Napoleon III be convinced about the grim plight of the Trans-Mississippi Department, and that he be urged to occupy the east bank of the Rio Grande. General Smith added that French assistance must come quickly; he feared that in one year the cause would be lost. Smith emphasized in his letter that his department was the only organization protecting the access of France to cotton and he said the department could "act as a buffer between the French protectorate in Mexico and the hostile United States."[273] In a missive forwarding a copy of the Slidell letter to President Davis, Smith spoke of "the almost hopeless condition of our affairs in this department." He added, "The prospects of the department are presented in a gloomy light, but I do not think it a too exaggerated picture of what may occur."[274] On September 4, 1863, Kirby Smith had a duplicate of this important letter to Mr. Slidell forwarded to Superviele through Major General Magruder and Brigadier General Bee. The importance of the letter is highlighted by the fact that a second copy was forwarded to Magruder for him to transmit by a reliable officer or agent to Mr. Slidell. Specific instructions for Superviele were included in the copy of the letter entrusted to him. Specifically, the Southern emissary was to go to Mexico and contact French General Elie Forey as well as the French minister to Mexico. These individuals were to be allowed to read the letter. Next, Superviele was instructed that after the French authorities read the letter, he was to deliver it to Slidell. If, for some reason he could not do this, he was to select "some good, reliable, and intelligent man" to hand-deliver the letter.[275]

A month later, on October 14, 1863, the same Smith letter, along with a forwarding letter from General Magruder, commanding the District of Texas, New Mexico, and Arizona, was hand-carried to John Slidell by Major George A. Magruder, Jr., his aide-de-camp. Magruder's forwarding letter makes a forceful case for further involvement by France in the Confederate cause. He says, "It will be impossible for France to hold her possessions in Mexico if the United States troops overrun Louisiana and Texas. I have been endeavoring to induce General Forey to order the occupation of Matamoras [sic], offering to throw the cotton of Texas into the hands of French merchants in return for the convenience to us of such occupation."[276]

At about the same time, Kirby Smith decided to make further use of the diplomatic skills of Superviele by sending him to Veracruz because there was a most delicate matter for him to resolve. Relationships with France did not always proceed in such an amicable manner as had been enjoyed of late. The Confederacy was riding something of a tightrope in late 1863 because now she had two blockades with which to contend. The U.S. blockade had become increasingly active in the gulf because the United States had more ships available after the fall of Vicksburg and Port Hudson in July. Furthermore, the United States had become greatly concerned with an increasing volume of goods leaving Texas and was determined to strengthen the barrier. The Confederacy not only had to be concerned about legal seizures of her vessels by the United States, but about illegal captures as well. Her vessels were being illegally apprehended in neutral waters of Mexico because, in some instances, U.S. Navy vessels were failing to properly compensate their compasses for magnetic variation off the Rio Grande. With embarrassment, they were required to release these Confederate blockade runners when they ascertained that improper compass bearings had been used. To further complicate matters for the C.S.A., the French had now established their own blockade off the coast of Mexico to seize vessels bringing in contraband to aid the Mexican armed forces.

Superviele had been dispatched to Veracruz to negotiate the release of impounded cargo from the English schooner *Love Bird*. It had been seized in a most unloving manner by the French off the mouth of the Rio Grande, who ascertained that she was carrying armaments for the Mexican army. They were mistaken. *Love Bird* had been loaded under contract between the Confederacy and Nelson Clements in London, and the cargo was consigned to the C.S.A. in care of Hale & Co. in Matamoros. She had sailed from London on July 29, 1863. The Confederacy had contracted a huge and important cargo: 10,000 Enfield rifles, 156 revolvers, 2,000,000 cartridges, and 5,000,000 percussion caps. After *Love Bird* anchored off the mouth of Rio Grande on September 26, C.S.A. General Bee sent lighters to the vessel to transfer cargo to Point Isabel, fourteen miles to the north. He had brought 4,200 rifles (210 boxes) to C.S.A. territory when a French frigate captured *Love Bird* near sunset. The frigate left at daybreak the next day, bound for Veracruz, with the vessel in tow.

Superviele's first mission on this trip was to get this cargo released and returned to Point Isabel. His second mission, after contacting certain French officials in Mexico, was to proceed to Paris carrying the letter from Kirby Smith to John Slidell. On October 13, 1863, General H. P. Bee amplified the instructions given Superviele on September 4. The revised requirements were, first, the admiral of the French navy was to be interviewed, and only if he was friendly to the Confederate cause was he to be allowed to read the Kirby Smith letter to Slidell, but he was not permitted to keep a copy. Second, he was instructed to find an officer who "would have the power to control the movements of the French army" and allow him to read a copy of the letter. Further, the Confederate agent was "instructed to keep this matter a profound secret, and allow no intimation of your business to escape you. Your dispatches will be concealed on your person or otherwise, prepared for immediate destruction should there arise any emergency involving their capture by the enemy." To continue the subterfuge, he was to communicate back to Kirby Smith by representing himself as an agent of the firm of Droege, Oetling & Co. of Matamoros.[277]

According to Ella Lonn, Superviele showed the Smith letter to the French admiral about December 20, 1863. "The London Times shortly afterwards carried a notice of the arrival in Paris of a M. Superviele, who had sailed from Veracruz in a French steamer, as a special envoy to secure recognition for the Confederacy."[278]

Love Bird was not the only vessel the Confederacy "temporarily" lost to the French blockade. Two other ships were loaded under similar arrangements and contracts with the Nelson Clements firm at about the same time as *Love Bird*. They were the English schooners *Caroline Goodyear* and *Nancy Dawson*. Particularly alarming to the Confederates was the *Caroline Goodyear*, because she arrived at the mouth of the Rio Grande with 10,000 more English rifles that were badly needed by many unarmed soldiers of the Trans-Mississippi Department. She too was seized and sent to the Veracruz prize court. General Bee clearly became disgruntled over the behavior of the blockading French warship *Magellan*, and advised Captain Duval, commanding the *Magellan* on October 13, 1863, that *Nancy Dawson* departed London on September 1, 1863, under the same set of circumstances as did *Caroline Goodyear* and *Love Bird* earlier. He asked Captain Duval "to prevent a repetition of the disastrous and lamentable consequences to my country which she suffered with the other cargoes." In his reply, Captain Duval is equally miffed and says, "I regret infinitely having received the communication which you addressed to me concerning the *Nancy Dawson*; but I am under the obligation of following the instructions which have been given me." Then he adds a tart P.S., "I shall hereafter find myself under the necessity of not taking any cognizance of any letters which may have reference to vessels laden with arms, and request you to indorse on the letters which you may write me that they are not relative to that matter."[279]

Clearly, the two officers were becoming a bit testy with one another. Before these incidents could erupt into a major impediment in the generally good and friendly relationships between the two sides, John Slidell was able to defuse the matter through negotiations with officials in France. He succeeded by getting the seized cargoes released to the Confederates, and establishing procedures that would ensure that such incidents would not recur.[280]

Obviously, the Department of the Trans-Mississippi was dealing directly with France and was encouraging that nation to expand her involvement in Mexico. Whether or not the "Kirby-Smithdom" had ever been given any explicit authority by Jefferson Davis to engage in foreign policy to this extent is arguable, but it did not seem to make any difference. Kirby Smith proceeded to shape foreign policy as far as the Trans-Mississippi Department was concerned, and President Davis did not intercede. The president was well aware of the impossibility of governing the west from Richmond because of Union occupation of the Mississippi River. He asked the Confederate Congress on December 7, 1863, to "delegate to the commanding general [of the Trans-Mississippi] so much of the discretionary power vested in them by law as the exigencies of the service shall require." The Congress agreed and delegated some administrative functions. For example, Smith was permitted to appoint a treasury agent who was to report to the C.S.A. secretary of the treasury, P. W. Gray. The selected agent did report to Gray, but frequently he consulted with, and deferred to, Kirby Smith. In February 1864, General Smith got a deputy postmaster general, and Congress even considered establishing an assistant secretary of war for the Trans-Mississippi. That did not pass because of the concern about civilian control over the military, but many military functions were delegated to Smith. These included suspension of the writ of habeas corpus and employment or impressment of free or enslaved Negroes as laborers for the army.[281]

On April 28, 1864, President Davis assured Smith that "as far as the Constitution permits, full authority has been given to you to administer the wants of your department, civil as well as military."[282] It was clear that both Congress and the president were to treat the Trans-Mississippi Department as a detached province of the Confederacy.

Chapter 6

The Rio Grande Expedition

In November 1861, Winfield Scott retired as general in chief and General George B. McClellan replaced him. Meanwhile, over at the U.S. Navy Department, Commander David D. Porter had come to Secretary Gideon Welles proposing an expedition to capture New Orleans. Secretary Welles concurred and said New Orleans was "the most important place in the insurrectionary region and the most difficult to blockade."[283] It was one of the prime components in Scott's Anaconda Plan; Assistant Secretary of the Navy Gustavus Fox turned his attention to devising a detailed plan for capturing the Crescent City.

On November 14, 1861, Fox met with President Lincoln about the project and Lincoln doubted its feasibility. Nevertheless, he kept an open mind on the subject and the next evening the president was head of a delegation that went to General McClellan's headquarters for a consultation. Others in the delegation included Porter, Fox, Welles, and Secretary of State William H. Seward. The group listened to Fox's detailed plan for capturing New Orleans. Following questions and answers, the plan was approved, although McClellan "had little faith in the venture."[284] The president endorsed the plan, indicating he wished the invasion force to be launched by mid–January 1862.

Major General Benjamin F. Butler, commanding the Department of New England, wrote to Major General George McClellan on December 2, 1861, urging that he be allowed to lead an army of 15,000 New England troops to invade Texas. He favored landing a force at Indianola on Matagorda Bay, and then marching to San Antonio, where the loyal German population could be expected to assist the United States force. From there, he would go to Brownsville and the Rio Grande to prevent commerce between Texas and Mexico.[285] Butler was unaware of the naval plan for capturing New Orleans that had been approved the previous month. Subsequently, it was decided that General Butler should lead his army to New Orleans, not Indianola, as he had suggested. Although Butler had wished to go to Texas, he agreed to the change of destination, feeling that he could gain glory in Louisiana as well as in Texas.[286] The New Orleans campaign was successful and that town fell to the U.S. Navy on April 25, 1862. General Butler and his army occupied the Crescent City on May 1, 1862. However, the hoped for flow of cotton from that port did not materialize; due to a dearth of the staple, the textile mills of New England were idle. It appeared that the only way to get cotton would be to conquer Texas.

Butler's original plan to land in Texas was reconsidered. Pressure increased for a Texas incursion when a delegation of Bostonians came to Washington in October 1862 urging an invasion of the Lone Star State in order to obtain cotton. The Boston contingent called upon Secretary of War Stanton and President Lincoln; both men indicated there was a paucity of troops available for implementing this plan. The group then visited Secretary of State Seward to gain his support for a Texas campaign. He told them he had been considering occupying at least part of the Rio Grande line for some time. On October 10, 1862, Horace Greeley's *New York Tribune* reported there had been "the distinct promise of an expedition at an early day for the relief of Texas."[287]

While entreaty for a Texas invasion increased, there was mounting enthusiasm for wresting control of the Mississippi River from the Confederacy. This interest arose because Southern sections of Ohio, Indiana, and Illinois historically had traded goods down river, and those states wished to have their trade route—the Mississippi—once more open for commercial ventures. Of course, Lincoln, originally from Illinois, realized the importance of that great river to commerce. In October, Democrats won state and congressional elections in Ohio and Indiana; this was due in part to failure of the Federal government to open the Mississippi for trade. In response to the election results in these two states, on October 21 Major General John A. McClernand was authorized to raise soldiers for an expedition to capture Vicksburg and clear the Mississippi all the way to New Orleans. By the next spring, McClernand would lead a corps in the Vicksburg campaign under the command of General Grant.

Next, on October 28, 1862, Secretary of War Stanton sent a confidential dispatch to the governors of New York and the New England states announcing, "General Banks has established his headquarters in New York to organize a Southern expedition."[288] It was Stanton's intent that Banks would land on the coast of Texas. Furthermore, it was assumed by the public that Banks's "Southern expedition" was headed for the Lone Star State, although there was no public announcement to this effect. After all, Nathaniel P. Banks, a three-term governor of Massachusetts, represented a state with idle textile mills needing cotton that could be obtained in Texas. On November 1, 1862, Assistant Secretary of the Navy Gustavus Fox wrote to Rear Admiral Farragut, "An army force is preparing on a large scale to move into and take possession of that country [Texas]."[289]

President Lincoln found himself trapped between the conflicting goals of clearing the Mississippi or invading Texas. He thought he might resolve this dilemma by sending Banks's army to Texas for the purpose of gaining control of cotton, while General McClernand's army moved downstream toward Memphis and Vicksburg. However, this notion was tentative and upon further reflection, he made countermoves.

Military plans began to change on November 9 when, by order of General in Chief Henry W. Halleck, General Banks was given command of the Department of the Gulf, now expanded to include the State of Texas. The order changed his destination from Texas to New Orleans. His new assignment was to move north and open the Mississippi River, after which he was to capture Vicksburg and destroy the railroads at Jackson and Marion, Mississippi. Next he was to ascend the Red River in Louisiana to establish a cotton and sugar outlet as well as a base of operations for an attack upon Texas.[290] On November 11, President Lincoln (not the secretary of the navy) sent a communication to Rear Admiral Farragut ordering him to cooperate with General Banks. The president said Banks was "in command of a considerable land force for operating in the South."[291]

Between October 28 and November 9, Banks's destination had changed from Texas to New Orleans, and clearing the Mississippi River assumed priority over a Texas incursion. Two things had happened to cause this and both events were political in nature. First, Lincoln had experienced a setback in his home state when Illinois voters, on November 4, repudiated his party and voted Democratic. Behind this Republican defeat was dissatisfaction with the lack of progress made by the Union in opening the Mississippi River to unobstructed traffic. The earlier congressional elections in October that rejected the Republican Party in Ohio and Indiana likewise mirrored concerns about this same issue. Second, Indiana Governor Morton had written President Lincoln a letter about that state switching to the Democratic camp. Morton emphasized that not only must the Mississippi River be cleared for navigation, but states on the west bank must be secured for the Union as well.

These two incidents had a profound impact upon the political soul of Abraham Lincoln. The president believed it would not take long to open the river, and thereafter Banks could invade Texas. "Texas was in this way abandoned for the time being but the administration did nothing to correct the prevailing impression that Banks was headed there."[292] The press announced that the expedition was on its way to Texas and the administration did not contradict these reports. Further heightening the deception was the November 14 appointment of Andrew J. Hamilton as Texas military governor by Secretary of War Stanton, who also gave him authority to raise two regiments of Texas volunteers.[293] At about the same time, General Butler had heard rumors that General Banks was headed for New Orleans and, in private correspondence Secretary of the Treasury Salmon P. Chase, assured him that "Gen. Banks goes to New Orleans, not, as I understand, to supersede you; but to conduct an expedition to Texas."[294] A few days later, President Lincoln became impatient with Banks's delayed departure for New Orleans and he probably feared that information about the true destination of the expedition would be discovered. On November 22, Lincoln wrote to Banks that the postponement of the sailing date "will be our final ruin if it is not abandoned.... You must be off before Congress meets."[295] Banks put to sea on December 4. Various state officials and New England merchants, who were looking forward to the flow of Texas cotton for empty spindles in their mills, saw him off.

Why did the Lincoln administration make no effort to correct the impression that this fleet was sailing for Texas, not New Orleans? There was ample time to do so between the decision to go to New Orleans and the sailing date. Perhaps part of the answer lies in the character of Lincoln. Early in 1864 he wrote a letter saying, "I claim not to have controlled events, but confess plainly that events have controlled me." David Donald suggests that Lincoln always had a sense that some larger force controlled events, and perhaps that was why he did not intervene in this situation.[296]

Nevertheless, General Banks's fleet arrived, to the surprise of most, at New Orleans on December 14. Banks reported, "Not a soul here anticipated our arrival, and scarcely a man on board ship suspected our destination until we were steaming up the Mississippi."[297] Hangers-on and politicians on board were thoroughly agitated about this state of affairs and Banks tried to placate Andrew Hamilton by informing him that a small expedition would be sent to Texas. Subsequently, naval ships and army troops were sent there and Southerners, at the Battle of Galveston, defeated them on January 1, 1863. Thus the first so-called "Rio Grande campaign" was aborted, not to be re-launched until the following November.

This cancelled invasion of Texas by land and sea presents an opportunity for a brief examination of some of the strategic and tactical factors involved in a combined operation by the Union army and navy. We start by looking at the role assumed by the commander in chief. There is no better illustration of how President Lincoln imposed political objectives over military objectives. He diverted forces originally scheduled to invade Texas to a new priority—clearing the Mississippi River—because of congressional election results. Political factors gained ascendancy eleven months later when the Rio Grande expedition was actually launched. Strategic elements guiding this invasion of the Lone Star State included showing the flag to the French in Mexico, occupying the east bank of the Rio Grande to signal the French of the possible consequences of violating the Monroe Doctrine, and interruption of the flow of cotton. The president supported these factors. The secondary objective was the only true military goal and this involved invading Houston and Galveston from the west in order to close the port of Galveston. This goal was never seriously pursued because troops were withdrawn to participate in another military objective.

This aborted Texas invasion illustrates a problem in command structure as well. The army had General in Chief Henry Halleck in overall command. The navy had no parallel figure such as chief of naval operations or commander of the blockading fleet. This encouraged a "hands on" commander in chief to issue a direct order to Rear Admiral Farragut. Lincoln apparently bypassed the secretary of the navy while leaving army operational details in the hands of Halleck. This might have led to confusion, conflict, and competing objectives. For example,

Halleck issued Banks a host of specific objectives, but Farragut only received a vague order to support Banks in his military activity in the South. This complicated any effort to have a well-coordinated operation. Furthermore, some politicians were placed in high military positions and continued to have their own constituents' demands to meet. Banks had a New England constituency to satisfy and, of course, Lincoln and his cabinet had their constituents as well. Consequently, compromises were required to deal with conflicting goals, and this also complicated efforts to develop strategic planning.

As we shall see below, the actual Rio Grande expedition was successful. Why was this so when the Union had suffered ignominious defeats in January 1863 at the Battle of Galveston and in September 1863 at the Battle of Sabine Pass? The Union had developed a good tactical plan and placed adequate resources at the disposal of General Banks. Furthermore, the Yankees had excellent intelligence about rebel defenses and struck when it was learned that most of the C.S.A. forces had been transferred to the Houston-Galveston area to defend against an expected strike there. The Union also correctly estimated the strength of the principal fortification they would encounter—Fort Esperanza—and were well prepared and equipped to deal with that obstacle. There was good coordination between the army and the navy because close attention had been paid to detailed planning in the pre-engagement phase. As a result a sound operational plan had been prepared and the force was well organized, trained, and equipped. Also, the Banks expedition had developed contingency planning in the event things should not go as expected. While sailing to the Rio Grande, the combined force encountered a severe storm at sea and it reacted promptly and correctly to deal with the potential disaster. This was remarkable in itself in an era when "failure to anticipate and provide for contingencies was characteristic of most Civil War combined operations."[298]

In short, the Union had applied lessons learned from their defeats at Galveston Bay and at Sabine Pass. In these two earlier engagements, the Federal navy had been restricted to narrow, shallow channels that deprived the fleet of necessary maneuverability to unleash superior firepower. Because of poor planning, the army component at Sabine Pass never participated in the battle; at Galveston the army group was forced into a defensive position because it was not of sufficient strength to carry out its mission nor did the navy properly support it. These mistakes were not repeated at the Rio Grande.

When the French occupied Mexico, the Confederacy found them sympathetic to their cause. In 1863, the French agreed to occupy Matamoros to clean out the grafting warlords and to facilitate a free flow of goods. In addition, there were rumors that France intended to take Louisiana and Texas under her protection. During July and August 1863, there were numerous communications between and among President Lincoln and Generals Banks and Halleck regarding an invasion of western Texas, but for the most part, they allowed Banks to choose an invasion location in Texas.[299] The Federal secretaries of navy, war and treasury all displayed their interest in Texas when Gideon Welles wrote to them that "in reference to the constant and extensive traffic that appears to be carried on ... through the port of Matamoras [sic] the only sure means of checking this illicit and injurious intercourse seems to be in occupying with our military forces the left bank of the Rio Grande, in Texas." In a dispatch dated June 9, 1863, Welles wrote, "I apprehend the naval force alone will be insufficient to either blockade or protect our interests.... [T]he left bank of the river shall be occupied by our troops."

Charles Francis Adams, the United States minister in London, wrote to Secretary of State Seward on May 1, 1863, and told him that the British were reorganizing their scheme for smuggling by way of the Rio Grande. He said he did not know "whether anything short of the possession of the eastern bank of the river will avail to defeat these machinations." Rear Admiral David Farragut supported this thinking when he added that there was increased "illegal traffic ... with the rebels through Mexico ... and [he] knew of but one mode to stop this trade, viz, to occupy the Rio Grande either with small, light-draft steamers or to send a land force to take and hold Brownsville and the banks of the river for some miles."[300]

President Lincoln clearly displayed his intent on July 29, 1863, when he wrote Secretary of War Stanton: "Can we not renew the effort to organize a force to go to Western Texas? ... I believe no local object is now more desirable."[301] Lincoln was still feeling the old pressure from the cotton lobby but now was also responding to the pressure of the French in Mexico. Two days later, General in Chief Henry Halleck sent a note to General Banks saying, "It is important that we immediately occupy some point or points in Texas."[302] General Nathaniel Banks reviewed his activities in the Department of the Gulf for the period December 16, 1862, to December 31, 1863, in his report to the secretary of war. He summarized his difficulties in progressing up Sabine Pass, and the problems inherent in moving westward across Southern Louisiana toward the Sabine River. He concluded that the only option open to him was to do an about-face and attempt to isolate Texas from the Confederacy by an approach from the west. Specifically, he says he decided to "attempt the occupation of the Rio Grande, which I had suggested on the 13th September as an alternative if the land route was found impracticable."[303]

Things were beginning to fall into place for an invasion of the Rio Grande Valley. Top government leaders supported such an operation, and the C.S.A. seemed to be spontaneously cooperating by pulling its ground units toward the east to protect the Galveston–Sabine Pass area. Commodore Bell indicated on June 2, 1863, that the USS *Brooklyn* reported all Texas troops left Brownsville on May 29, and probably had marched toward Louisiana. He added that the French threat in the area was increasing and that General Miramon was in Matamoros. The United States vice-consul at Monterrey, Mexico, M. M. Kimmey, wrote Secretary of State Seward on June 4, 1863, reporting that "all the troops from the western frontier of Texas have been ordered east. The line of the Rio Grande is now nearly deserted by the rebels." Secretary Seward forwarded a copy of this dispatch on July 28, 1863, to Secretary of War Stanton, who in turn referred it to the general in chief. In October 1863, the USS *Tennessee* cruised down the coast to chart fortifications and water depths; C.S.A. General Bee reported that three U.S. gunboats were surveying off the Rio Grande bar. Bee expressed his concern about an invasion and stated he was removing public property and cotton toward the north.[304]

General Banks decided it was time to launch the Rio Grande Expedition. He did so on October 26, 1863, when a group of transports, supply ships, light draft vessels, and escort ships departed New Orleans. The flagship was *McClellan*, which was accompanied by major transports *General Banks*, *Saint Mary's*, *Clinton*, and *Crescent*. Most of these transports could carry up to 900 men, or 100 horses and 500 men; the initial invading force consisted of 4,400 officers and men and 16 artillery pieces. More troops were to follow that would swell the size of the force to about 7,000 men. The total invasion fleet consisted of twenty-six transports and gunboats, but the group was delayed by a storm at sea during the afternoon of October 30 which disabled some of the vessels, requiring that they be towed. A Texas norther also caused the steamer *Union* to sink, but no lives were lost. Finally, on November 2, 1863, a successful landing was made upon Brazos Island, just north of the mouth of the Rio Grande. Opposition was light, with only James Duff's cavalry of approximately 100 men making token resistance. As predicted, nearly all rebel soldiers had been drawn to the east near Houston and Galveston. Banks announced, "The Flag of the Union floated over Texas to-day at meridian precisely. Our enterprise has been a complete success."[305]

On November 6, the expedition occupied Brownsville, thirty miles inland, finding that rebel General Bee, who had retreated north with his small force toward King's Ranch, had burned most of the remaining public property, including cotton. The Federal provisional governor, Andrew J. Hamilton, arrived with his staff and he was installed in office. Yankee soldiers planned to scout upriver for cotton; Hamilton's staff eagerly looked forward to their return with confiscated bales since they were anticipating their profits from factoring this commodity.

General Banks then initiated the second phase of his plan, which was to occupy passes on the coast between the Rio Grande and Galveston Bay before marching on Galveston. Banks commenced his operation up the coast, leaving General Napoleon J. T. Dana in charge of Brownsville with instructions to send a force up the Rio Grande. This task was assigned to Colonel Edmund J. Davis, whose soldiers included, among others, the First Texas Cavalry that consisted of many German volunteers from the Texas Hill Country. Davis's group sallied forth on the morning of November 23 with the goal of reaching Rio Grande City, over 100 miles upriver. The unit departed with 100 mounted men, 2 howitzers, 100 infantry troops in wagons, and an additional 150 men and 1 howitzer on board the steamer *Mustang*. Their route was on land and water, but the water passage was troublesome because of low water and sandbars. The group on land was able to make better progress, especially the cavalry. The land and river forces met no resistance and were able to round up a quantity of cotton on numerous forays away from the river. The detachment had secured a presence on the river and accumulated 82 bales of the staple. The force concluded its return trip on December 2 without experiencing any casualties or loss of property. General Dana happily reported to General Banks that 500 bales of cotton, which had been collected in Brownsville and along the river, would replenish the U.S. treasury.[306]

Meanwhile, Banks was sailing up the coast. At sunset on November 16, lead elements of his army landed outside Corpus Christi Bay at the south end of Mustang Island. During the night, they marched to the north end of the island and the next day the troops overpowered the fort and three heavy guns guarding the bay's entrance. To the north, across Aransas Pass from Mustang Island, was St. Joseph Island. These ground forces landed on St. Joseph Island and moved toward Cedar Bayou, where they arrived at noon on November 23. Troops were ferried across the bayou and encamped about seven miles up Matagorda Island. Fort Esperanza, the principal C.S.A. fortification in the area, was constructed at the Northern end of Matagorda Island. It guarded Pass Cavallo, the entry to Matagorda Bay, where two important ports (Indianola and Port Lavaca) were located.

Fort Esperanza was a well-manned and armed stronghold that had nine guns, including eight 24-pounders and one 128-pounder. Federal General Thomas E. G. Ransom reached Fort Esperanza on November 27; a two-day battle ensued, resulting in rebels evacuating the fort after they were outflanked and outnumbered. Thereafter, the bastion was occupied by U.S. forces to be used as a base of operations for the remaining campaign to the east. The army group spread out from there, occupying Port Lavaca and Indianola.[307] That was as far as they got; the mission was changed.

The next move was to be inland toward the mouth of the Brazos River and onward to Galveston Island. It was expected that Banks would meet a concentration of Confederate forces as he moved toward Galveston, and he requested additional men for the attack. General Henry Halleck, recalling the fate of the Union at Galveston on January 1, 1863, refused his request; the chief of staff decided he needed these troops for another operation (the Red River expedition in Louisiana the next spring). Banks was ordered to hold ground he had taken, and then slowly shrink his perimeter throughout winter and spring. His troop strength was diminished during this period until finally there was only a small defensive strip around the Brownsville area.

Critics of the Rio Grande expedition contend little was gained except some dusty border towns and sandy barrier islands. Furthermore, faultfinders complain that the campaign drew materiel and manpower so far westward that they could not be utilized elsewhere. These are narrow and shortsighted criticisms.

Two important objectives were achieved. One gain was securing more than 500 bales of cotton and forcing trade of that commodity out of the Brownsville-Matamoros area and upriver 235 miles to Laredo and beyond. Because of this military intervention, the transport of cotton from east Texas became much more difficult, time-consuming, and expensive. The presence of U.S. forces impeded the flow of cotton and disruptions were severe enough that some drayage companies complained that hauling bales was no longer profitable.[308]

The second and more important object achieved was discouraging the French from taking Matamoros and occupying the Mexican bank of the Rio Grande. The French were fearful of getting involved in a war with the United States at a time when they were occupied with the Mexican army. Additionally, they perceived arrival of the U.S. Army to be a clear signal of what could happen should France fail to heed the warnings implicit in the Monroe Doctrine. John Slidell, the Confederate minister in Paris, saw all this quite clearly. On February 3, 1864 he wrote to General Kirby Smith and said, "I fear that Matamoras [sic] will not soon be occupied by a French garrison ... while the eastern bank of the Rio Grande is occupied by the enemy.... I had long since been aware of the vast importance of a French occupation of Matamoras [sic]. The reason given [by the French] for not having taken possession of that port was the want of troops. There is undoubtedly much truth in this, but an indisposition to come in contact and possible collision with Federal troops had perhaps also a certain influence."[309]

As 1863 closed, General Banks's troops were being gradually withdrawn for use in the planned spring offensive in Louisiana's Red River Valley. Remaining Union troops in Texas were pulled back to Fort Brown and the lower Rio Grande Valley. By July 1864, all U.S. soldiers had been removed from the mainland offshore to Brazos Santiago. With the diminution of threat from Federal troops in Texas, numerous Confederate units were transferred to the Red River Valley to counter General Banks's advance in March 1864.

At this point, Texas authorities concentrated their efforts in keeping their major ports open to support blockade runners that increasingly were operating out of Havana because of closure of other Southern harbors. These primary ports were Velasco, Sabine Pass, and Galveston. Union vessels began probing the defenses in the Velasco area in February 1864. On February 9, the *Sciota* and *Aroostook* attacked the batteries at Velasco and they determined that the rebel artillery consisted of six 32-pounder guns. At nearby Caney Creek, they found that the Confederate battery consisted of one 30-pounder Parrott and four 32-pounder guns along with a force of 4,000 to 5,000 troops. Lieutenant Commander G. H. Perkins of the *Sciota* reported blockade running activity near Velasco.[310] United States naval and army forces had previously tested rebel defenses at Sabine Pass and Galveston; they found them to be formidable. Confederate military officials continued to strengthen all these positions throughout 1864. In the opening days of 1865, Secretary of the Navy Gideon Welles sent a message to Acting Rear Admiral Thatcher directing him to assume command of the West Gulf Blockading Squadron. In his missive dated January 24, 1865, Welles instructed Thatcher to "lose no time in closing that port [Galveston], so far as it can be done without actual possession, to the ingress and egress of vessels. It is feared that there is already an extensive trade carried on there. Rear admiral Porter has been instructed to send four of his swiftest steamers to the West Gulf Squadron for blockade duty off Galveston." Furthermore, the number of blockading vessels off the Texas coast was increased to 20 ships in 1865, where previously only six or seven ships had been on station.[311]

Chapter 7

The Confederacy Collapses

Throughout 1864, conditions in west Texas became gloomy, not from military activity but from civil disorder. Roving groups of "jayhawkers, bushwhackers, recusant conscripts, deserters, and 'blanket' Indians grew increasingly bold."[312] These gangs seized control of significant portions of territory; Texas state and Confederate contingents assigned to police the area were not up to the given task. Matters became so bad that the Texas state government declared unorganized land in the west to be closed until the war's end. This freed men in that area to come to the defense of Texas against Federal incursions. One such encroachment was at Brownsville, where Yankee troops were still garrisoned following the withdrawal of Banks's forces at the end of the Rio Grande expedition. During the spring and summer of 1864, "the state's Rio Grande border was liberated, reoccupied, and pacified by an irregular Confederate expeditionary force assembled for the task by John S. Ford."[313] He was to liberate Brownsville as well.

John "Rip" Ford was a legendary character who had served in the army of the Republic of Texas and in the U.S. army during the Mexican War. Earlier in the Civil War, he was commandant of conscripts. In addition to his military experience, Ford had been a politician, legislator, Texas Ranger, and newspaper editor. In his latter capacity, he would publish death notices captioned with "Rest in Peace" and later this was abbreviated during battle conditions to "R. I. P.," thereby earning him his nickname.[314]

General John Magruder, on December 23, 1863, ordered John Ford to go to San Antonio and raise himself a small army in order to drive the U.S. Army from Brownsville and the lower Rio Grande Valley. He immediately went there and recruited anyone willing to fight as long as that fellow had a horse and gun. His resulting "Cavalry of the West" was a nondescript collection of militiamen, bushwhackers, bandits, mixed blood Indians, old men, adolescent boys, and the like.

They had nothing in common except they were adventurous and wanted to defend their homes against a "mongrel force of Abolitionists, negroes, plundering Mexicans, and perfidious renegades." He had collected a brigade of 1,300 men who, "if not made up of the flower of Southern chivalry, at least contained a large number of hard and wiry gunslingers."[315]

The Cavalry of the West set out for the lower Rio Grande Valley and Brownsville to face the United States army. The Yankee group was a formidable force of well-equipped and seasoned veterans composed of 2,700 men and 28 pieces of artillery. They defended their beachhead at Brazos Santiago and were deployed along the Rio Grande. On June 25, 1864, Ford led 400 cavalrymen to explore the Union perimeter; he found that two companies of First Texas Cavalry were at Las Rucias Ranch. He engaged these units in a skirmish, beat them badly, and captured wagons, horses, saddles, and guns. Ford then progressed to within five miles of Brownsville and Fort Brown, where he found the defending force too large to attack. He retired thirty miles away and purchased additional ordnance for a push on the Union position.

However, on July 5, 1864, orders were issued to the U.S. force to abandon Fort Brown and garrison 1,200 men at Brazos Santiago to prepare a proper defense at that island location. Remaining troops were to return to New Orleans.[316] The Brownsville defenders apparently were in no hurry to depart because, on July 19, Ford launched an offensive operation and had sharp engagements with outlying U.S. forces. There was a standoff and the Union concluded on July 29 that Brownsville could not be effectively defended. They evacuated the town, declared it an open city, and pulled back to their strong defensive position at Brazos Santiago, where they remained for the rest of the war.

On July 30, Ford occupied Brownsville and French forces in Mexico quickly reacted. A French military contingent made an amphibious landing at Bagdad on August 22, 1864, and fortified the Mexican bank of the Rio Grande. John Ford sent envoys to the commander at Bagdad, Captain A. Vernon of the French navy, to secure an agreement with the French "by which our supplies can be passed over the Rio Grande." On August 25, Captain Vernon replied, "I shall see that all persons and property covered by the flag of your nation are duly respected. With regard to the facilities I might offer you in the transportation of supplies to your camp, you may be sure that I will bestow all my care upon this matter, and that you shall not suffer in anything on account of my presence here."[317] This French position set off another Mexican revolution in the area that was settled through cooperative military action by Captain Vernon on the Mexican side of the river and John Ford on the Texas side.

By the end of September 1864, there were no United States soldiers on the Texas mainland and the contingent occupying Brazos Santiago was reduced to a force of 950 men. Ford instructed his small force to keep a wary eye on them, but for the most part, the two sides ignored one another. The United States reinstated its token blockade with only one ship north of the mouth of the Rio Grande. Captain Vernon's expeditionary force seized Matamoros and gained control of the state of Tamaulipas. Relationships between the French and Confederates remained amicable and trade flourished across the river.

Matters returned to normal in the area—normal being the status of affairs before the Union incursion into the Rio Grande Valley. The rebel flag was flying over Brownsville; this pointed to a return of the hundreds of cotton wagons kicking up dust on their routes. Brownsville and Matamoros were enjoying boom times one last time. Historian Robert Kerby reports, "During the months of October and November, more than 600,000 pounds of ordnance stores passed from Matamoros to Brownsville and on to San Antonio."[318]

Not only was southwest Texas enjoying an economic revival, so was Galveston. The major C.S.A. harbors in the east were experiencing a tightened blockade and occupation by land; consequently, high tonnage steamships sought alternative ports. The last major Southern port, Mobile, fell to the Union on August 5, 1864, and Galveston, though remote, was the blockade runners' only option because it alone was available. This port had begun as a minor location for blockade running at the beginning of the war because it was exposed on a neck of land that was viewed as difficult to defend against attack. Ship owners did not wish to assume this additional risk. A Union invasion had been anticipated and due to this and for other reasons, she had not been favored for blockade running. That all changed in August with the fall of Mobile. In the first three years of the war, about a dozen steam blockade runners had arrived in Galveston, but after August a blockade runner came into port nearly every week.

During late summer 1864, three ships tested Galveston waters and found them hospitable. *Denbigh*, *Francis Marion*, and *Susana* all sailed from Havana to Galveston and returned safely to Cuba. This announced to the world that the blockade could be run, that Texas was full of cotton for sale at reasonable prices, and that the military establishment in that region was willing to pay top dollar for supplies and ordnance. Six more steamers sailed for Galveston within days and by the end of 1864, steamers were coming to the only open port in the Confederacy from Belize, Tampico, Havana, and Veracruz. While the rest of the Trans-Mississippi Department was failing, boom times came to Galveston in addition to Brownsville. Galveston imported all kinds of military goods, including rifles, carbines, and gunpowder—all the things an army needs to keep fighting. Cotton paid for all these goods.[319] While this war materiel was of great value to Kirby Smith's army, it was of no value to the Confederacy heartland in the east that was effectively cut off by the Federal occupation of the Mississippi River.

The *Denbigh* became a renowned "runner" in and out of Galveston. She had been built by the famous shipbuilders John Laird, Sons & Co. of Birkenhead, England, and was launched in August 1860. The *Denbigh* was a 162-ton side-wheel steamer made of iron and measured 182 feet long and 22 feet wide.[320] In September 1863, the European Trading Company (a C.S.A. firm) purchased her to be used for the run from Havana to Mobile. She made that trip frequently beginning early in 1864, and her arrivals at Mobile became so routine that she was called a "packet" boat, denoting the regularity of her schedule. She made seven runs into Mobile

BLOCKADE RUNNER DENBIGH. This painting by Thomas C. Healy is dated at Mobile, Alabama, July 29, 1864. It is believed that the depiction accurately portrays the steamship on that date. The *Denbigh* was set on fire in Galveston Bay on May 24, 1865, and was the last blockade runner to be captured or destroyed in the Civil War. (From a private collection.)

and her last trip was on July 26, 1864. *Denbeigh*'s successful tactics were based primarily on stealth and piloting skills rather than speed, although she had plenty of that if needed. She was called the "Bold Rascal" as she continued her achievements by making six round trips between Havana and Galveston. She slipped through obstructions that sometimes consisted of a dozen vessels.

The charmed life of the *Denbigh* ended on the hot evening of May 23-24, 1865, when she ran the blockade into Galveston Bay loaded with contraband from Cuba. While attempting to enter Galveston harbor through a narrow, but relatively deep, swash channel north and east of the Bay, strong currents carried her against a sandbar from which she could not free herself. The mostly British crew escaped in a smaller boat by rowing about one-quarter mile to Bolivar Point. At daylight, a blockading vessel, *Fort Jackson*, commanded by Captain B. F. Sands, discovered the *Denbigh* aground on Bird Key Spit. Captain Sands dispatched two vessels to fire upon her and sent boats to board and destroy her. This was accomplished by 7 A.M., when the blockade runner was enveloped in flames. Just before dawn, the blockade runner *Lark* had slipped into Galveston; she picked up *Denbigh*'s crew and returned to sea that evening. *Denbigh* was the last vessel captured or destroyed by blockading ships and *Lark* was the last boat successfully running through the blockade. This closed the book on blockade running during the Civil War.[321]

The May 1865 burning of the *Denbigh* was a metaphor for the impending collapse of the Confederate States of America.[322] General Robert E. Lee had surrendered to General Ulysses S. Grant at Appomattox Court House on April 9, 1865; General Joseph Johnston obtained an armistice from General William T. Sherman near Hillsborough, North Carolina, that led to the surrender of Johnston's army on April 26, 1865. Jefferson Davis held his last full cabinet meeting on April 24, 1865, and left with 2,000 cavalrymen intending to join Generals Richard Taylor and Nathan Bedford Forrest in Alabama. United States soldiers near Irwinsville, Georgia, arrested President Davis on May 11, 1865. General Grant was pleased to hear that Davis had been captured since he feared that Davis "might get into the trans–Mississippi region and there set up a more contracted confederacy." Indeed, Davis may have had something like that in mind. Confederate Major General Joseph Wheeler was part of the plot to help President Davis elude Federal capture. In the May 1898 edition of *The Century*, Wheeler reported, "We supposed it was Mr. Daviss [sic] purpose or hope to attain safety among the large body of troops still in arms west of the Mississippi. We fancied he also put some faint trust in rumors then circulating, namely, that France or England might do something to revive the chances of the Confederacy."[323] Although Grant did not know it, he had no need for angst because the end was also near for "Kirby-Smithdom."

Collapse of the Confederacy had been signaled by events occurring months earlier. The first and strongest indicator of despair of the Confederate States of America, and of her realization of the nearness of her collapse, pertained to availability of men to fight the war. The C.S.A. was running out of white men to fight and die for the cause; she had become desperate enough to turn to black men to do so. On January 2, 1864, a C.S.A. officer, Major General Patrick R. Cleburne, had written a letter that was signed by 13 other officers recommending that slaves be armed to fight for the C.S.A., and afterwards freed. In this letter, he suggested

> that we immediately commence training a large reserve of the most courageous of our slaves, and further that we guarantee freedom within a reasonable time to every slave in the South who shall remain true to the Confederacy in this war. As between the loss of independence and the loss of slavery, we assume that every patriot will freely give up the latter—give up the Negro slaves rather than be a slave himself.... [W]hen we make soldiers of them we must make free men of them beyond all question, and ... [i]f we arm and train him and make him fight for the country in her hour of dire distress, every consideration of principle and policy demand that we should set him and his whole race who side with us free.[324]

Cleburne had been severely chastised for daring to openly suggest the unthinkable. Slaves had been used in army labor battalions, and in Texas had been "borrowed" from plantations to build fortifications, but they rarely had been used as regular soldiers.

To put a gun in the hands of a slave in order to fight the Union was fraught with dangers and posed many questions, not the least of which was where he would end up pointing the gun. An unspoken fear (sometimes articulated) always had been apprehension about slave insurrection. This was a realistic concern. There had been uprisings of slaves against their masters in the United States as well as elsewhere in the world, and everyone remembered John Brown and Nat Turner. Therefore, the Southern soldier could never be certain that Negro C.S.A. soldiers would be able to distinguish Southern whites from Northern whites while firing their weapons. Further, there was always the question of whether whites and blacks could fight alongside one another in a cooperative and effective manner. Additionally, could a black man who had fought as a soldier for the Confederacy return to bondage at war's conclusion?

The most serious issue, however, was the implication involved in employing a Negro as a soldier. Making a soldier of a slave signaled moral collapse of the Confederacy. The change of a black man's status from slave to soldier announced to the world that the South was abandoning its basic and most important social institution. The South had seceded for the purpose of preserving and perpetuating slavery, and to abandon this "peculiar institution" was to discard justification for continuing the secession struggle.

Nevertheless, there was so little white civilian manpower available in the South that the venerable Robert E. Lee had made such a suggestion. The Confederate government acknowledged the depth of this problem—and the extent of its despair—by deciding to make soldiers of slaves on March 13, 1865. The act signed by President Davis authorized raising of up to 300,000 able bodied men between the ages of eighteen and forty-five, "irrespective of color." Manumission of veteran slaves was not an option and "nothing ... shall be construed to authorize a change in the relation which the said slaves shall bear to their owners, except by the consent of the owners and of the States in which they reside."[325] The C.S.A. War Department then issued implementing regulations to carry out the law and authorized commissions to any white man willing to command ex-slaves in the field. One Texas white man, Isaac Dennis, applied for a commission on April 8, 1865; his petition was never processed because the next day Lee surrendered to Grant.

Confederate states had begun to disintegrate by the spring of 1864, when wives were pleading for their husbands to return home to put in the crop, and some did. On January 1, 1865, the *Galveston News* and *San Antonio Herald* carried "a column and a half of the names of men, who are officially published as deserters."[326] Soldiers were seeking legal ways of detaching themselves from the military arm by securing a detail to a needed civilian occupation. By the end of 1864, perhaps 10,000 men were detailed away from military activity in the field into occupations such as commissary clerks, farmers, printers, teamsters, hospital workers, and postmen. Kirby Smith cancelled all such furloughs and prohibited the detail of more men in February 1865, but men reacted by deserting.[327]

Army desertions were only one indication of imminent collapse of the Confederate States of America. The breakdown of morale undermined social order, and the judicial system began to give way to vigilante justice in many areas of Texas. For example, "The Weathersford County minutemen lynched as least fourteen victims; the vigilantes in both Parker and Gillespie counties killed numerous others; ... an armed mob of eighty men ... collected at Tyler, stormed the jailhouse, kidnapped four notorious bandits who were awaiting trial, and hanged them all from a single tree."[328]

Despite obvious disintegration of the Confederacy, "Kirby-Smithdom" gamely carried on with a modicum of Confederate authority that brought a sense of order out of chaos, generating a glimmer of hope. General Magruder called upon his men to resist the expected Yankee invasion. Texas Governor Murrah urged the populace to rally around the battle-scarred rebel flag; he promised, "With God's blessing, it may yet be the proud privilege of Texas, the youngest of the Confederate Sisters, to redeem the cause of the Confederacy from its present perils."[329] All the rhetoric in the world, however, could not re-ignite the will to fight and could not provide necessary men, money, and war materiel with which to fight.

The situation had become so gloomy in the Trans-Mississippi Department that Kirby Smith sent one of his generals to Paris on a remarkable mission. Major General Camille Polignac was a native of France who was a successful division commander in the Red River campaign. On January 9, 1865, Smith wrote a letter for General Polignac to carry to John Slidell, the C.S.A. diplomat. The communication called Slidell's attention to the "state of affairs in this department.... Our cause has reached a crisis to call for foreign intervention." He stressed the importance of France coming to immediate aid of the department and suggested that Polignac may be helpful in discussions with them. To encourage the French, Smith implied that slaves might be freed. He wrote, "I have formed the opinion from careful observation that in the great slave districts of this department nineteen-twentieths of the planters would at this time willingly accept any system of gradual emancipation to insure our independence as a people." Of course, such an offer would have been unthinkable earlier and it highlights the despair felt by Kirby Smith. Polignac arrived in France in March but the mission was a failure because it was obvious to all that the Confederacy was on the verge of defeat.[330]

At Brazos Santiago near Brownsville, both the Yankees and rebels reached an informal agreement that senseless slaughter would have no effect upon the outcome of the Civil War, so they simply stopped fighting. The two sides were overseeing the fall of the Confederacy and both were favorable to finding some way of ending it all. It was like a death knell. The bell was tolling for the Confederacy and all was quiet in the west. In January 1865, General Grant authorized a leave of absence for General Lew Wallace's travel to Brazos Santiago. The purpose of the trip was to meet with John Ford to determine whether a formal truce, or perhaps some surrender of Confederate forces in that area, might be arranged. Ford, his commander, General James Slaughter, and General Wallace met under a flag of truce on March 11. They concluded their discussions by drafting a written agreement stating the terms of surrender of the Trans-Mississippi states and territories. This draft was forwarded to departmental headquarters and was angrily rejected because those drafting the document had no authority to speak on behalf of the Trans-Mississippi Department; the terms were not acceptable. The war in the department would continue for another two months.

General Lee surrendered to General Grant on April 9, 1865, and this stimulated Kirby Smith to begin negotiations in May with U.S. General John Pope for surrender of his troops. Pope had been authorized by General Grant to offer to the Trans-Mississippi Department the same surrender terms that Lee had accepted when Grant proffered them. Smith replied that he found the terms unacceptable, but he temporized and asked Pope's chief of staff to remain in Shreveport while he met one more time in Marshall, Texas, with the Trans-Mississippi governors. The governors (or their representatives) met between May 9 and 11 with General Smith and developed a set of proposals that provided for cessation of hostilities and preservation of civil order, while maintaining honor and avoiding the humiliation of a formal surrender. Simultaneously, a number of prominent C.S.A. army officers were also meeting and they determined that they would "fight unto the end" or "at least until President Davis reaches this department."[331] If Kirby Smith resisted, they intended to take over the government. On May 11, the Union captured President Davis, but communications were such that no one knew that at the time.

The Federal chief of staff was presented the proposals resulting from the Marshall Conference. He rejected them because he had no authority to accept the right of the department to disband its troops without the formality of surrender. General Grant reacted by initiating steps to send an expeditionary force to crush Texas into submission. General Pope suggested that Grant exercise patience and let events run their natural course. Pope knew that the department's army was already disintegrating and whether he surrendered or not, Smith would soon find he had no army to command. Kirby Smith would not relent, and he proposed to continue the fight.

However, nearly by accident, the last battle of the Civil War erupted on May 10, 1865. When U.S. forces were reduced at the conclusion of the Rio Grande campaign, they established a garrison at Brazos Santiago on Brazos Island to symbolically fly the U.S. flag on Texas soil and let the French know they occupied a portion of that Southern state. In addition, they could cooperate with the Union barrier offshore by informing blockading vessels of approaching small boat traffic that was sailing on the Intracoastal Waterway. The commander of the U.S. force, Colonel Theodore H. Barrett, reported to his superiors that he was maintaining a good defensive position, and in addition could take Brownsville. On May 1, 1865, some Confederates at Palmito Ranch, located midway between Brownsville and the sea, had seen a copy of the *New Orleans Times* that announced

Lee's surrender to Grant, Lincoln's death, and surrender negotiations between Generals Sherman and Johnston in North Carolina. Within the next ten days, hundreds of rebels deserted the army and returned home, but those that remained were "hard core" and were determined to continue to fight for Texas as a matter of honor.

In the meantime, Colonel Barrett had received reports that the rebel army had numerous deserters and was preparing to evacuate Brownsville and move east of Corpus Christi. Considering this intelligence to be valid, and perhaps wishing to gain some glory before the end of the war, he ordered 300 men of the Sixty-second U.S. Colored Infantry and the dismounted Second Texas U.S. Cavalry to cross to the mainland and occupy Brownsville. This force, along with a reinforcing body of 200 men of the Thirty-fourth Indiana Infantry, was defeated by a contingent of John "Rip" Ford's "Cavalry of the West" at Palmito Ranch on May 13, 1865. The defeated Yankees retreated to the safety of Brazos Santiago.[332] The United States had the dubious distinction of making the last retreat of the war, while the Confederate States of America could claim the final victory of the Civil War. Ford proclaimed to his men, "Boys, we have done finely."[333]

This singular victory, however, did little to stem a tide of desertions or increase morale. Everyone knew it was all over, or would be in a matter of days. By this time the "whole state of Texas was fast becoming indifferent to the war.... The fortunes of the entire Confederacy were ebbing fast.... Gloom and uncertainty, soon to pass into despair, settled quickly over Texas."[334] In wholesale numbers, rebels began to leave their posts throughout Texas to return to their homes. Those who did not return to their homes reported to their commanders that they would lay down their arms at the first appearance of U.S. soldiers. Others engaged in insurrection. For example, on the night of May 14, four hundred members of the Galveston garrison mutinied and attempted to desert their post while armed; only the force of the Eighth Texas Infantry put down insurrection.[335]

Not surprisingly, Federal prisoners at Camp Ford four miles northeast of Tyler had a different perspective. Living conditions there had become difficult after 3,000 prisoners taken during the Red River campaign had been transferred to this POW compound. One of the Yankee prisoners there was Sergeant Arthur E. Gilligan, Third Rhode Island Volunteer Cavalry, who had been captured near Bayou Goula in Louisiana. He wrote in his diary of his last days at Camp Ford and his entry for Sunday, April 23, 1865, says, "The news came again that Richmond was taken, that Lee had surrendered with 45,000 men, also that Johnson [sic] with 25,000 men had surrendered, but I don't believe a word of it." On May 15, 1865, Sergeant Gilligan was told he was to be paroled and he writes, "The guards have all deserted, but Sweets [sic] men and they are all drunk, officers and all. In the evening the Band got together and went to headquarters and played to the Rebs and our officers. The whiskey was passed around and I partook freely." On May 17, 1865, the sergeant and the remaining prisoners were released from Camp Ford and walked toward Shreveport, Louisiana. On Sunday, May 21, 1865, he records in his diary, "Today we passed a good many nice hours and crossed the Texas line. I hope I shall never have occasion to cross it again." He died in 1922 without ever again having crossed the Texas boundary.[336]

General Smith left Shreveport on May 18 to go to Houston, where he hoped to make a last ditch effort with Magruder's corps to sustain the Confederacy. While en route, he received a telegram from Magruder saying he had lost control of his command. Everyone, everywhere was demobilizing throughout the whole of the Department of the Trans-Mississippi. Slowly, General E. Kirby Smith came to realize that he was in command of a Confederate force that did not exist.[337]

Most of the remaining stragglers of the once-mighty Trans-Mississippi army were formally surrendered to U.S. General Edward R. S. Canby on May 26, 1865, under the same terms that Lee had accepted from Grant a month earlier. Nevertheless, Kirby Smith had not yet surrendered. He decided to shift his headquarters to Houston to take charge of the army of the District of Texas, New Mexico, and Arizona, but before arriving there, he learned of the capture of C.S.A. President Jefferson Davis by the Union. That did it! General Smith decided it was hopeless and he reopened negotiations with General Canby, who was en route from Mobile to New Orleans. Canby had led the assault on Mobile, and on May 4, he had accepted the surrender of Richard Taylor and his troops near there. General Smith delegated negotiations to his chief of staff, Lieutenant General Simon Buckner, who, at Fort Donelson three years earlier, had surrendered the first Confederate unit to lay down its arms. Now he was to surrender the last Confederate army in the land. Buckner was told to accept whatever terms were offered and on May 26, Buckner signed a surrender agreement in New Orleans that contained in substance the same terms that General Lee had accepted.

The day after Buckner had signed the accord, Kirby Smith arrived in Houston to take charge of his army, but an army simply was not there. Smith's reaction was astounding. On May 29, he issued a special order convening a Court of Inquiry to learn why the troops had been disbanded, and the court made a cursory report after a brief meeting. Smith then wrote a farewell address to his men on May 30: "Soldiers! I am left a Commander without an army—a General without troops. You have made yr. Choice. It was unwise & unpatriotic, But it is final. I pray you may not live to regret it."[338]

The agreement for capitulation called for a formal surrender ceremony to take place in Galveston on June 2, 1865. The U.S. steamer *Fort Jackson* was dispatched to Galveston with General Canby and his staff on board. General Smith arrived in Galveston, boarded the *Fort Jackson* in the harbor, and signed the surrender document that finally ended the terrible four-year conflict.

A prominent resident of Galveston had served the Confederate States of America in several capacities, most recently as a member of the C.S.A. Congress. Previously a Brigadier General, Louis T. Wigfall was unaware of this ceremony on Galveston Bay as he was walking with Texas troops back home from Montgomery, Alabama. His daughter, Louise Wigfall Wright, had started home ahead of her father and waited for him at the house of friends. She wrote a book about her experiences and describes meeting her father:

One evening, about dark, I was standing at the gate, watching down the road, with hardly a thought or hope of his appearing, when, far up the dusty highway, I saw him coming. He walked slowly, unlike the brisk step I knew of old; absolute dejection was in his mien, and he had no joyous greeting to give me. His uniform was worn and soiled, and he had taken from his collar the gold stars of his rank. Somehow I had no word to say. We stood and looked at each other. Finally, we found speech, and to my query, "What are you going to do?" he answered, "I am on my way across the river to join Kirby Smith." I laid my hand upon his shoulder, and paused a moment, "Have you not heard," I said, "Kirby Smith has surrendered."[339]

Major General Gordon Granger was placed in command of all Federal troops in Texas. In Galveston on June 19, 1865, he released General Order Number 3 that declared,

The people of Texas are informed that, in accordance with a proclamation from the Executive of the United States, all slaves are free. This involves an absolute equality of personal rights and rights of property between former masters and slaves, and the connection heretofore existing between them becomes that between employer and hired labor. The freedmen are advised to remain quietly at their present homes and work for wages. They are informed that they will not be allowed to collect at military posts and that they will not be supported in idleness either there or elsewhere.[340]

It is noted that the last two sentences of the order somewhat dampen the spirit of the message, since former slaves are admonished to be quiet and not become idle. Nevertheless, slaves were free. The Civil War had ended.

Chapter 8

Blockade Revisited: An Evaluation

There are probably as many views as to the effectiveness of the blockade as there are historians. The efforts here will be to make some sense out of all the conflicting views; to evaluate and discuss certain blockade-related data and factors; to present a summary of diverse views without promoting one position or the other; to discuss shortcomings of blockade evaluations appearing in the literature; and finally, to summarize and reach conclusions.

The difficulty in assessing blockade efficiency lies in clearly defining its purpose, and then measuring results against this objective. The first critical task is to define what constitutes a blockade. According to a definition in *Webster's Collegiate Dictionary*, a blockade is "the isolation of a warring nation or a particular enemy area (as a harbor) by means of troops or warships to prevent passage of persons or supplies."[341] Using this definition, it is helpful to recall that blockades, or threats of blockades, had been utilized in America before the Civil War. Additionally, we are prone to believe that only ships apply a blockade when by definition troops may be involved.

In 1774 Great Britain passed the Boston Port Act that barricaded Boston in order to coerce payment of a tea tax. During the War of Independence, England blockaded our coast. France was a principle blockade runner, and in 1781, the French fleet broke a British blockade off Chesapeake Bay. One of many causes of the War of 1812 was America's contention that Great Britain had declared the coast blockaded when in fact it was not blockaded (a polemic often voiced by the Confederacy during the Civil War). In response, the British expanded their barrier in 1813 and 1814 to encompass Delaware and Chesapeake bays, New England, and the important seaports of Norfolk and New York. The effect of this was to contain the U.S. Navy. Moreover, the nullification crisis in South Carolina twenty years later carried with it a threat of secession should the Federal government try to blockade Charleston harbor. Consequently, before mid-century the blockade concept was well established in the United States.

A blockade, to be legal, must be broad enough so that shipping feels threatened by its presence; otherwise, it cannot be considered effective. The United States had no intention, at the commencement of the blockade, to seal off 3,500 miles of coastline. That was an impossibility; consequently, blockade implementation concentrated on closing specific ports. The C.S.A. government always contended that relative disregard of coastal shipping in favor of sealing off specific ports made the barrier a "paper blockade"—an ineffective barrier—because ships could always slip in an out of unguarded coastal ports. While it was true that rebel vessels could do so, that in itself did not make the plan ineffective from a legal standpoint. A reading of the law and review of some of its interpretations (as discussed below) may serve to clarify this issue.

Any sovereign nation may declare a blockade, and to be sufficient it first must be publicized by some reasonable means. A nation must receive due notice of such action and must be made aware of consequences should the blockade be ignored. The country erecting the obstruction must communicate this information to other countries either by "a formal notice from the blockading power, by notice to his government, or by the notoriety of the fact."

The next step for construction of a competent blockade is to make it effective. This matter is central to proper evaluation. For a blockade to be effective, "it is required that there should be a number of vessels stationed near enough to the port to make the entry apparently dangerous." In the Civil War, the United States had to present a "competent force, stationed and present, at or near the entrance of the port," in order for the blockade to be considered effective. However, the "accidental absence of the blockading force" is not sufficient to consider the barrier removed unless there is "negligence or remissness." A violation of the blockade occurs "by going into the place blockaded or by coming out of it with a cargo laden after the commencement of the blockade. Additionally, placing himself so near a blockaded port as to be in a condition to slip in without observation is a violation of the blockade and raises the presumption of a criminal intent. The sailing for a blockaded port, knowing it to be blockaded ... may be a breach of the blockade. When the ship has contracted guilt by a breach of the blockade, she may be taken at any time before the end of her voyage ... and when taken, the ship is confiscated and the cargo is always, prima facie, implicated in the guilt."[342]

United States Secretary of State William H. Seward was careful to see that the letter of the law was observed. According to historian David Paul Crook, Seward "ensured that the blockade was punctiliously notified and set up according to the canons of international law."[343] The issuance of the proclamation met requirements for proper notification to the world of the blockade and of consequences for its violation. From a reading of law, it seems clear that blockade of a port, not a coastline, is sufficient for existence of a legitimate blockade. Moreover, the law distinguishes between the blockading nation, which has extensive rights and responsibilities, and the country violating the blockade, which has few rights or responsibilities. It is important to keep these legal principles in mind when examining blockade effectiveness because we are assessing a legal concept that has evolved since the days of Napoleon. This introductory material establishes a framework for inquiry. From this point onward, we will investigate practical and functional aspects of the blockade.

The doctrine of continuous voyage affected the Civil War blockade. This doctrine means that a neutral ship and her cargo are subject to seizure if that cargo is ultimately destined for an enemy port, even if landing at a neutral port interrupts the trip. A ship engaged in an illegal voyage (carrying contraband destined for a blockaded port) could not make the trip lawful by the mere touching of the vessel at a neutral port. This principle emerged from English prize court decisions during the Napoleonic wars. The British applied it in the first decade of the nineteenth century to United States ships that brought Cuban sugar to New England and reshipped it as U.S. goods to Spain (which was blockaded by the English). The critical question always was whether the cargo originally was bound for a blockaded port, irrespective of interruptions in the voyage. The United States objected to this doctrine in 1805, but then reversed itself, using the same principle against blockade runners during the Civil War. The British hardly were in any position to object since they had initiated the concept.

Throughout the Civil War, the United States often interrupted merchant shipping on the high seas for inspection of papers to determine if contraband cargo was bound for the Confederacy. Frequently, papers would reveal the legitimacy of a voyage; cargo and ship would continue the voyage after a slight delay. This was only a minor nuisance. However, in one celebrated case, a ship was seized under the continuous voyage principle, and this created both a precedent and an untoward incident with Great Britain.

On February 25, 1863, British steamer *Peterhoff* was stopped off Saint Thomas in the Caribbean by the U.S. warship *Vanderbilt*. This began as a routine stop and ships' papers were found to be in order for her journey to Matamoros, Mexico. An interview with a crew member revealed, however, that this cargo ultimately was bound for the Confederate town of Brownsville, Texas. The cargo was inspected and was found to consist of gray blankets, boots, horseshoes, nails, leather, and large quantities of drugs including morphine, quinine, calomel, and chloroform.[344] The vessel was seized with the justification that it was on a continuous voyage from Great Britain to the neutral port of Saint Thomas, and on to Matamoros with a cargo destined for the enemy.

The *Peterhoff* was taken to prize court in New York. This court upheld the seizure, stating that the continuous voyage concept could be expanded to include transshipment of contraband across land frontiers. The cargo was sold at auction with proceeds going to the U.S. Treasury. The ship was turned over to the U.S. Navy and ultimately it sunk after a collision with *Monticello* on March 6, 1864. Great Britain objected to interruption of commerce, but it was largely a *pro forma* action; the Brits did not file a formal protest. Lord Earl Russell, the British foreign secretary, on another occasion had instructed Lord Lyons, the British minister to the United States, to tell U.S. Secretary of State Seward that the British government "considered trade between England and Matamoras [sic] perfectly legitimate; if some of the goods were later shipped across the frontier, that was beside the question. He intimated that there was as much of this trade from New York to Matamoras [sic] as from London and Liverpool."[345] Moreover, Great Britain looked to the future and correctly anticipated that the doctrine might be useful to them in future wars. The owners of the *Peterhoff* were in an uproar nevertheless, and they seethed about it throughout the war. After the Civil War, they appealed the verdict of the prize court to the United States Supreme Court, which overturned the ruling. The owners were reimbursed for the vessel and its cargo.[346]

Continuous voyage is just one of many factors that must be considered in assessing the efficacy of a blockade. A reasonable person would never dismiss this type of action on the grounds that it had no bearing on the conduct of the blockade or success of blockade running. Other similar incidents have been mentioned earlier: U.S. Navy ships making illegal seizures off the Rio Grande because they captured vessels in neutral waters as a result of using incorrect compass bearings; and claims on seized vessels being overturned by prize court due to legal technicalities. The impact of these and other incidents must be taken into account.

When President Lincoln proclaimed imposition of a blockade on April 19, 1861, the Federal navy was "in a dilapidated state: caught flatfooted" by his announcement.[347] The Federal establishment instituted a crash building program and purchased nearly any vessel capable of floating in order to get equipment on station quickly. Although the navy quickly rose to the task at hand, the Confederates rather aptly called the obstruction a "paper blockade." It would be fair to say that there was little semblance of a blockade until late that year; the Confederacy constantly reminded France and Britain of this fact in the hope they would be recognized as an independent nation. In fact, however, there was not that much shipping to interfere with, because few foreign vessels were attempting to enter or leave our ports during the first year of war. This occurred for several reasons. One was the C.S.A. decision to embargo cotton in order to force European powers to come to their aid. England and France did not respond as the South had hoped because they believed the South would defeat the North. If that were the case, they did not wish to risk war with the United States. Furthermore, these foreign powers would not come to the aid of the South until the new confederation displayed its capability to maintain its independence. Since most Europeans felt the war would not last long and the South would win, because there was an adequate initial supply of cotton on hand in England at the beginning of the war, and because of the South's cotton embargo, there was little blockade running in 1861.

According to Mahin, "During 1862, however, an effective blockade running system was established."[348] The most active port for such activity during this period was Charleston, South Carolina. To understand how blockade running traffic increased, it is useful to look at data from this port. In 1861, Charleston had one steam blockade runner arriving there, but the next year 27 steamships got through the barrier, and most had departed from Nassau. Data for vessels running from Charleston are similar. In 1861, four steamships slipped out of Charleston, but in 1862 the number leaving from that port increased to 30 vessels. Again, the favorite destination was Nassau.[349]

Frank L. Owsley contends that in 1861 and 1862, "the blockade was nothing more than the plundering of neutral commerce en route to the Confederacy under the cover of a nominal blockade." British Consul Bunch at Charleston reported on August 6, 1861, that privateers were "sending their prizes into all the ports quite unmolested by any of the ships of the United States." About this same time, a privateer left Charleston in daylight and "there were no blockading vessels in sight." In addition, in August 1861 Bunch wrote, "The blockade of this port [Charleston] continues to be conducted with the same laxity which has hitherto distinguished it. Vessels of various sizes enter and sail almost at pleasure."[350] Regarding the Georgia and Florida coastal area, Fullerton, the acting consul at Savannah, reported on July 10, 1862, that the obstruction was ineffective. He said, "The blockading vessels still continued to depend upon an occasional cruise up and down the coast."

Thus there was widespread reporting and agreement as to ineffectiveness of this barrier on the East Coast through 1862, and the situation in the gulf was not much different. Consul Arthur T. Lynn at Galveston reported that blockade running was uninterrupted in that area. A Union blockading vessel guarded the main channel of Galveston, but Pass San Luis to the west was unguarded, and blockade runners used it regularly. An east channel was unguarded as well. In addition, in December 1861 nearby Sabine City had a blockade runner that delivered 91,000 pounds of gunpowder to that port. The vessel had loaded her cargo at Havana, and from Sabine City she went to New Orleans without any challenge from a United States vessel on either leg of her voyage.[351] Tans concludes, "the blockade was ineffective in the early stages of the war, but it did eventually tighten as more ships were added to the blockading fleet."[352]

Using episodic events and statistical counts to evaluate the effectiveness of a blockade can lead one to improper conclusions when using this material in isolation of less obvious factors such as governmental policies. The Confederacy developed "King Cotton" policy to place an embargo on cotton exports to England and France, and related to this was the Confederates' decision to burn excess cotton through 1861 and the first half of 1862. The magnitude of this destruction, however, is seldom compared with the amount of cotton getting through the blockade. Historian David M. Potter places this in perspective when he suggests that much more cotton was destroyed or smuggled through the lines than was run through the blockade. Specifically, Potter states, "At the end of the war, 2,500,000 bales had been destroyed to prevent them from falling into the hands of the enemy; less than 1,000,000 probably had been exported through the blockade; and an incalculable amount had been smuggled through the lines."[353]

Opinion has been nearly unanimous that during at least the first year of the war, the Union blockade was ineffective against light blockade running traffic. Although blockade violations were prevalent, especially in 1862, there was no serious effort by France and Britain to challenge the legality of the naval barrier. These nations likely were exercising caution to avoid entanglement in a war with the United States. Moreover, the Union's victory over Lee at Antietam in September 1862 suggested to Europe that the North might win the war. Also, Lincoln's Emancipation Proclamation in January 1863 injected a moral tone into the conflict that resonated with the British, who likewise had abolished slavery. Although France favored the Confederacy, it was unlikely she would engage in any unilateral action that might antagonize Great Britain.

The Federal barrier did not remain ineffective throughout the war. At the end of 1861 only one-tenth of blockade runners were captured or destroyed. By 1863, the barriers had become tighter and one-quarter were captured; by the end of 1864, the capture rate rose to one-third. East Coast ports were effectively closed by 1865 and at gulf ports only one-half of blockade runners successfully made their runs. Throughout the Civil War, on the average, one in six blockade runners failed in their attempt. Of course, this also means that on the average, five of six ships that attempted to penetrate the barrier were successful.

These odds were good enough to entice many individuals into a lucrative career of blockade running. Rewards were phenomenal. A ship running cotton could show a profit of a quarter-million dollars from each one-way voyage, and a firm often considered financial gain was such that it could afford to lose a vessel after two successful runs.[354] It was easy to find good captains who cherished visions of becoming rich, and enjoyed living an adventurous life as well. A captain could be paid $5,000 in gold for a round trip from Nassau to a Southern port, but he could gain much more than that because space might be allotted to him for carrying his private cargo. It is reported that one enterprising captain sailing from Glasgow, Scotland, to Wilmington, North Carolina, had 1,000 pairs of corset stays as his private cargo that he sold at Wilmington at a profit of 1,100 percent. About the same return was enjoyed on a load of toothbrushes that he carried back to his homeport.[355]

This type of lucrative career was unintentionally encouraged by Southern cultural factors that were inclined to be antiauthoritarian and individualistic. Evidence of this propensity in the mores of the South is found in the support of rights of individual states as opposed to promotion of a strong central government. There was a tendency to insist upon due process of law and writ of habeas corpus to protect the freedom of the individual. Therefore, even disloyal activities that were harmful to the Southern cause were tolerated. Blockade runners brought in high profit goods—such as linens, perfumes, and liquor—that were officially prohibited. The Confederate Congress passed a law on February 6, 1864 that made it illegal to import such luxury goods. The act enumerated a long list of prohibited goods, such as "brandy, wines, or other spirits ... beer, ale, and porter ... bananas, coconuts, plantains and oranges ... coins, medals, gems, pearls, rubies, and other precious stones." If the person importing these prohibited goods was caught and convicted, the punishment entailed forfeiture of the goods and payment of a fine amounting to double the value of the goods. Of course, a ship's captain would be undeterred by this inconsequential punishment because he was taking a greater risk in running the blockade. The amount of money he could make in a successful run more than offset the punishment he might receive for violating the law. The statute was unpopular and seldom was enforced; the blockade runner carrying such goods could do so with impunity. However, cotton smuggling and importation of luxury goods worked to the detriment of the Southern cause because it diverted cotton that was badly needed to finance the war effort, and limited cargo space that was needed for medicines and other items required by the military. In fact, one writer sees the emphasis upon retaining these self-indulgences in wartime as a principle reason for the collapse of the Confederacy.[356]

During the first two years of war, there was a dearth of steamships going to and from Galveston, but this activity began increasing by 1864 as the East Coast ports of Savannah, Charleston, and Wilmington faced stronger barriers. In 1861 and 1862, only four steamships ran the blockade into Galveston and two of these vessels came from other Texas ports. The reason for so little activity was that the cotton embargo did not terminate until mid–1862. Also, most shipments were made by private firms that preferred running from Nassau to southeastern ports because shorter distances meant less cargo space had to be devoted to coal and more cargo space could be dedicated to high-profit goods. As the East Coast blockade became more effective, European ship owners tended to switch their transshipping port from Nassau to Havana to decrease the distance to Galveston. Consequently, there was a noticeable increase of traffic going in and out of Galveston. In 1863 and 1864, there were twenty-three arrivals and twenty-two departures to and from Galveston and most of them had come from, or were bound for, Havana. Six of these arrivals and five of these departures were by the same steamship, *Alice*. She made her last departure from Galveston on September 10, 1864, and was captured the same day by *Magnolia*.[357]

American consuls at various gulf ports provided rich pictures of blockade running through their regular reports. Consul-General R. W. Shufeldt at Havana wrote on April 26, 1863, that the steamer mentioned earlier (*Alice*) was so successful running the blockade between Havana and Mobile that her captain was earning $5,000 for each round trip. In late 1863, Consul Chase at Tampico, Mexico, reported that this port was a regular stop for sailing vessels transporting cotton from Galveston, Sabine Pass, and the Brazos River. Blockade runners formed a steady stream of ships carrying cotton from Texas. British as well as New York cotton buyers would take possession of the fiber in Tampico for shipment to the ports of New York or Liverpool. Consular agents at Veracruz, Mexico, reported a similar flow of cotton from that port and returning traffic of munitions. Comparable traffic occurred between Texas and Belize, British Honduras, during 1863. Blockade running in the gulf region was active throughout 1863, and it increased in volume in the second half of 1864 as the siege of Mobile materialized. After

Mobile fell, Galveston traffic became even larger because it was the only C.S.A. port still open.

By September 9, 1864, Consul Savage at Havana reported that the composition of the blockade running fleet was changing from sailing ships to steamships. Shippers had thought that profit on this run would not be too generous because of the need to carry a large supply of coal for the round trip. However, after Mobile fell, there was little choice. Larger and faster steamships were necessary for this run and they proved to be successful. On September 14, Savage reported that two blockade runners that had left Havana with supplies on September 9 were already back from Galveston with cotton. Further, it was reported that 14 sailing vessels waited at Galveston and ten paused at the Brazos River for favorable weather in order to make runs to sea laden with cotton. At this same time, six steamers were loading at Havana and would depart for the Texas coast. In this part of the Gulf of Mexico, the sea literally was swarming with blockade runners through the end of 1864. The sum of this evidence indicates that blockade running in the gulf was similar in character to that on the Atlantic coast. As on the East Coast, the only way to stop the flow was to capture a port, and this clearly was the case with the Mobile-Galveston experience. When Mobile was closed down, nearly all of its traffic was transferred to Galveston.[358] This important port was not captured by war's end, and historian Edward T. Cotham, Jr., contends that most ships running the Galveston blockade prevailed. He says "Shipping records confirm that during 1864, approximately 87 percent of all of the steamers that attempted to run the blockade on the Gulf Coast were successful."[359]

Obviously, many vessels were successfully running the blockade. The question arises as to why Great Britain did not challenge the legality of the barrier. After all, England was arguably the greatest sea power in history and France would follow her lead. Early in the war, the Confederacy attempted to convince England and France that Union naval obstructions constituted a mere "paper blockade." Confederate diplomats and agents constantly emphasized the ineffectiveness of the blockade; nevertheless, European nations respected the barrier. The conventional reason given for Britain and France not challenging the legality of the blockade is that these nations did not desire to become involved in war with the United States. Norman A. Graebner presents another interpretation of why Britain respected the barrier. He asserts, "In undermining the principle of the Declaration of Paris that blockades to be binding must be effective, the United States was releasing England in a future conflict from this burdensome feature of the past. American action weakened the stand of the smaller maritime powers in their perennial effort to force Great Britain to recognize neutral rights in time of war."[360] Similarly, David Paul Crook examines Great Britain's experience with imposing blockades, especially during the Napoleonic wars. Given this history, he suggests it would be hypocritical for Britain to deny the Union its right to impose an effective blockade during the de facto war with the South. Furthermore, he contends it was in Great Britain's long-term naval interests to affirm the Union's use and expansion of a blockade because it would establish precedents that might serve England well in its future blockades.[361]

In most evaluations of the blockade, traffic through Matamoros and Bagdad, Mexico, is infrequently mentioned. It is important to understand that Bagdad was not a port subject to our obstruction because Mexico was not a belligerent. The United States scrupulously observed the neutral status of Mexico and never stopped a ship in her waters except by error. Of course, the Confederate state of Texas moved volumes of cotton out of Mexico with the aid of Mexican merchants; military supplies and light armament were shipped back through Bagdad-Matamoros and ferried across the Rio Grande to Brownsville. The United States would not impose a blockade on a neutral country because that action would have been illegal and unsupportable. The Confederacy evaded the blockade through this avenue, but technically did not violate this barrier. It is true that the French obstructed Mexican shipping because of its belligerent status with that nation, but C.S.A. blockade running through the French obstruction caused few problems. Confederates were shipping items out of Mexico through contracts with Mexican firms, but the items were intended for nations other than Mexico, and therefore were not subject to the French blockade. The French seized some British ships loaded with rifles that anchored off Bagdad because they thought the arms were destined for Mexico. Instead, the transshipment was to be through Mexico and on to the Confederacy as provided in a contract with a Mexican merchant. Initially, the French did not understand this to be the case, but the matter finally was settled through the diplomatic efforts of a Confederate agent in Paris.

The C.S.A. and Texas did not take full advantage of opportunities offered them through the "back door of the Confederacy." Throughout the war, little was done to make any improvements in the transportation system to and from Brownsville, but this problem was nearly unsolvable without a nearby railroad. In addition, it should be noted that because of the transportation problems, most of the artillery came in through Galveston. Vast quantities of other military supplies and small armaments did come through Bagdad and Matamoros.[362]

The Confederacy was very successful in avoiding the blockade of Texas by going around it through neutral Bagdad, Mexico. This circumvention strengthened Texas and the Confederacy because most imported materials supplied the requirements of state and C.S.A. troops, and met at least a portion of needs of the civilian population. At the end of the Civil War, most of the states in the Deep South were destitute and barren, but that was not the case in Texas. A May 1865 report by Union scout C. S. Bell reveals:

> Arkansas is literally starved out. There is not enough to feed the people on the route between Little Rock and Shreveport, via either Camden or Washington. Louisiana is better supplied; still an army could by no means subsist off the country, and it is problematical whether a small column of cavalry would not starve their horses on a scout of 250 miles in any direction. Texas is full to repletion. Cattle, hogs, and horses, immense graneries [sic] of corn, and abundant forage may be found within 100 miles of the Arkansas or Louisiana borders.[363]

On the military side of the equation, although the Bagdad-Matamoros-Brownsville supply line was inefficient, it became almost the only source of military supplies for the "Kirby-Smithdom," especially after the fall of Vicksburg. "Without this vital artery of supplies from the Rio Grande, the Trans-Mississippi might have conceivably collapsed before Appomattox."[364]

We turn next to a survey of selected expert opinions on the efficacy of the blockade. Frank L. Owsley wrote in 1931 regarding the ineffectiveness of the blockade in his classic text, *King Cotton Diplomacy*. He records that the barrier was so ineffective that it "made the old-fashioned English blockade look like a stone wall in comparison." He states that the blockade "flew in the face of all American precedents, all American permanent interests and doctrines of neutral maritime rights, [and] vitiated the principles in the Declaration of Paris that a blockade to be binding must be effective."[365] Obviously, Owsley believed the blockade was not in our national interests, was patently ineffective, and therefore illegal.

In *History of the Confederate States Navy*, J. Thomas Scharf devotes most of Chapter 16 to an extended exposition of the illegality of the Federal blockade. In Chapter 17 he provides good coverage of navy activities in east Texas waters, particularly Galveston and Sabine Pass, while failing to discuss similar activities to the west and south of Galveston Bay.[366]

In 1962, retired Rear Admiral Bern Anderson published *By Sea and By River: The Naval History of the Civil War*. As might be expected, he takes contrary views to those expressed by J. T. Scharf. He not only finds the blockade to be legal, but effective as well. Anderson concentrates upon the economic collapse of the Confederacy and writes, "Sole credit for the economic chaos ... cannot, of course, be given to the Union blockade. Yet it should be recognized that it was the chief instrument for bringing about that condition. ... The blockade ... was one of the major factors that brought about the ultimate collapse and defeat of the South."[367]

Jochem H. Tans, in his fine paper "The Hapless Anaconda: Union Blockade 1861–1865," reaches conclusions similar to that of Owsley. He states, "The Confederates were, however, able to survive for a long time while dependent on blockade-running for most of their supplies, and this is in itself a proof of the ineffectiveness of the blockade." He continues, "On the whole, the blockade was under-enforced. After an exceptionally slow start, the blockade was never able to seal off Southern shipping."[368]

The ineffectiveness of the blockade is also advanced in *Why the South Lost the Civil War*. The authors describe this barrier as "only a serious nuisance" and they contend that "clearly, Confederates could get whatever they wanted or needed through the blockade, if they wanted it badly enough. The efficacy of the blockade off Galveston meant little after the fall of Vicksburg." They acknowledge that the barrier did have some detrimental effect upon supplies for the Confederacy and disruption of the Southern economy. They believe, however, that this Federal action was not a decisive factor in the South's loss of the war. The authors contend, "The South did not lose the Civil War because of the blockade. The net was too loose." Their thesis is that the South lost the war because the Southerner's morale was sapped and he lost the will to continue the struggle. There is acknowledgement that the blockade was an important factor contributing to this loss of morale. The writers claim the armies surrendered because "they did not want an independent Confederacy badly enough to continue the struggle."[369]

Marcus Price published a series of articles in *American Neptune*, and one article published in 1951 was "Ships That Tested the Blockade of the Gulf Ports, 1861–1865." According to his data, a total of 2,960 vessels tried to get through the blockade during the period April 20, 1861, to June 4, 1865. In 1862 and 1863, nearly two-thirds of these ships made successful runs in and out of blockaded ports. In Part III of this article, he presents data for specific ships testing the blockade in 1863. He concludes that during that year, 254 vessels attempted 428 runs and 266 of these runs were successful. Examination of these data further reveals that 30 of these 254 vessels ultimately were captured or destroyed off the Texas coast, or near Texas ports. These 30 ships had attempted 46 runs, of which 16 were successful. The author concludes that in 1864 and 1865, around ninety percent of the ships challenging the blockade made it through. He attributes a higher failure rate in 1862-1863 to the fact that a higher percentage of sailing ships were used in that period. He makes a convincing argument that the barrier was readily breached.[370]

Another historian taking a stance similar to that of Marcus Price is Robert Warren Glover. Dr. Glover concludes in his doctoral thesis (*The West Gulf Blockade, 1861–1865: An Evaluation*) that the blockade was effective enough to create scarcity and inflation of prices, but it was ineffective in terms of seriously impeding the flow of trade through the barrier. In particular, he cites evidence of successful blockade running through Galveston in the last months of the war. The author judges the performance of the West Gulf Blockading Squadron as mediocre.[371]

The anonymous author of Section 2.2 of the *U. S. Naval Landing Party Handbook*, in a section entitled "The U.S. Navy in the Civil War," comes to a different conclusion. The writer says, "On the face of the above data, it is perhaps a justifiable argument that the Federal blockade was a failure. Certainly the U.S. Navy was never able to make good on its promise to close the Southern ports; blockade running did not stop until these rebel harbors were actually taken by mixed Army-Navy assault forces. But the blockade was marvelously effective in sapping the will and ability of the Rebel states to make war." Additionally, "even in hindering the supply line, the Navy's blockade played a major role for the Union."[372]

James Daddysman has concentrated much of his research in evaluating trade through Matamoros and Bagdad. He judges that during the three-year period from 1862 to 1865, about 320,000 bales of cotton were exported from Matamoros and "this represents more than 20 percent of the total Confederate cotton exports, making the Rio Grande port one of the largest single outlets for Confederate cotton during the war."[373] Daddysman's conclusion is that the Matamoros trade was "essential to the war effort in the Trans-Mississippi Department.... Without it, the Trans-Mississippi might have collapsed before Appomattox."[374]

Another important contribution to blockade literature is *Lifeline of the Confederacy* by Stephen R. Wise. Dr. Wise presents data on which to base his conclusion that "imported supplies were vital to the Confederacy's existence" because home production could not supply even one-half of the C.S.A. military needs. He goes on to quantify by writing, "The South imported at least 400,000 rifles, or more than 60 percent of the nation's modern arms. About 3 million pounds of lead came through the blockade ... and over 2,250,000 pounds of saltpeter, or two-thirds of this vital ingredient for powder, came from overseas. Without blockade-running the nation's military would have been without proper supplies of arms, bullets, and powder. Blockade-running also supplied countless other essential items such as food, clothing, accouterments, chemicals, paper, and medicine." Because of blockade running "a supply lifeline was maintained until the very last months of the war. The Confederate soldiers had the equipment and food needed to meet their adversaries."[375]

Dean B. Mahin echoes this sentiment in *One War at a Time*. He concludes, "Despite the determined efforts of the U.S. Navy, blockade-runners kept the Confederate war effort going for at least a year longer than would have been possible if the Confederate ports had been effectively sealed." He then amplifies this point by quoting from Hamilton Cochran, author of *Blockade Runners of the Confederacy*, who enthusiastically states, "The benefits of blockade running to the Southern cause were incalculable. The business it carried to the South, the life and activity it brought, the news it told and carried away, the sympathy it communicated, the money it left behind—all these were sinews of war, without which the war must have ceased from twelve to twenty-four months earlier than it did."[376]

On the other hand, James M. McPherson deals with the effectiveness of the obstruction in a more sympathetic manner in *Battle Cry of Freedom*. Dr. McPherson concedes that five out of six blockade runners got through the barrier, but contends this is not the crucial statistic. "Rather, one must ask how many ships carrying how much freight *would have* [emphasis in original] entered Southern ports if there had been no blockade." He adds that many of these successful runs were accomplished by craft "merely redistributing freight from one part of the South to another, and could scarcely be termed 'running' the blockade. From June through August 1861, for example, of 178 ships entering or clearing five major Southern ports, only eighteen were involved in foreign trade." McPherson continues:

> Eight thousand trips were made through the blockade during the four years of war, but more than twenty thousand vessels had cleared into or out of Southern ports during the four prewar years. The blockade reduced the South's sea borne trade to less than a third of normal. And of course the Confederacy's needs for all kinds of supplies were much greater than the peacetime norm.... To maintain that the blockade "won the war" for the North ... goes entirely too far. But it did play an important role in Union

victory. [Those who say the blockade] did not have a "decisive effect" on the outcome of the war may go too far in the opposite direction. The impact of the blockade was certainly significant, though of course it did not alone win the war.[377]

Richard N. Current advances another favorable view of the blockade in his essay, "God and the Strongest Battalions." Current states, "While Union military power was weakening the Southern economy, Union naval power had the same effect in perhaps even greater degree. The blockade, by bringing about serious shortages in strategic items, not only added to the inflationary trends but also frustrated efforts to maintain the transportation network and to increase industrial output.[378]

Professor James R. Soley advanced another positive assessment of the blockade when he wrote:

> As to the legal efficiency of the blockade after the first six months, there can be no question; and by the end of the second year its stringency was such that only specially-adapted vessels could safely attempt to run it. If proof of its efficiency was needed, it could be found in the increased price of cotton and in the scarcity of manufactured goods at the South. In the last year it became as nearly perfect as such an operation can be made. Taking its latest development as a type, it is probable that no blockade has ever been maintained more effectually by any State; and it is certain that no State ever had such a blockade to maintain.

Soley goes on to quantify his argument by stating that a total of 1,504 vessels trying to run the blockade were either taken as prizes or destroyed. He adds that these ships and their cargoes were conservatively valued at $31 million.[379]

David Paul Crook believes the barrier deterred many foreign merchantmen from making even a token attempt to run the blockade. He emphasizes that these vessels quickly gave up the attempt to enter major ports and confined their trade to intermediate destinations such as Nassau, from which cargo was off-loaded to smaller vessels. He contends that statistics on successful runs are less impressive when taking into consideration the light tonnage of these ships. Not only was the South deprived of strategic materials, but their flow of intelligence, dispatches, and instructions were likewise interrupted (and sometimes, to their chagrin, published in the Northern press). Crook concludes, "The blockade forced the Confederacy to breathe through a constricted windpipe, and the effort became more debilitating with time. Runners brought in large quantities of essential arms and supplies, but greed for maximum profits caused many shippers to waste space on luxury items."[380]

Historian Francis B. C. Bradlee has much to say about the blockade in his classic study that was originally published in 1925. In *Blockade Running During the Civil War and the Effect of Land and Water Transportation on the Confederacy*, Bradlee contends that the blockade was unprecedented in its magnitude and difficulty. He stresses that during the war, 1,504 blockade running vessels were captured or destroyed and the value of the ships and their cargoes amounted to $31 million. The author believes that "As a military measure the blockade was of vital importance in the operations of the war; and there is no doubt that without it the South would have won its independence."[381]

In *A Naval History of the Civil War*, Howard P. Nash, Jr., writes, "The blockade made the Confederate States into a land besieged, a land unable any longer to procure the materiel with which to continue the war or even to obtain the very necessities of life." He quotes J. Thomas Scharf as writing in the preface to his *History of the Confederate States Navy* that "the blockade 'shut the Confederacy out from the world, deprived it of supplies, weakened its military and naval strength, ... compelled exhaustion by requiring the consumption of everything grown or raised in the country.'"[382]

One of the most influential students of naval history was Alfred Thayer Mahan, who wrote a series of books on sea power around the turn of the 20th Century. In *The Influence of Sea Power Upon History 1660–1805*, he makes a lucid argument that the Union blockade was effective not so much because it was a great feat (he concedes it was), but because of the weaknesses of the South. Mahan goes on to explain that the South did not have an adequate navy with which to make its long coastline a fortress rather than a liability. The Federal navy was able to station its blockading ships singly or in small detachments with little fear of attack by the South, and the C.S.A. was unable to capitalize upon its numerous bays, inlets, and estuaries from which to launch counterstrikes. Mahan maintains this was so because the South's population was inadequate to produce a garrison of its extensive seacoast and it was not a nation of seamen, in the sense that it was "unused to the sea."[383]

Dr. David G. Surdam of Loyola University of Chicago has provided us with a balanced assessment of the blockade through the publication of two articles that deal with Union successes and Confederate opportunities. They are "The Union Navy's Blockade Reconsidered," and "The Confederate Naval Buildup: Could More Have Been Accomplished?" In the first article, Surdam argues that the blockade's contribution to the war effort has been underestimated because, among other things, it consisted of a lengthy period of slow strangulation of the Confederacy that ultimately led to the South's inability to sustain its military operations. Since there are few dramatic and decisive moments in the naval campaign, the contributions have been undervalued but the author asserts that the blockade was necessary to assure Union victory. Surdam states that previous analyses of the blockade have focused heavily upon imports that "ran" through the barrier but have not paid sufficient attention to the reduced exports of cotton resulting from the blockade. He claims that these exports were far below the level of antebellum cotton exports and this contributed significantly to the cash flow problems experienced by the Confederate government. Further, Dr. Surdam argues that the blockade stunted the growth of the Confederate navy and prevented it from growing strong enough to seriously challenge the Union navy.

In the second article, Professor Surdam answers his question in the positive by generalizing that too little was done at an early stage. He points out that initially the North was little better prepared for operating a blockade than was the South in blunting it and suggests the Southern states had the opportunity after secession and before the beginning of the war to begin building a Confederate navy. He argues that the South lost this opportunity through inaction and the North was able to begin building its navy with impunity. Surdam identifies the disadvantages the South experienced in building a strong navy (scarcity of iron products and iron ore, lack of funds, shortage of skilled labor, and other factors) and maintains that the South's most important deficiency was the lack of time (and money) to purchase warships in England and Europe and to otherwise develop a viable war plan to counteract the Federal blockade. By 1862 the Anaconda Plan had begun to squeeze the life out of the Confederacy, and the moment to gain maritime superiority was lost forever.[384]

Finally, the recent observations of a military man, United States Air Force Colonel David J. Murphy, may be instructive. He examines naval strategy during the Civil War and concludes:

> Overall, the Union Navy played a major role in winning the Civil War, although it was not the most important factor. The naval blockade of the South ... was never able to completely seal off the Confederacy and strangle it to death. However, the blockade was able to put a large dent in Southern commerce and severely hamper the Confederates' ability to carry on the war effort. In particular, the blockade was effective in curtailing Southern exports of staple goods [and it] severely altered the movement of internal goods, which put added burdens on the overtaxed Southern rail system.[385]

After all the palaver, perhaps historian Dave Horner, author of *The Blockade-Runners*, has made the most candid and succinct observation: "Blockade-running was only a temporary means by which the South prolonged the agony of facing the decision of defeat."[386]

In summarizing views of recognized authorities on blockade efficacy, it should be noted that there is seldom any reference to, or connection with, goals of the blockade. In the process of measuring effectiveness, it seems reasonable to identify these objectives.

President Lincoln's blockade proclamation imposes "a blockade of the ports within the States ... so as to prevent entrance and exit of vessels from the ports aforesaid." From the U.S. point of view, the primary goal of barricading specific ports is pragmatic. Attainment of this objective makes a dramatic statement to foreign nations as to the effectiveness of the obstacle, notwithstanding Confederate statistical counts to the contrary. Furthermore, progressing toward this goal maintains efficient use of limited resources by intercepting larger cargoes while not wasting assets on smaller ones.

The Blockade Strategy Board expanded blockade goals. This group's highest priority was to interpose a barrier between major Southern ports and oceangoing, deep-draft, large cargo capacity ships coming from or going to Europe; a secondary objective was assigned to obstructing light-draft, smaller cargo coastal vessels that were traversing interior waters.

Navy Secretary Welles addressed the scope of the blockade in his 1861 annual report to Congress. While recognizing the importance of the primary goal of blockading specific Southern ports, he extended the objective by applying the blockade to the entire Southern coast. Moreover, he specified that escaping vessels would be pursued on the high seas. Finally, he established an additional responsibility for his vessels—that of performing important support activities in conjunction with joint Army-Navy coastal operations. The blockade objectives in December 1861 are considerably more comprehensive than those enunciated in April 1861, and this fact requires clarity on the part of scholars when evaluating the blockade's efficacy. The examination must consider both Lincoln's narrow blockade concept and Welles's broadened outlook. Much of the research cited above evaluates blockade effectiveness without taking into full account these disparate goals.

Except for the first few months, the naval blockade was of sufficient force to make harbor entry and egress appear to be dangerous and therefore effective; it was never legally challenged by European powers. Early in the war, foreign shipping continued to run the blockade on the Atlantic coast. Eventually, this shipping became obstructed to a significant degree and was forced to interrupt its trips to and from ports such as Savannah, Charleston, and Wilmington. As the blockade strengthened, Great Britain began running its large seagoing vessels to intermediate ports such as St. George, Bermuda, Nassau, Saint Thomas, and (less frequently) Havana, where the cargo was off-loaded to smaller ships that would assume the greater risk of violating a coastal blockade. Other than trying to draw Federal ships off the blockade, this barricade was not physically challenged by the Confederate Navy that, for the most part, assumed a mode of coastal defensive.

The main goal of the blockade was to completely close down major Southern ports—to strangle them so that no more supplies or personnel could reach the interior. Many who evaluate the blockade emphasize failure of the navy to single-handedly shut down these important port facilities. They stress that these ports were closed only when the army occupied the site, or threatened to do so, suggesting the navy failed to achieve its goal. Overlooked is the fact that Secretary Welles, in his December 1861 blockade message, explicitly enunciated the goal of using "combined naval and military expeditions to operate in force against various points of the Southern coast." Although one is conditioned to think of a blockade as a purely naval matter, in fact by definition a blockade may employ both troops and warships. This is precisely what Gideon Welles had in mind and it was admirably achieved (with one exception) before the end of the war. The obstruction of Southern seaports increased in effectiveness as time went on and it was supplemented by army land action. Eventually the sea blockade, in coordination with army action, was converted into military occupation of the major Confederate ports. Galveston was the only deep-water port still in Confederate hands at war's closure and she remained an active port for blockade runners as late as May 1865. This fact, however, had little impact on ending the war beyond delaying its conclusion in the Trans-Mississippi Department.

The goal of closing designated Southern ports was substantially achieved. In contrast, many lower priority targets associated with vessels redistributing cargo through interior waters continued unimpeded throughout the war. Thus the secondary goal was never totally achieved.

What the review of literature reveals is diversity of opinion as to blockade efficacy. There is little consensus beyond the agreement to disagree. It is quite probable that researchers will never agree with one another on this subject because there are so many factors and imponderables that must be considered. Some of these are discussed below.

The blockade is difficult to assess not only because insufficient attention has been addressed to objectives, but also because the researcher is working with a shifting target. The blockade was not a stagnant entity—it was a dynamic force always in a state of flux, always stimulating differing responses, and in turn, being shaped by these reactions. The blockade of 1861 and the Confederate reaction to that event were different from that in 1862. Similarly, these dynamics continued throughout the Civil War. Consequently, the examiner is always trying to capture something that is inherently elusive. One example of this evasive target is the nature of the vessels themselves. This era was in a state of progression from sailing ship to steamer, requiring drastic changes in design and construction of both blockading vessels and ships running the blockade and development of suitable tactics to deal with changing circumstances. A concomitant factor was the character and training of crews, and leadership qualities and skills of captains of these vessels.

Also, the literature usually does not address the ultimate reason for a blockade beyond obstructing shipping. In his blockade proclamation, President Lincoln opens with a mention of the interruption in ability to collect the revenue. It is unlikely that the president expected only to collect the revenue through imposition of a blockade. The main purpose was to interfere with commerce, but for what reasons: to decrease the means to wage war through seizure of contraband; to interfere with food imports in order to foster hardships; to impose psychological warfare on the Southern population; to deny European luxury items to the South; to encourage inflation and financial distress; to diminish the availability of capital to the South; to create havoc for the Confederacy? All of these factors applied at one time or another but were selected and weighted according to strategic needs at the moment.

The use of statistics and data in evaluation require thoughtful consideration. Much of the available data is incomplete due to loss of records. This is particularly so for Confederate documents, because they were not always carefully preserved after the war. Some of the data simply are inaccurate and there is limited opportunity to cross-check information to determine its validity. Also, it is difficult to identify which data may have been manipulated in order to support a certain position, develop a viewpoint for propaganda purposes, or for self-aggrandizement.

Statistics were sometimes intentionally inflated or distorted in order to improve morale of troops and citizens, or to further political aims. The ultimate problem with statistics is that they can be carefully selected and interpreted in such a way as to support any argument or preconceived notion.

Often, data manipulation may be quite subtle and not readily apparent. To illustrate the problem for the researcher, let us examine a speech made by President Jefferson Davis to the Confederate House of Representatives on December 20, 1864. The congress had challenged him on whether some new regulations had effectively reduced foreign commerce. Davis replied that trade with foreign vessels had actually increased, not decreased. The president substantiated his position by claiming, "The number of vessels which arrived at two ports of the Confederacy between the 1st of November and 6th of December was forty-three, averaging more than one per day, and indicating no check in trade." Obviously, the researcher has a considerable problem in evaluating this statement since (among other things) the ports are not identified, the time period is short, there is no comparison with other time periods, and the cargo capacity of the ships is not identified. Obviously, there is quite a stretch to make in concurring with the president's conclusion. The task becomes even more difficult when reviewing Davis's next sentences. He said, "further and conclusive" proof of the profits of vessels engaged in foreign commerce "is afforded by the fact that the shares of the companies engaged in it have greatly advanced in value. The shares of one company, originally of $1,000 each, were selling in July last for $20,000 each, and now command $30,000. Those of another company have increased in the same period from $2,500 to $6,000; and all exhibit a large advance."[387] What a conundrum for the reviewer. What are the names of the companies? What is the time period involved? Do the advances outpace the rate of inflation? If so, to what degree? This example is meant only to illustrate the potential traps for a researcher.

Beyond difficulties in assessing raw data, the probative value of documents must be considered by examining the reputation, integrity, life experiences, maturity, educational level, and other similar factors of the person who wrote the document being reviewed. In addition, a researcher must be alert to the authenticity and accuracy of the document itself. For example, if the document was reported in a newspaper of the times, did that newspaper accurately print the entire document and, if it was excerpted, did that segment fairly represent the whole?

A number of other factors must be considered and these, in themselves, make it difficult for researchers to reach agreement on the blockade question. For example, for any military force—but especially for two navies—the forces of nature play an important part. Did an event occur at night or day, in calm seas or a gale, in a full moon or new moon, what was the effect of a particular coastline, what about currents and tides, how did temperatures, salt air, and humidity affect men and machines? Another consideration is the nature of the order or objective provided the skipper. Was it realistic and attainable under the circumstances? If not, did the captain improvise in such a way as to maximize the potential of the vessel and crew? To what degree did uncommon bravery and courage play a significant part in the episode? What was the effect of the type and grade of coal used in steamships, the condition of sails, the crews' motivation of patriotism versus prize money, the type of cargo carried? The list is endless.

Given the diversity and multitude of concrete factors and imponderables suggested above, it is no wonder that scholars and researchers can reach no consensus as to the efficacy of the blockade. There is merit to most views expressed by these researchers and they should not be peremptorily dismissed.

It seems wise to evaluate effectiveness of the blockade against two distinct goals enunciated by the Union: Lincoln's limited goal of closing specified ports and Welles's broader concept of blockading the entire Southern coast. Lincoln's prudent goal of port closures was a remarkable success. All of the specified major Southern ports (and many minor ones as well) were closed to commerce before the end of the war, save Galveston. This port continued to operate well into May 1865. It remained an open port probably because the Union perceived it as no more than a nuisance since all other ports had been closed. Another consideration was yellow fever. Again in mid–September until mid–October 1864, the city of Galveston was under quarantine because of an epidemic of the disease and this probably gave Union planners pause in considering another invasion of the peninsula. The Federal government was content to commit no more resources there and Galveston's 1865 blockade running had no bearing on the outcome of the war, other than delaying its conclusion.

Evaluating Welles's goal—the attempt to blockade the entire Southern coast—is problematic: it was both a success and a failure. It clearly was a failure in terms of totally blocking the Southern coast. Blockade running was continuous and successful even after Appomattox. However, in the last two years of the war much of this activity took place using coastal vessels with limited cargo capacity. This constricted pipeline had little impact upon the South's ability to wage war beyond extending the combat period. The Confederacy fared no better in the last year of the war than it did earlier. In the end, the success of blockade running through Galveston and blockade evasion through Mexico only contributed to more bloodletting by both sides.

In some respects, the blockade of the entire coast was a success. There seems little doubt that it discouraged European powers from intervening on behalf of the Confederate States of America. Additionally, it is likely that the blockade contributed to inflation in prices of manufactured goods and foodstuffs. Furthermore, the blockade probably had a significant negative impact upon the Southern psyche, becoming a heavy burden for the citizen to carry. In the end, it, along with other factors, sapped the will of Southerners to continue the struggle. This was evident in Galveston where in May 1865 blockade running was successful, while army men were deserting in droves and returning to their homes.

Finally, it is necessary to make a clear distinction between violating the blockade and evading or going around the obstacle. Successful blockade running occurred all along the Texas coast. There was no blockade running south of the mouth of the Rio Grande, and down the coast of Mexico, because the barrier did not extend beyond Texas. Of course, there were thousands of bales of cotton going across the river from Brownsville to Matamoros and then to sea from Bagdad. The blockade, however, was being evaded, not violated, by using this back door to the Confederacy. Future blockade evaluations should make a clean distinction between blockade running and blockade evasion.

What is certain is that the blockade directly or indirectly affected the lives of everyone in this nation, civilian and military, and many foreign nations, especially Great Britain, France, and Mexico. Without a doubt, the Union blockade played a significant role in the defeat of the Confederate States of America.

Chapter 9

Epilogue

When General Granger released his General Order Number 3 in Galveston on June 19, 1865, Texas slaves reacted to this profound news with both shock and immediate jubilation. A great sense of joy remained after the shock wore off and black citizens of Texas came to regard June 19 as the date of their freedom from bondage. Thereafter, June 19 was coined as "Juneteenth" in celebration of the event, and that date became a day for thanksgiving, prayer, and a gathering of family members. Many decades later Juneteenth continued to be revered by ex-slaves, and today their descendants make an annual pilgrimage to Galveston. Juneteenth is now the oldest celebration still in existence that stimulates celebration by many citizens who acknowledge the end of slavery in Texas as of June 19, 1865.[388]

While some Texans were elated, the majority was in despair. In her diary, a Southern belle wrote an entry dated November 10, 1865, from her family's plantation near Houston. Her view probably was typical of most white citizens living in east Texas at that time. She says, "Heroically the South struggled against adverse fate, and endured all ills till exhausted and 'overpowered' by numbers, she surrendered her gallant little army, and the Confederacy was no more. The bitter suffering, the sacrifice during four long years of bloodshed, has all been in vain; all is lost save honor.... The proud Southerner is humbled. We are but dust."[389]

For some Southerners, their feelings of despair were only the first stage of growing hate and anger. Following the April 9, 1865, surrender of Lee to Grant at Appomattox, U.S. Brigadier General Joshua L. Chamberlain remarked to C.S.A. Brigadier General Henry A. Wise of Virginia that in the future perhaps many brave men on both sides might become friends. Wise railed at him and said, "You're mistaken sir, ... There is rancor in our hearts ... which you little dream of. We hate you, sir."[390]

A popular song of the era was "O, I'm a Good Old Rebel" and some of the lyrics are:

> O, I'm a good old Rebel
> Now that's just what I am,
> For this "Fair Land of Freedom"
> I do not care at all;
> I'm glad I fit against it—
> I only wish we'd won,
> And I don't want no pardon,
> For anything I done.
> I hates the nasty eagle,
> With all his brags and fuss,
> The lyin', thievin' Yankees,
> I hates 'em wuss and wuss.
> Three hundred thousand Yankees
> Is stiff in Southern dust;
> We got three hundred thousand
> Before they conquered us;
> They died of Southern fever
> And Southern steel and shot,
> I wish they was three million
> Instead of what we got.[391]

For the United States, the French army in Mexico remained as unfinished business. Many leaders in Washington still considered that army to be a serious threat to our national interests due to its violation of the Monroe Doctrine. President James Monroe had formally presented that doctrine at his annual message to Congress on December 2, 1823. Two important parts of the foreign policy statement were: (1) "The American continents ... are henceforth not to be considered as subjects for future colonization by any European powers," and (2) "The political system of the allied [European] powers is essentially different ... from that of America.... We should consider any attempt on their part to extend their system to any portion of this hemisphere as dangerous to our peace and safety."[392] This statement of American foreign policy had stood firm for 42 years and was to be enforced across the Rio Grande.

Following Lincoln's assassination, Andrew Johnson succeeded him and William Seward remained as secretary of state. Seward maintained his policy of increasing the diplomatic pressure on France to leave Mexico, and avoided any direct intervention. Other governmental leaders wished to take action that was more drastic. General U. S. Grant was one of those. The Mexican minister, Mattias Romero, reported that Grant told him "his major desire is to fight in Mexico against the French, that the Monroe Doctrine has to be defended at any price." General Grant ordered General Phillip Sheridan with 50,000 soldiers to Texas to occupy that state and provide a show of force to the French along the Rio Grande, in order to demonstrate the resolve of the United States to enforce the Monroe Doctrine.[393] The Navy Department kept a reduced gulf squadron, consisting of 16 vessels, headquartered at Pensacola, Florida, until May 1867 in the event it might be needed to support troops along the Rio Grande.[394] Seward continued to put diplomatic pressure on Napoleon III and Emperor Maximilian. The French people, who were not happy with the Mexican war, likewise were pressuring Napoleon at home. The French emperor formed an opinion that this army might better be used to meet a growing Prussian threat. In October 1865, he began discussing bringing his army home, and a year later there were signs that Maximilian's empire was beginning to totter.[395] Finally, Napoleon withdrew all his men from Mexico by March 16, 1867, and without that support, Emperor Maximilian's rule was doomed. The ruling Juarez party captured Maximilian, a military court tried him, and he was executed by a firing squad on June 19, 1867.[396] Thus the French occupation of Mexico was concluded and the last chapter of the Civil War was closed.

Appendix I

Blockade Proclamation

By the President of the United States of America.—A Proclamation.

Whereas an insurrection against the Government of the United States has broken out in the States of South Carolina, Georgia, Alabama, Florida, Mississippi, Louisiana, and Texas, and the laws of the United States for the collection of the revenue can not be effectually executed therein, conformably to that provision of the Constitution which requires duties to be uniform throughout the United States; and

Whereas a combination of persons engaged in such insurrection have threatened to grant pretended letters of marque to authorize the bearers thereof to commit assaults on the lives, vessels, and property of good citizens of the country lawfully engaged in commerce on the high seas and in waters of the United States; and

Whereas an Executive proclamation has been already issued requiring the persons engaged in these disorderly proceedings to desist therefrom, calling out a militia force for the purpose of repressing the same, and convening Congress in extraordinary session to deliberate and determine thereon:

Now, therefore, I, Abraham Lincoln, President of the United States, with a view to the same purposes before mentioned, and to the protection of the public peace and the lives and property of quiet and orderly citizens pursuing their lawful occupations until Congress shall have assembled and deliberated on the said unlawful proceedings, or until the same shall have ceased, have further deemed it advisable to set on foot a blockade of the ports within the States aforesaid, in pursuance of the laws of the United States and of the law of nations in such case provided. For this purpose a competent force will be posted so as to prevent entrance and exit of vessels from the ports aforesaid. If, therefore, with a view to violate such blockade a vessel shall approach or shall attempt to leave either of the said ports, she will be duly warned by the commander of one of the blockading vessels, who will endorse on her register the fact and date of such warning, and if the same vessel shall again attempt to enter or leave the blockaded port she will be captured and sent to the nearest convenient port for such proceedings against her and her cargo as prize as may be deemed advisable.

And I hereby proclaim and declare that if any person, under the pretended authority of the said States, or under any other pretense, shall molest a vessel of the United States, or the persons or cargo on board of her, such person will be held amenable to the laws of the United States for the prevention and punishment of piracy.

In witness whereof I have hereunto set my hand and caused the seal of the United States to be affixed.

Done at the city of Washington this nineteenth day of April, in the year of our Lord one thousand eight hundred and sixty-one, and of the Independence of the United States the eighty-fifth.

ABRAHAM LINCOLN.

By the President:

WILLIAM H. SEWARD,

Secretary of State.

[Source: Official Records Navy, series 1, vol. 4, 156–157.]

Appendix II

Excerpted Report of the Blockade Strategy Board

Second report conference for the consideration of measures for effectually blockading the coast bordering on the Gulf of Mexico.

WASHINGTON, September 3, 1861.

5. Coast of part of Louisiana and the whole coast of Texas, from Grande Pass, Vermilion Bay, to the Rio Grande del Norte: From Vermilion Bay to the Sabine River is about 100 nautical miles, and the coast of Texas, from the Sabine to the Rio Grande, extends about 325 miles.

The chief interest of this section centers at Galveston entrance, 55 miles from the Sabine River and 270 from the Rio Grande. Galveston entrance itself is but the analogue of Charleston [S. C.], in its depth of water, having 12 feet at low water over a shifting bar. This chief maritime city of Texas had, in 1860, but 8,117 inhabitants and a small foreign trade. The number of vessels which arrived at Galveston in 1856, from beyond the limits of the collection district, was 269, of which 27 were foreign vessels. New Orleans is the great entrepôt which it uses, from which it is distant 280 miles by the steamer route to Berwick Bay, and thence by the Opelousas, New Orleans [and Great Western] Railroad.

There are small steamers trading from Galveston up the bay and Trinity River, and to the various rivers and bays of the coast by a precarious navigation, part of which is exposed to the dangers arising from the storms of the Gulf. An efficient blockade of Galveston is, in fact, the blockade of the coast of Texas. Of the six other entrances, one, the Rio Grande, has but 4 feet on its bar at low water, and 4.9 feet at high water; Aransas Pass, 9 feet; Matagorda, 9 feet; Brazos River, 8 feet; San Luis Pass, 8 feet; Sabine Pass, 7½ feet at low water, with a rise of tide of less than one foot and a half at the several ports.

The smooth-water navigation, to be effected by connecting the sounds by artificial means, has been begun by the State of Texas, but not completed even for the minimum proposed depth.

Three or four efficient Vessels, which can take care of themselves at sea against storms and enemies, are required for the blockade of this portion of the coast, three being the least number which it would probably be safe to trust, considering the northers and hurricanes to which the coast is exposed, and the possible presence of fevers among the unacclimated crews. One of the vessels, besides, should be of the lightest draft, free to move up and down the coast, to interrupt the small commerce carried on by the interior sounds, which are nearly continuous from Galveston to the Rio Grande. A visit to Galveston, Corpus Christi, and Aransas to recover the United States movable property seized there from the Revenue and Coast Survey services, or to obtain indemnity for the seizures, would also form [one] of the objects of such an expedition. The Coast Survey hydrographic notes which we attach to this memoir are accompanied by maps and sketches showing the general character of this coast, and giving minute information in regard to the harbors and passes. We take this occasion earnestly to recommend that a Coast Survey vessel be attached to each of the principal blockading squadrons to complete, under general instructions from the Superintendent, the examination of such parts of the coast not yet surveyed in detail. The importance of this measure can not be overrated. Protection may readily be afforded to the surveying vessels without interfering at all with the regulations of the strictest blockade.

We have the honor to be, very respectfully, your most obedient servants,

S. F. DU PONT,
Captain, U. S. Navy, President.

A. D. BACHE,
Superintendent U. S. Coast Survey, Member.

J. G. BARNARD,
Major, U. S. Engineers, Member.

C. H. DAVIS,
Commander, U. S. Navy, Member and Secretary.

[Source: Official Records Navy, Series 1, vol. 16, 651–655. Extracted here is item 5 that specifically addresses the Texas coastline and is found on pages 654–655.]

Notes

ABBREVIATIONS USED IN NOTES

HTO *The Handbook of Texas Online*

LSBG *Lone Star Blue and Gray*

ORA *The War of the Rebellion: A Compilation of the Official Records of the Union and Confederate Armies.* (CD-ROM). In the citations, all references are to Series 1, unless otherwise indicated. Standard abbreviations are used. Thus, "vol. 11. pt.1. 571" refers to Series 1, Volume 11, Part 1, page 571.

ORN *Official Records of the Union and Confederate Navies in the War of the Rebellion.* (CD-ROM). In the citations, all references are to Series 1, unless otherwise indicated. Standard abbreviations are used. Thus, "ser. 2. vol. 1. 431" refers to Series 2, Volume 1, page 431.

TDC *Texas, the Dark Corner of the Confederacy: Contemporary Accounts of the Lone Star State in the Civil War*

1. Blockade Genesis

1. "Sallie McNeill's Diary, 1858–1867," *Levi Jordan Plantation*, September 28, 2000, <http://www.webarchaeology.com/Html/direxrpt.htm>.

2. Shelby Foote, *The Civil War, a Narrative. Fort Sumter to Perryville* (New York: Vintage Books–Random House, 1986), 48–49. Other authorities state that Edmund Ruffin did not fire the first shot of the war. For example, Bruce Catton claims that Lieutenant Henry S. Farley, who was ordered to do so by his battery commander, Captain George S. James, fired the shot. (See Catton, *The Coming Fury*, 312–313.)

3. James M. McPherson, *Battle Cry of Freedom* (New York: Oxford University Press–Ballantine Books, 1988), 308.

4. Foote 55.

5. Howard P. Nash, Jr., *A Naval History of the Civil War* (South Brunswick: A. S. Barnes; London: Thomas Yesloff, 1972), 13.

6. McPherson, *Battle Cry of Freedom*, 313.

7. William H. Seward to Abraham Lincoln, April 1, 1861. Available at *Abraham Lincoln Papers at the Library of Congress*, Manuscript Division (Washington, D.C.: American Memory Project, 2000–02).

8. John S. D. Eisenhower, *Agent of Destiny: The Life and Times of General Winfield Scott* (New York: The Free Press, 1997), 430 (note 1). The General would die on May 30, 1866, 405.

9. "Confederate Letters of Marque." (Taken from "History of the Confederate States Navy" by J. Thomas Scharf, the "American Civil War

Naval War Page.") June 2, 2001 <http://civilwar home.com/lettersofmarque.htm>. For various reasons, the use of privateers did not work out well, but they led to the establishment of commerce raiders that were official Confederate state naval vessels.

10. Dean B. Mahin, *One War at a Time: The International Dimensions of the American Civil War* (Washington, D.C.: Brassey's, 1999), 45–46; Ivan Musicant, *Divided Waters: The Naval History of the Civil War* (New York: HarperCollins Publishers, Inc., 1995), 51–52.

11. France demonstrated its interest in this objective through later movements in Mexico toward Texas.

12. Two years later the United States Supreme Court spoke on the issue of the legality of the blockade, in *Prize Cases 67 U. S. 635 (1863)*. In a 5–4 decision, the court held that the blockade was legal. Justice Grier wrote the majority opinion and he indicated a state of war existed in April 1861 in spite of the fact that there was no declaration of war. He viewed the rebellion as a de facto war, a civil war, and said the president had the authority to determine if suppressing an insurrection required the imposition of a blockade.

13. Donald, *Lincoln*, 303.

14. Samuel Eliot Morison, *The Oxford History of the American People* (New York: Oxford University Press, 1965), 632–633.

15. ORA vol. 51, pt. 1, 338–339. "The War of the Rebellion: A Compilation of the Official Records of the Union and Confederate Armies" (abbreviated hereafter as ORA), The Civil War CD-ROM. CD-ROM v.1.0 (Carmel, IN: Guild Press of Indiana, Inc., 1996). (All references hereafter are to series 1, unless otherwise indicated.)

16. ORA vol. 51, pt. 1, 369–370.

17. ORA vol. 51, pt. 1, 386–387. The organization of this letter is of interest because it begins with a rebuke and concludes with a request for McClellan's input in implementation of the plan. It is amusing to note that in the midst of this entire grand planning, General McClellan must attend to insignificant minutiae. On May 22, he wrote to Secretary of War Simon Cameron: "Will you please authorize me to use boards to put up places for worship at Camp Dennison. Parties furnish nails and labor." Cameron replies, "The Lord's will be done." (ORA vol. 51, pt 1, 388.)

18. Catton, *The Coming Fury*, 469. A more thorough discussion of the "Anaconda Plan" and its application is found in Dr. Rowena Reed's *Combined Operations in the Civil War* (Annapolis: Naval Institute Press, 1978), 3–32.

19. Donald, *Lincoln*, 302–303.

20. Nicholas Kiersey, "The Diplomats and Diplomacy of the American Civil War," diss. University of Ireland, Limerick, Ireland, 1997. August 1, 2000 <http://www.iol.ie/~kiersey/civ war.html>.

21. Abraham Lincoln, "Proclamation of Blockade Against Southern Ports," *The History Place*. June 13, 2000 <http://www.historyplace .com/lincoln/proc-2.htm>.

22. Kevin J. Weddle, *"There Should Be No Bungling About the Blockade:" The Blockade Board of 1861 and the Making of Union Naval Strategy*, "International Journal of Naval History," from the U. S. Army War College, Princeton University. September 9, 2002 <http://www.ijnhon line.org/volume1_number1_Apr02/article_wed dle_blockade_board.doc.htm#_ednref24>; Albert E. Theberge, Captain NOAA Corps (Ret.), *The Coast Survey in the Civil War 1861–1865*, Volume I of the History of the Commissioned Corps of the National Oceanic and Atmospheric Administration, "The Strategic Contribution." September 9, 2002 <http://www.lib.noaa.gov/edocs/ TITLE.htm#TITLE>.

23. These six reports are found in the Navy Official Records as follows: "Official Records of the Union and Confederate Navies in the War of the Rebellion." *The Civil War CD-ROM II*. CD-ROM. Carmel, Indiana: Guild Press of Indiana, Inc., 1999. (Abbreviated hereafter as ORN. All references are to series 1, unless otherwise indicated.) Vol. 12, 195–198 (first conference report—South Atlantic coast), 198–201 (second conference report—South Atlantic coast), 201–206 (third conference report—South Atlantic coast); vol. 16, 618–630 (first conference report—Gulf of Mexico), 651–655 (second conference report—Gulf of Mexico, including Texas), 680–681 (third conference report—Gulf of Mexico). These reports primarily deal with naval matters. Also see ORA vol. 53 (report of a conference in reference to the occupation of points on the Atlantic coast) dated July 5, 1861, 64–66. This report concentrates on affairs of a "purely military character" and deals with permanent occupation of certain east coast locations.

24. ORN vol. 12, 201.

25. ORN vol. 16, 651–655.

26. Weddle, *"There Should Be No Bungling About the Blockade:" The Blockade Board of 1861 and the Making of Union Naval Strategy*.

27. ORN vol. 12, 207.

28. Richard E. Beringer, Herman Hattaway, Archer Jones, and William N. Still, Jr., *Why the South Lost the Civil War* (Athens and London: The University of Georgia Press, 1986), 54.

29. "The Union and Confederate Navies." (Taken from an article by James R. Soley, "Battles and Leaders of the Civil War," by the "American Civil War Naval War Page.") June 3, 2001. <http://civilwarhome/unionconfednavies.htm>; "The U.S. Navy in the Civil War." *The United States Navy Landing Party Handbook: Guide to Naval Reenacting, Section 2.2, Basic Naval History of the Civil War* (The Navy and Marine Living History Association, Inc). June 13, 2000 <http://www.nmlha.org/unit192/usnrole.html>.

30. The navy had ten yards before the war and eight of them were distributed in the north. Two navy yards—at Norfolk, Virginia, and Pensacola, Florida—were taken by the Confederacy before or at the outbreak of war. However, they later reverted to Federal control.

31. Jochem Tans, "The Hapless Anaconda: Union Blockade 1861–1865," *The Concord Review: Advanced Placement Essays* (Concord, Maine). Fall, 1994. June 13, 2000 <http://www.tcr.org/advpl_7.html>; "U. S. Navy in the Civil War." *The United States Navy Landing Party Handbook: Guide to Naval Reenacting, Section 2.2, Basic Naval History of the Civil War* (The Navy and Marine Living History Association, Inc). June 13, 2000 <http://nmlha.org/unit192/handbook.html>; Silverstone 68; Nash 20.

32. Beringer 61.

33. ORN vol. 9, 191.

34. Boatner 503, 504; Musicant 67–71.

35. Beringer 57, 58. According to the authors, President Davis showed little interest in the blockade except for its international implications. He generally left naval operational matters in the hands of Secretary Mallory. One exception to this general rule was on January 15, 1865, when he issued an order to Commodore Tucker, commanding C.S.A. vessels at Charleston. The order reads, "The movements of Sherman render it important that you should, if practicable, attack the enemy's force off the harbor. I trust that you can do so, and, if successful, that you may be able to destroy his depot at Hilton Head and render the most valuable aid to General Hardee." (Source: ORA vol. 47, pt. 2. 1014.)

36. Nash 29, 30.

37. "Overview of the Civil War Naval War." *American Civil War Naval War Page.* June 4, 2001. <http://civilwarhome.com/navalwaroverview.htm>.

38. The navy yard was abandoned by the Confederates on May 9, 1862, and was reoccupied by the Union. It then became headquarters for the West Gulf Squadron. (Source: Boatner, *The Civil War Dictionary*, 641.)

39. Boatner 582–583; Musicant 28–29; McPherson, *Battle Cry of Freedom*, 279–280, 427; Jones, *The Civil War at Sea, January 1861–March 1862: The Blockaders*, vol. I, 97. When Gosport navy yard was abandoned in April and then occupied by Virginia militia, Virginia had not yet seceded because the ordinance of secession would not be official until it was ratified in a referendum on May 23. Similarly, in Texas, General Twiggs had surrendered Federal property to Texas militia on February 18 (the state had not yet seceded) while the popular vote for secession was scheduled to take place on February 23.

40. "Confederate Forces Afloat" (Appendix II) and "Texas Marine Department, Confederate States Army" (Appendix II, Annex III). *Dictionary of American Fighting Ships, Vol. II*. Washington, D.C.: Navy Department, Office of the Chief of Naval Operations, Naval History Division. Electronic edition. June 2, 2001. <http://www.hazegray.org/danfs>.

41. "The Union and Confederate Navies, Confederate Navy." Exhibit, September 5, 2001, Port Columbus National Civil War Naval Museum, Columbus, Georgia.

42. "The Union and Confederate Navies, U.S. Naval Academy." Exhibit, September 5, 2001, Port Columbus National Civil War Naval Museum, Columbus, Georgia.

43. James Morris Morgan, *Recollections of a Rebel Reefer*. Electronic Edition. First Edition, 1999, University of North Carolina at Chapel Hill Libraries. October 7, 2000 <http://www.ibiblio.org/docsouth/morganjames/morgan.html#morgan1> 204–206. For further information on the remarkable institution of learning, see *Academy on the James: The Confederate Naval School* by R. Thomas Campbell (Shippensburg, Pa.: Burd Street Press, 1998).

44. "The Union and Confederate Navies, Confederate Navy."

45. "The Union and Confederate Navies, U.S. Naval Academy." Additionally, in April 1861 the academy was moved to Newport, Rhode Island, for security purposes.

46. "The Union and Confederate Navies." Interestingly, because of a long tradition of ethnic diversity, 15 to 20 percent of crews aboard ships in the U. S. Navy were of African-American descent. (Source: "Crew of the USS Hunchback, ca. 1864," Exhibit at Port Columbus National Civil War Naval Museum.)

47. Harold D. Langley, "The Sailor's Life," article taken from *The Image of War: 1861–1865, Volume IV, Fighting for Time*, June 12, 2000 <http://www.civilwarhome.com/sailorlife.htm>.

48. Langley.

49. ORN ser. II. vol. 1, 40; ser. I, vol. 13, 226–227; Robert Warren Glover, *The West Gulf Blockade, 1861–1865: An Evaluation.* Diss. North Texas State U, 1974 (Ann Arbor: Xerox University Microfilms, 1975) 241. Horatio Wait, who was a paymaster in the U.S. Navy, claims the total prize awarded for *Memphis* was $510,000. (Source: *Century Magazine*, 1898, quoted in " Chapter XXIV, 1. The United States Navy Blockades the Confederacy." Henry Steele Commager, ed., *The Blue and the Gray*, vol. II (New York: Bobbs-Merrill Company, 1950, p. 853).

50. ORN vol. 18, 672–673.

51. "U. S. Navy in the Civil War." Albert E. Theberge. He adds, "It is difficult to trace amounts of prize money awarded during the Civil War [but] over 1,300 prize cases were eventually adjudicated in United States courts." As of 1867, J.T. Headley in *Farragut and Our Naval Commanders* (E.B. Treat and Co., New York, p. 604) stated: "Payment has already been made to nearly ten thousand different claimants, in sums varying from twenty-five cents to thirty-eight thousand dollars. There still remain to be adjudicated about six hundred prizes, the most of which will be condemned and the proceeds paid to the captors." Although these statements do not preclude the possibility that there was a single higher prize award, it does make it very improbable. However, the flag officers commanding the various blockading squadrons received a share of each capture made by their squadron. Consequently, their total prize awards sometimes amounted to over $100,000. (From *The Coast Survey in the Civil War*, "The Volunteer Naval Officers.") Further, Horatio Wait states, "the value of prizes captured [during the war] was $31,000,000."

52. Ludwell H. Johnson, *Red River Campaign: Politics and Cotton in the Civil War* (Kent, Ohio: Kent State University Press, 1993) 101. It is noted that the two formulas for distribution of prize money differ in content and presumably this is due to differences in legislation. Interestingly, the Supreme Court ruled in the spring of 1865 that prize law did not apply to inland seizures. (Reference: Johnson 287, footnote 28.)

53. Major General H. W. Halleck wrote a letter on March 1, 1862, to Senator M. S. Latham pointing out "the injustice of the distinction in our laws in regard to captures made by the Army and Navy." He suggested that a law be passed "putting the Army and Navy on an equality in regard to prize-money." (Source: ORA vol. 10, pt. 2, 26–27.)

54. ORN vol. 21, 351.

55. ORN vol. 20, 486–489.

2. Blockade Growth

56. Glover 89, 90. By September 1862, Great Britain acknowledged that all Confederate ports were effectively blockaded.

57. The revenue cutter *Harriet Lane* (a steamer) was named for the niece of President Buchanan and had been secured from the Treasury Department's Revenue Marine, which later became the Coast Guard. (Reference: Musicant, footnote, page 13.)

58. ORN vol. 4. 180; vol. 5. 629–631, 682; vol. 18, 500.

59. Cotham 30–31.

60. ORN vol. 16, 595; Alwyn Barr, "Texas Coastal Defense, 1861–1865" LSBG 154; Silverstone 80–81; "The Western Gulf Blockade," May 23, 2001 <http://www.brownwaternavy.com/wg-main.htm>.

61. ORN vol. 16, 605–610; Cotham 33–34.

62. ORN vol. 16, 666.

63. Ronald Baxter, "Naval-U.S. Gunboat South Carolina." Barnstable (Mass.) Patriot, September 3, 1861 (Electronic edition, June 5, 2001 <http://www.brownwaternavy.com/7-31-61k.htm>).

64. Tans 2. Quoting Frank L. Owsley, *King Cotton Diplomacy: Foreign Relations of the Confederate States of America* (Chicago: University of Chicago Press, 1959), 229–231.

65. Tans 2–3. Quoting O'Flaherty, Daniel. "The Blockade That Failed," *American Heritage*, Vol. 6 (August 1955), 104.

66. Silverstone 128.

67. ORN vol. 17, 29.

68. ORN vol. 16, 759–762, 844; "Confederate States Navy," May 24, 2001 <http://www.ibiblio.org/pub/academic/history/marshall/military/civil_war_usa/C.S.N.r.txt>; Jones *The Civil War at Sea, January 1861–March 1862: The Blockaders*, vol. I, 291.

69. ORN vol. 16, 749–750.

70. Milledge L Bonham, Jr., *The British Consuls in the Confederacy* 1911 (New York: AMS Press, Inc., 1967), 184–186.

71. ORN vol. 16, 734; TDC, Appendix III, 245.

72. Barr 158, 174.

73. "Dated Dispatches," *Galveston Weekly News*, September 14, 15, 1864 <http://nautarch.tamu.edu/projects/denbigh/news02.htm>.

74. "The Galveston Blockade," *Galveston Weekly News*, January 11, 1865. June 15, 2001

<http://nautarch.tamu.edu/projects/denbigh/news04.htm>; *Dictionary of American Naval Fighting Ships*, June 15, 2001 <http://www.hazegray.org/danfs/steamers/bienvell.htm>.

75. William F. Hutchinson, M.D., "Monotony and Excitement on the Texas Blockade," TDC 213–217; Silverstone 43.

76. Stephen R. Wise, *Lifeline of the Confederacy: Blockade Running During the Civil War* (Columbia: University of South Carolina Press, 1988), 28–29, 119; Norman Shavin, *Illustrated Stories of the Century* (4th ed.) (Atlanta, Ga.: Capricorn Corporation, 1974), 16.

77. ORN vol. 17, 108; vol. 20, 429.

78. McPherson, *Battle Cry of Freedom*, 612–613.

79. Ralph J. Smith, "Reminiscences of Life on the Gulf Coast with the Second Texas Infantry," TDC 191.

80. Ralph A. Wooster, *Civil War Texas: A History and a Guide* (Austin: Texas State Historical Association, 1999), 32.

81. Ralph A. Wooster, *Texas and Texans in the Civil War* (Austin: Eakin Press, 1995), 123.

82. Wooster, *Civil War Texas* (Quoting Amelia Barr), 32.

83. McNeill, "Sallie McNeill's Diary, 1858–1867."

84. B. P. Gallaway, ed., *Texas, The Dark Corner of the Confederacy: Contemporary Accounts of the Lone Star State in the Civil War*, 3rd ed. (Lincoln, Neb.: University of Nebraska Press, 1999), 13–14.

85. "Civil War," HTO June 14, 2001 <http://www.tsha.utexas.edu/handbook/articles/view/CC/qdc2.html>.

3. Blockade Running and Blockade Evasion

86. C. Vann Woodward, ed., *Mary Chesnut's Civil War* (New York: Quality Paperback Book Club, 1981), 101, 306, 308.

87. Wise 25.

88. ORA vol. 1, 413.

89. Francis B. C. Bradlee, *Blockade Running During the Civil War, And the Effect of Land and Water Transportation on the Confederacy*, 1925 (Philadelphia: Porcupine Press, 1974), 21–22.

90. Wise 46–52; ORN vol. 6, 49, 216, 286; "George Alfred Trenholm," *The Trenholm Company Runs the Blockade*. June 5, 2001 <http://www.awod.com/gallery/probono/cwchas/trenholm.html> (Civil War @ Charleston website.)

91. James Morris Morgan, *Recollections of a Rebel Reefer*. Electronic Edition. First Edition, 1999, University of North Carolina at Chapel Hill Libraries. October 7, 2000 <http://www.ibiblio.org/docsouth/morganjames/morgan.html#morgan1> 100–101.

92. J. Wilkinson, *The Narrative of a Blockade-Runner*. Electronic Edition. June 14, 2001 <http://www.civilwarancestor.com/store/files/Ebook 0106.htm>. Chapter V.

93. Wise 107–111.

94. Wilkinson n. page.

95. Bradlee 34.

96. Thomas E. Taylor, *Running the Blockade*. 2nd Ed. London: John Murray, 1896. Electronic edition. June 6, 2001 <http//www.civilwarancestor.com/STORE/files/Ebook 0100.htm>; Wise 289. "The Crew of the Banshee: A Profile," *Blockade Runners*, Archives of NARA, September 5, 2002 <http://www.archives.gov/publications/prologue/fall_1999_blockade_runners_3.html>.

97. Bradlee 60.

98. William Watson, "Running the Union Blockade," TDC 136–145.

99. ORN vol. 20, 842–845; Bonham 188–190.

100. William Watson, "Running the Blockade Into Galveston: A Personal Narrative." *The Denbigh Project: Archaeology of a Confederate Blockade-Runner*. June 18, 2000 <http://nautarch.tamu.edu/projects/denbigh/Watson.htm>. n. page.

101. Wise 74–75, 80.

102. Bradlee 144, 145.

103. Glover 188, 189; "House, Thomas William," HTO August 29, 2001 <http://www.tsha.utexas.edu/handbook/articles/view/HH/fho68.html>.

104. Glover 191, 192; "Swisher, John Milton," HTO August 31, 2001 <http://www.tsha.utexas.edu/handbook/articles/view/SS/fsw20.html>.

105. ORN vol. 16, 768; vol. 17. 654; vol. 19, 158, 159; Glover 180–182.

106. ORN vol. 22, 30, 190, 194; vol. 48, pt. 2, 230; ser. II, vol. 2, 720–722.

107. ORN vol. 48, pt. 2, 230.

108. Glover 215, 218, 219.

109. ORN vol. 22, 190.

110. ORN vol. 22, 126.

111. Wilkinson n. page.

112. W. T. Block, "The Romance of Sabine Lake," June 29, 2000 <http://block.dynip.com/wtblockjr/sabine1.html>.

113. W. T. Block, "Blockade Runs at Sabine Pass Commonplace in Civil War," June 7, 2001 <http://block.dynip.com/wtblockjr/blockade1.htm>.

114. W. T. Block, "Sabine Pass and Galveston Were Successful Blockade-Running Ports," June 25, 2000 <http://block.dynip.com/wtblockjr/blockade.htm>.

115. Wise 83–86.

116. James Arthur Irby, *Line of the Rio Grande: War and Trade on the Confederate Frontier, 1861-1865*. Diss. University of Georgia, 1969 (Ann Arbor: University Microfilms, Inc., 1981), xiii, xxii, 2–3; James Arthur Irby, *Backdoor at Bagdad: The Civil War on the Rio Grande*, Southwestern Studies, Monograph No. 53 (The University of Texas at El Paso: Texas Western Press, 1977), 5, 6.

117. ORN vol. 18, 51, 78.

118. ORN vol. 18, 83–86.

119. Wise 88; ORN vol. 18, 82.

120. ORA ser. III, vol. 2, 948–949. Documents of the period often spell "Matamoros" as "Matamoras." However, the town was named for a patriot priest, Mariano Matamoros. Consequently, the correct spelling should be "Matamoros." (Source: Irby, *Line of the Rio Grande: War and Trade on the Confederate Frontier, 1861-1865* 2, footnote 5.)

121. ORN vol. 18, 79.

122. Irby, *Backdoor at Bagdad: The Civil War on the Rio Grande* 23, 24; ORN 19. 265.

123. ORN vol. 19, 159.

124. Irby, *Backdoor at Bagdad: The Civil War on the Rio Grande* 26–27; ORN vol. 17, 402.

125. Mahin 84.

126. Jefferson Davis, "Inaugural Address," *The Papers of Jefferson Davis*, Reprinted in C.S.A., Congressional Journal 1:64–66, Lynda L. Crist and Mary S. Dix, ed. (Baton Rouge, Louisiana: LSU Press, 1992). June 21, 2000 <http://sunsite.utk.edu/civil-war/jdinaug.html>.

127. Eugene H. Berwanger, *The British Foreign Service and the American Civil War* (Lexington: University Press of Kentucky, 1999), 20.

128. "Brazos Santiago, Texas," HTO, February 2, 2000 <http://www.tsha.utexas.edu/handbook/online/articles/view/BB/rrb12.html>.

129. Irby, *Line of the Rio Grande: War and Trade on the Confederate Frontier, 1861-1865*, 13.

130. The hamlet disappeared from the map after being struck by a hurricane in 1867. (Source: Irby, *Line of the Rio Grande: War and Trade on the Confederate Frontier, 1861-1865*, xxi–xxii, 5–6.)

131. Irby, *Line of the Rio Grande: War and Trade on the Confederate Frontier, 1861-1865*, 14; James Arthur Irby, *Backdoor at Bagdad: The Civil War on the Rio Grande*, Southwestern Studies, Monograph No. 53 (The University of Texas at El Paso: Texas Western Press, 1977), 9.

132. ORN vol. 1, 368, 369; vol. 17, 99–115; vol. 18, 66, 67. Four months later *Labuan* again was loading cotton from Matamoros (Glover 34).

133. Irby, *Line of the Rio Grande: War and Trade on the Confederate Frontier, 1861-1865*, xxi–xxii, 5–6.

134. Arthur J. L. Fremantle, *Three Months in the Southern States: April–June 1863*. Introd. Gary W. Gallagher (New York: J. Bradburn, 1864; Lincoln: University of Nebraska Press, 1991), 8–9.

135. Irby, *Backdoor at Bagdad: The Civil War on the Rio Grande*, 7, 23.

136. ORN vol. 17, 404.

137. Irby, *Line of the Rio Grande: War and Trade on the Confederate Frontier, 1861-1865*, 5–6.

138. Irby, *Line of the Rio Grande: War and Trade on the Confederate Frontier, 1861-1865*, 69–70; 138, footnote 187.

139. "Alleyton, Texas," HTO, June 23, 2000 <http://www.tsha.utexas.edu/handbook/online/articles/view/AA/hna25.html>.

140. Fremantle 63.

141. "Richard King," HTO, June 24, 2000 <http://www.tsha.utexas.edu/handbook/online/articles/view/KK/fki19.html>.

142. Ronnie C. Tyler, "Cotton on the Border, 1861–1865," *Lone Star Blue and Gray: Essays on Texas in the Civil War* (Abbreviated hereafter as LSBG), Ralph A. Wooster, ed. (Austin: Texas State Historical Association, 1995), 216.

143. Glover 203–206.

144. Irby, *Line of the Rio Grande: War and Trade on the Confederate Frontier, 1861-1865*, 94–95.

145. Glover 67.

146. Glover 133, 136.

147. Kerby, Robert L., *Kirby Smith's Confederacy: The Trans-Mississippi South, 1863-1865* (New York: Columbia University Press, 1972), 180–181.

148. Tyler 218.

149. Kerby 182.

150. James W. Daddysman, *The Matamoros Trade: Confederate Commerce, Diplomacy, and Intrigue* (Cranbury, N.J.: Associated University Presses, Inc., 1984), 155.

151. Daddysman 156.

152. Irby, *Line of the Rio Grande: War and Trade on the Confederate Frontier, 1861-1865*, 8–19.

153. This town no longer exists. During the Civil War it was located in Jackson County, above Lavaca Bay, near the present county seat.

154. Daddysman 155–158.

155. Fremantle 15–16.

156. ORN Vol. 18, 456–457.
157. ORN Vol. 20, 469.
158. Wooster, *Texas and Texans in the Civil War*, 120.

4. Moves and Countermoves

159. ORN vol. 21, 164–166; *Dictionary of American Fighting Ships, Vol. II.* "D." Washington, D.C.: Navy Department, Office of the Chief of Naval Operations, Naval History Division. Electronic edition. June 1, 2001 <http://www.hazegray.org/danfs>; Paul H. Silverstone, *Warships of the Civil War Navies* (Annapolis, Maryland: Naval Institute Press, 1989), 192, 49. See also Ralph W. Donnelly, "The Confederate States Marine Corps: The Rebel Leathernecks" (Revised February 1990). It is interesting to note that just after *Henry Dodge* was surrendered to rebel forces, one of the U.S. coast surveyors working near Galveston became nervous. He ceased his operations on March 19, 1861, because of "the unfortunate and excited state of the country." (Source: Captain Albert E. Theberge, "The Coast Survey in the Civil War," Section I, Introduction. <http.www.lib.noaa.gov.edocs/CW1# INTRODUCTION>.)
160. *Dictionary of American Fighting Ships, Vol. II*, Appendix II, Annex III; Cotham 13–14.
161. Barr 152–154.
162. ORA vol. 4, 92.
163. Barr 154–157.
164. ORN vol. 17, 166, 167.
165. ORN vol. 17, 79–81, 166; Glover 172, 176; "The Western Gulf Blockade," n. pag.
166. ORA vol. 4, 117, 148.
167. ORA vol. 9, 729.
168. ORA vol. 15, 834–835.
169. Block, "The Ghostly-Silent Guns of Galveston"; ORA vol. 15, 853–854, 865.
170. Block, "The Ghostly-Silent Guns of Galveston," n. pag.
171. Donald S. Frazier, *Cottonclads! The Battle of Galveston and the Defense of the Texas Coast* (Abilene: McWhiney Foundation Press, 1998), 18.
172. ORN vol. 18, 672–673; "The Western Gulf Blockade," n. pag.
173. ORN vol. 18, 672–673. vol. 19, 151–152, 780–783; "The Western Gulf Blockade."
174. ORN vol. 19, 201–204; Wooster, *Civil War Texas*, 14.
175. Edward Steers, Jr., *Blood on the Moon: The Assassination of Abraham Lincoln* (Lexington: University Press of Kentucky, 2001), 240–241; Robert N. Macomber, "Yellow Fever Assaults the Fleet in Florida," Parts 1 and 2, Civil War Interactive, September 4, 2002 <http://www.civilwarinteractive.com/myworstfear1.htm>.
176. ORN vol. 19, 217–237 (In these accounts there is conflict about the date Fort Sabine was bombarded. Crocker says the fort was bombarded on September 25, while Hooper and Pennington contend this action took place on September 24); Wooster, *Civil War Texas*, 14.
177. Wooster, *Civil War Texas*, 13.
178. ORN vol. 19, 213.
179. ORN vol. 19, 255–258. Commodore Renshaw had good cause to be concerned about the spread of yellow fever to his ship. Two years later, near Galveston, another Union blockading ship (*Arkansas*) saw the fever spread among her crew. A 21-year-old surgeon's steward, C. Marion Dodson, nursed the yellow fever victims and in his journal wrote an informative account of his experience treating the ill sailors. See C. Marion Dodson, *Yellow Flag: The Civil War Journal of Surgeon's Steward C. Marion Dodson*, ed. Charles Albert Earp (Baltimore: Maryland Historical Society, 2002), 71–85.
180. Frazier 16.
181. ORN vol. 19, 253–263.
182. Frazier 32; Wooster, *Texas and Texans in the Civil War*, 63–64.
183. ORA vol. 15, 183.
184. Frazier 51.
185. *Star of the West* had been chartered by the U.S. Army to transport troops to New York that had been surrendered by General Twiggs in February 1861.
186. Frazier 50; Wooster, *Texas and Texans in the Civil War* 65; Virgil Carrington Jones, *The Civil War at Sea, March 1862–July 1863: The River War.* Vol. II, 1961 (Wilmington, N.C.: Broadfoot Publishing Company, 1990), 319.
187. Frazier 57.
188. ORA vol. 15, 201–202.
189. ORA vol. 15, 204.
190. ORA vol. 15, 213–214.
191. ORA vol. 15, 214.
192. Frazier 60, 62.
193. ORN vol. 19, 437–444, 456, 457; Frazier 64–85; Wooster, *Texas and Texans in the Civil War*, 64–68; Jones, *The Civil War at Sea, March 1862–July 1863: The River War.* Vol. II, 323–325.
194. Barr 165; Frazier 82, 84–85.
195. ORA vol. 15, 201–207, 210–216; Barr 165; ORN vol. 19, 439–445.
196. ORA vol. 26, pt. 1, 6–7.
197. Frazier 93; Wooster, *Texas and Texans in the Civil War*, 68.
198. According to Kell, *Alabama* and *Hatteras* became engaged in a running fight on parallel courses with the C.S.A. vessel firing from

her starboard broadside and the Union vessel firing from her port broadside. He reports the firing lasted 13 minutes. After rescuing the *Hatteras* personnel, *Alabama* quickly left the scene because of concern that other Federal gun ships would pursue them. (Source: Kell, John McIntosh, *Recollections of a Naval Life: Including the Cruises of the Confederate States Steamers "Sumter" and "Alabama."* Electronic Edition, First Edition, 1998. University of North Carolina at Chapel Hill Libraries. October 10, 2000 <http://www.ibiblio.org/docsouth/kell/kell.html> 207–209.); Nash 281–283.

199. ORN vol. 19, 479, 504–506. Vol. 2, 18–21; Frazier 94–98; Wise 169; Boatner 4.

200. ORN vol. 20, 157.

201. ORN vol. 2, 639; Frazier 98.

202. Frazier 102–104; Wooster, *Texas and Texans in the Civil War* 69–70; Block, W. T. "Sabine Pass in the Civil War." Reprinted from East Texas Historical Journal, Vol. IX, No. 2 (October, 1971, 129–136), June 25, 2000 <http://block.dynip.com/wtblockjr/civilwar.htm>.

203. ORA vol. 34, pt. 3, 584.

204. ORA vol. 26, pt. 1, 672.

205. Andrew Forest Muir, "Dick Dowling and the Battle of Sabine Pass," LSBG 189– 192.

206. ORA vol. 26, pt. 1, 287–288.

207. Virgil Carrington Jones, *The Civil War at Sea, July 1863–November 1865: The Final Effort*, vol. III, 1962 (Wilmington, N.C.: Broadfoot Publishing Company, 1990) 40–41.

208. Muir 192–193. ORA vol. 26, pt. 1, 18–19, 281–288, 290–293, 294–295, 298–299, 309, 311.

209. In one report, Dowling refers to 47 men, but this figure is probably the maximum number of men that were in the fortification at any one time, the minimum number being 43. In an interview just after the battle, Dowling was asked how many men he had and he replied, "'We had forty-three men.'" Dowling was an Irish-born saloon keeper and the Davis Guards consisted of Irishmen who had been recruited in Houston. The Davis Guards was formed as a state militia in the summer of 1860 and on October 26, 1861, "it became Company F of Cook's (or the First Texas) Regiment, Heavy Artillery, Confederate States Army." (Source: Muir 184, 196 [footnote 115], 199.); Virgil C. Jones in *The Civil War at Sea, July 1863–November 1865: The Final Effort*, vol. III, page 43, contends that only five guns were fired because a brass 24-pounder lacked ammunition, and he lists cannon of different calibers.

210. Block, "Battle of Sabine Pass—Its Causes and Effects"; Wooster, *Texas and Texans in the Civil War* 87; ORA vol. 26, pt. 1, 311.

211. Pierce, David W. "Dick Dowling and the Battle of Sabine Pass." June 25, 2000 <http://rampages.onramp.net/~jtcreate/cofc/dowling.htm>; Muir 194–198; ORA vol. 26, pt. 1, 308, 295, 307.

212. Muir 196–200; ORA vol. 26, pt. 1, 297; Wooster, *Texas and Texans in the Civil War* 87–92; Barr 169–170.

213. Block, "Sabine Pass in the Civil War" 3; Wooster, *Texas and Texans in the Civil War* 91, 92; Muir, 178 (footnote 1).

214. Frazier 125–127, 130. Data are based upon armament as of January 1863.

215. ORA vol. 26, pt. 1, 288–290; Shelby Foote, *The Civil War: A Narrative. Fredericksburg to Meridian* (New York: Random House–Vintage Books, 1963) 774–775; Wooster, *Civil War Texas* 70, endnote 31 (Quoting from Harrington's book, *Fighting Politician* 131.); Muir 192.

216. Bonham 188.

217. ORN vol. 19, 452, 465, 548–549.

218. Bonham 188.

5. A Snarl: Cotton, Politics...

219. "King Cotton," *Encyclopaedia Britannica* July 22, 2000 <http://www.britannica.com/bcom/eb/article/printagle/5/0,5722,46575,00.html>. According to this source, this concept was first suggested in the book *Cotton Is King: or, The Culture of Cotton, and Its Relation to Agriculture, Manufacturers, and Commerce* by David Christy.

220. Wigfall, "Cotton is King." *Great Debates in American History*. New York: Current Literature Publishing Company, 1913. Vol. 5, 348–350. September 28, 2000 <http://www.adena.com/adena/usa/cw/cw112.htm>.

221. "French Legation," HTO, May 17, 2000 <http://www.tsha.utexas.edu/handbook/on line/articles/view/FF/ccf3.html>.

222. "French," HTO March 10, 2000 <http://www.tsha.utexas.edu/handbook/on line/articles/view/FF/pmf1.html>.

223. "Henri Castro, 'Empresario,'" June 29, 2000 <http://www.castroville.com/henricastro.htm>.

224. With the 1854 Gadsden Purchase, the United States obtained 30,000 square miles of Mexican territory for $10,000,000. This land is now part of southwestern New Mexico and Southern Arizona.

225. Crook 92.

226. Mahin 115–116.

227. Steven C. Topik, "When Mexico Had the Blues: A Transatlantic Tale of Bonds,

Bankers, and Nationalists, 1862–1910," *The American Historical Review* vol. 105, no. 3 n.d., September 20, 2000 <http://www.historycooperative.org/journals/ahr/105.3/ah000714.html>.

228. ORN vol. 1, 368, 369.
229. ORN ser. II, vol. 3, 684–686.
230. Cotham 55.
231. ORN ser. II, vol. 3, 671.
232. Mahin 224.
233. Gallaway 172.
234. Norman A. Graebner, "Northern Diplomacy and European Neutrality," *Why the North Won the Civil War*, David Herbert Donald, ed., 60.
235. David Paul Crook, *The North, the South, and the Powers, 1861–1865* (New York: John Wiley & Sons, 1974), 90, 336.
236. See Mahin, *passim*; Tyler 214, footnote 6.
237. "DRSC Focus: A 2000 Cinco de Mayo Primer," June 28, 2000 <http://www.cruzers.com/~cab/primer.html>. The defeat of the French at Puebla on May 5, 1862, is the source of the traditional Mexican independence holiday (Cinco de Mayo) celebrated today in the United States and elsewhere. However, true independence had been achieved on September 16, 1810, when Mexico overthrew the Spanish government. Cinco de Mayo symbolizes the right of people to self-determination and the ability of non–Europeans to resist incursions by modern military organizations. The holiday memorializes the victory of a weak army over a strong foe.
238. "Mexican Holidays: Cinco de Mayo," June 28, 2000 <http://www.mexonline.com/cinco.htm>; "Maximilian (1832–1867)," *World Book* June 28, 2000 <http://www.worldbook.com/fun/cinco/html/maximilian.htm>.
239. Tyler 229
240. ORN ser. 2, vol. 3, 202.
241. Daddysman 40.
242. Frank Lawrence Owsley, *King Cotton Diplomacy: Foreign Relations of the Confederate States of America* (Second edition, revised by Harriet Chappell Owsley) (Chicago: The University of Chicago Press, 1959), 89.
243. Owsley says the given name of Quintero is "Juan" and that he was an important and effective agent (Owsley 114). On the other hand, Daddysman says Quintero's given name is "Jose" (Daddysman, 68, footnote 68) and that "Quintero was the most effective agent sent to Mexico, and one of the most skillful and successful in the entire Confederate diplomatic corps." (Daddysman 46.) In the Navy OR and the Army OR, he consistently is identified as "J. A. Quintero." So as not to confuse, I shall refer to Quintero by his surname.
244. Daddysman 47.
245. Owsley 118.
246. Owsley 104.
247. Owsley 111; Daddysman 41; Mahin 110–114.
248. The United States Rio Grande Expedition in November 1863 temporarily reduced cotton trade, but most of the Union forces withdrew from mainland Texas early in 1864 (see Chapter 6). Revitalized cotton commerce emerged in 1864 and continued uninterrupted until the end of the war.
249. ORA ser. 3, vol. 2, 949–951.
250. ORA ser. 3, vol. 2, 949.
251. Edgar T. Welles, *The Diary of Gideon Welles* (3 Vols.), (Boston: Houghton Mifflin Company, 1911), vol. 1, 283.
252. Welles, vol. 1, 334.
253. Tyler 222.
254. Boatner 769–771, 845.
255. Kerby 136.
256. Kerby 136–137.
257. ORA vol. 22, pt. 2, 952–953.
258. Kerby 137–138.
259. Wooster, *Civil War Texas*, 36.
260. Wooster, *Texas and Texans in the Civil War* 99–100; "Marshall Conferences" HTO, April 18, 2001 <http://www.tsha.utexas.edu/handbook/online/articles/view/MM/nhm1.html>.
261. ORA vol. 22, pt. 2, 1003–1010; Wooster, *Texas and Texans in the Civil War*, 101.
262. Smith to McCulloch. Quoted in Kerby 155.
263. Kerby 161–162.
264. Kerby 154; Wooster, *Texas and Texans in the Civil War*, 106–108.
265. Kerby 199–207.
266. Kerby 156–160.
267. Ella Lonn, *Foreigners in the Confederacy* (Gloucester, Mass.: Peter Smith, 1965), 84–85.
268. "Woll, Adrian" HTO, July 3, 2000 <http://www.tsha.utexas.edu/handbook/online/articles/view/WW/fwo3.html>; ORA vol. 26, pt. 2, 142–143.
269. "Dubois De Saligny," HTO, July 26, 2000 <http://www.tsha.utexas.edu/handbook/online/articles/view/DD/fdu2.html>.
270. ORA vol. 26, pt. 2, 140–151.
271. ORA vol. 26, pt. 2, 181–182.
272. ORA vol. 26, pt. 2, 202.
273. Kerby 144.
274. ORA vol. 22, pt. 2, 992–994.
275. ORA vol. 26, pt. 2, 234–235.

276. ORA vol. 26, pt. 2, 314–315.
277. ORA vol. 26, pt. 2, 308–309, 272–274.
278. Lonn 84–85. This author was unable to glean any background information about one A. (or M.) Superviele. Perhaps this was a *nom de guerre?*
279. ORA vol. 26, pt. 2, 308–310, 314–315.
280. ORA vol. 53, 961; Irby, *Backdoor at Bagdad: The Civil War on the Rio Grande*, 27.
281. Kerby 146–148.
282. Kerby 149.

6. Rio Grande Expedition

283. James M. Merrill, *Battle Flags South: The Story of the Civil War Navies on Western Waters* (Cranbury, N.J.: Associated University Presses, Inc., 1970), 53.
284. Merrill 55.
285. ORA vol. 53, 507–509.
286. Ludwell H. Johnson, *Red River Campaign: Politics and Cotton in the Civil War* (Kent, Ohio, and London: Kent State University Press, 1993), 12–13.
287. Johnson 16.
288. ORA ser. 3, vol. 2, 691–692.
289. ORN vol. 19, 338.
290. ORA vol. 15, 590–591.
291. ORN vol. 19, 342.
292. Johnson 23–24.
293. ORA ser. 3, vol. 2, 782.
294. Johnson 25–26.
295. ORA ser. 3, vol. 2, 862.
296. Donald, *Lincoln*, 15.
297. ORA vol. 15, 613.
298. Rowena Reed, *Combined Operations in the Civil War* (Annapolis: Naval Institute Press, 1978), 385.
299. Kerby 186–188; Welles, vol. 1, 387–391.
300. ORN vol. 20, 155, 291, 201, 278–279.
301. ORA vol. 26, pt. 1, 659.
302. ORA vol. 26, pt. 1, 664.
303. ORA vol. 26, pt. 1, 19–20.
304. ORN vol. 20, 836, 606, 623, 284–285; ORA vol. 26, pt. 1, 656–657.
305. ORA vol. 26, pt. 1, 396; Nash 230.
306. ORA vol. 26, pt. 1, 411–416, 20–21.
307. ORA vol. 26, pt. 1, 416–423, 426–428; "St. Joseph Island," HTO, February 8, 2000 <http://www.tsha.utexas.edu/handbook/online/articles/view/SS/rrs9.html>; "Fort Esperanza," HTO, February 8, 2000 <http://www.tsha.utexas.edu/handbook/online/articles/view/FF/qcf2.html>.
308. Kerby 195.
309. ORA vol. 53, 961.
310. ORN vol. 21, 74–76; Barr 172–173.
311. ORN vol. 22, 20–21; Barr 174.

7. Confederacy Collapses

312. Kerby 363.
313. Kerby 365.
314. "Ford, John Salmon," HTO, July 7, 2000 <http://www.tsha.utexas.edu/handbook/online/articles/view/FF/ffo11.html>.
315. Kerby 366.
316. ORA vol. 41, pt. 2, 46–47.
317. Kerby 369.
318. Kerby 377.
319. Kerby 378–379. By fall 1864 there were more Union vessels blockading Galveston to try to stem the increased flow of blockade runners. The *Galveston Weekly News* reported that there were eleven blockaders guarding Galveston Bay on September 14, 1864, nine on September 15, eleven on October 19, twelve on October 21, and ten on October 24, 1864. (Source: "The Denbigh Project: Archaeology of a Confederate Blockade-Runner" June 18, 2000, October 23, 2002 <http://nautarch.tamu.edu/projects/denbigh>.) Frequently it is erroneously reported in popular literature that the first Confederate port to fall to the Union was Wilmington, N.C. For example, in the May 10, 2003, electronic publication *The Washington Times*, historian Thomas J. Ryan's article "The End of the confederacy's Safe Harbor" appeared. In the lead paragraph he incorrectly notes that in October 1864 Wilmington, N.C., was "the South's last lifeline to the outside world." He fails to note that Galveston continued to import military goods and export cotton through May 1865. However, Galveston and Texas were not transporting any of these supplies to the east because of the earlier Union control of the Mississippi River. (Source: http://www.washingtontimes.com/civilwar/20030512-103151-6750r.htm. May 20, 2003.)
320. Wise 296.
321. ORN vol. 22, 197; "The Denbigh Project: Archaeology of a Confederate Blockade-Runner," June 18, 2000, October 23, 2002 <http://nautarch.tamu.edu/projects/denbigh>. The wreck of *Denbigh* was located in 1997 and it is now a protected archaeological site. The remains of *Denbigh* lie in state waters and come under the stewardship of the Texas Historical Commission which has issued the appropriate permits and authorization to the Institute of Nautical Archaeology to conduct site surveys and testing. See also Grant, Mary Lee, "Re-

searchers Dive into Ship's History," *Daytona Beach Sunday News-Journal*, July 30, 2000, 8A.

322. To complete the metaphor, it should be noted that on the same day *Denbigh* was burning the grand review of the armies was taking place in Washington. On May 24 General Sherman's 65,000-man Army of Georgia passed in review for six hours.

323. Grant, *Personal Memoirs of U. S. Grant*, 648; Joseph Wheeler, "An Effort to Rescue Jefferson Davis," *The Century*, Vol. 56, Issue 1, May 1898. 87, September 16, 2001. American Memory, Library of Congress, The Nineteenth Century In Print: Periodicals. <http://memory.loc.gov/ammem/ndlpcoop/moahtml/title/lists/cent_V56I1.html>.

324. ORA vol. 52, pt. 2, 586–592.

325. Kerby 397.

326. Kerby 399.

327. Kerby 397–398.

328. Kerby 400.

329. Kerby 413–414.

330. ORA vol. 48, pt. 1, 1319–1320; Boatner 657.

331. Kerby 417.

332. Irby, *Backdoor at Bagdad: The Civil War on the Rio Grande*, 47.

333. "Palmito Ranch, Battle of," HTO, February 8, 2000 <http://www.tsha.utexas.edu/handbook/online/articles/view/PP/qfp1.html>.

334. Claude Elliott, "Union Sentiment in Texas, 1861–1865," LSBG 106.

335. Kerby 420.

336. Arthur E. Gilligan, "Ten Weeks in Texas as a Prisoner of War." *Texas, The Dark Corner of the Confederacy: Contemporary Accounts of the Lone Star State in the Civil War*. B. P. Gallaway, ed. Third edition (Lincoln, Neb.: University of Nebraska Press, 1999), 192, 194, 201, 204.

337. Kerby 423.

338. Kerby 426.

339. Louise Wigfall Wright, *The War-Time Memories of a Confederate Senator's Daughter: A Southern Girl in '61*. Electronic Edition. First Edition, 1997. University of North Carolina at Chapel Hill Libraries. September 28, 2000 <http://www.ibiblio.org/docsouth/wright/wright.html#wright221> 246.

340. ORA vol. 48, pt. 2, 929.

8. Blockade Revisited

341. *Webster's Ninth New Collegiate Dictionary* (Springfield. Mass.: Merriam-Webster, Inc. n.d.), 160.

342. "Blockade." *The 'Lectric Law Library's Lexicon* (Lexicon on Blockade). July 13, 2000 <http://www.lectlaw.com/def.htm>. n. pag.

343. Crook 66.

344. Bradlee 92.

345. Bonham 193.

346. McPherson, *Battle Cry of Freedom* 387; Mahin 185–188; Wise 184–186, 316. Interestingly, McPherson states that the British Foreign Office merely recorded this precedent and then cited it years later to justify seizure of American ships carrying contraband to a neutral country for overland transshipment to Germany.

347. "The U. S. Navy in the Civil War" 2.

348. Mahin 165.

349. Wise 251–252, 255–256.

350. Owsley 232–233.

351. Owsley 235, 237–238.

352. Tans 3.

353. David M. Potter, "Jefferson Davis and the Political Factors in Confederate Defeat," *Why the North Won the Civil War*, David Herbert Donald, ed. (New York: Simon & Schuster-Touchstone, 1996), 99.

354. Tans 4.

355. "The U. S. Navy in the Civil War" 3.

356. David Herbert Donald, "Died of Democracy," *Why the North Won the Civil War*, David Herbert Donald, ed. (New York: Simon & Schuster–Touchstone, 1996), 92; Bradlee 32, 62; ORA ser. IV, vol. 3, 78–80.

357. Wise 272–273, 274–275, 312.

358. Owsley 253–257.

359. Cotham 173.

360. Graebner, "Northern Diplomacy and European Neutrality," *Why the North Won the Civil War*, 67.

361. Crook 48, 49.

362. Irby, *Backdoor at Bagdad: The Civil War on the Rio Grande*, 51.

363. ORA vol. 48, pt. 2, 401.

364. Irby, *Line of the Rio Grande: War and Trade on the Confederate Frontier, 1861–1865*, 218.

365. Owsley 267.

366. J. Thomas Scharf, *History of the Confederate States Navy*, 1887 (New York: Random House–Gramercy Books, 1996), 428–493, 494–532.

367. Bern Anderson, *By Sea and By River: The Naval History of the Civil War* (New York: Alfred A. Knopf–Borzoi, 1962), 232.

368. Tans 9.

369. Beringer 62–63, 309, 425.

370. Marcus W. Price, "Ships That Tested the Blockade of the Gulf Ports, 1861–1865," *American Neptune* vol. 11, no. 4 (October 1951) 262–297 and vol. 12, no. 2 (April 1952), 154–

161. July 21, 2000 <http://www.pem.org/neptune>. One of the ships captured was *Sir Wm. Peel* on September 11 near Bagdad. The American officer took *Peel* as a prize because he believed the vessel was to be converted to a Confederate privateer. This provoked an extended controversy in prize court, which eventually determined that *Peel* was seized illegally. The ship was released. (See Irby, *Backdoor at Bagdad: The Civil War on the Rio Grande*, 28.)

371. Glover 3, 251.

372. "The U. S. Navy in the Civil War" 4.

373. Daddysman 160–162. On the other hand, Frank L. Owsley used different data to come up with a contrary conclusion while some regional historians have probably exaggerated the importance of the Matamoros trade.

374. Daddysman 187.

375. Wise 226

376. Mahin 173.

377. McPherson, *Battle Cry of Freedom* 381; footnote 11, 381; footnote 12, 382.

378. Richard N. Current, "God and the Strongest Battalions." *Why the North Won the Civil War.* David Herbert Donald, ed. (New York: Simon & Schuster–Touchstone, 1996), 33.

379. James Russell Soley, "The Blockade and the Cruisers" (*Blockade: The Blockading of the Southern Seaports in the Civil War*), September 2, 2002. <http://www.civilwar home.com/blockade.htm>.

380. Crook 174, 175, 211.

381. Bradlee 162, 163.

382. Nash 301. In a similar though unorthodox vein, Ekelund and Thornton did an economic analysis of the war in a recent article in which they contend that the Confederate government's economic and military policies closed down international trade and led to the destruction of the South. In effect, the South is said to have blockaded itself and unwittingly supported the Federal blockade. They cite the effect of the King Cotton embargo and they discuss the negative effects upon the Confederacy of impressments of steam-powered ships, the deterioration of the railroads, legislation restricting cargoes aboard blockade runners, and other policies that all harmed the Southern economy. (See Robert B. Ekelund, Jr. and Mark Thornton, "The 'Confederate' Blockade of the South," *The Quarterly Journal of Austrian Economics*, vol. 4, no. 1 [Spring 2001] 23–42. <http://www.mises.org/journals/qjae4_1_2.pdf> Accessed September 27, 2002.)

383. Alfred Thayer Mahan, *The Influence of Sea Power Upon History 1660–1805* (Englewood Cliffs, NJ: Prentice-Hall, Inc., 1980.), 40–41.

384. David G. Surdam, "The Union Navy's Blockade Reconsidered." *Naval War College Review* (Newport, RI), vol. LI, no. 4, sequence 364, Autumn 1998, 105–127. May 14, 2003 http://www.nwc.navy.mil/press/Review/1998/autumn/art5-a98.htm; David G. Surdam, "The Confederate Naval Buildup: Could More Have Been Accomplished?" *Naval War College Review* (Newport, RI), vol. LIV, no. 1, Winter 2001, 107–128. May 20, 2003 http://www.nwc.navy.mil/press/Review/2001/Winter/art7-w01.htm.

385. David J. Murphy, Colonel, USAF, *Naval Strategy During The American Civil War* (Research Report, Air War College, Air University, Maxwell Air Force Base, Alabama, April 1999). <http://papers.maxwell.af.mil/projects/ay1999/awc/99-175.pdf.>

386. Dave Horner, *The Blockade-Runners* (New York: Dodd, Mead & Company, 1968), 4.

387. ORA ser. 4, vol. 3, 952.

9. Epilogue

388. June 19 has been recognized as "Emancipation Day in Texas." This date has been designated as a legal state holiday effective January 1, 1980, as provided in House Bill no. 1016 that was passed in the regular session of the 66th legislature.

389. McNeill, "Sallie McNeill's Diary," n. pag.

390. Gary W. Gallagher, "There Is Rancor In Our Hearts ... Which You Little Dream Of," *Civil War Times*, n. d. October 5, 2000 <http://www.the history net.com/CivilWar Times/articles/2000/0500_side2.htm>.

391. "O, I'm a Good Old Rebel," *Poems and Songs of the Civil War Page*. October 5, 2000 <http://www.civilwarhome.com/pooroldrebel.htm>.

392. Morison 414.

393. Mahin 270.

394. Glover 81.

395. Mahin 276–277.

396. Mahin 281, 284; Boatner 521.

Bibliography

Books, Articles, Pamphlets, and Exhibits

Anderson, Bern. *By Sea and by River: The Naval History of the Civil War*. New York: Alfred A. Knopf–Borzoi, 1962.

Barr, Alwyn. "Texas Coastal Defense, 1861–1865." *Lone Star Blue and Gray: Essays on Texas in the Civil War*. Ralph A. Wooster, ed. Austin: Texas State Historical Association, 1995, 150–174.

Beringer, Richard E., Herman Hattaway, Archer Jones, and William N. Still, Jr. *Why the South Lost the Civil War*. Athens: The University of Georgia Press, 1986.

Boatner, Mark M. *The Civil War Dictionary* (Rev. Edition). New York: Random House–Vintage Books, 1988.

Bonham, Jr., Milledge L. *The British Consuls in the Confederacy*. 1911. New York: AMS Press, Inc., 1967.

Bowden, J. J. *The Exodus of Federal Forces from Texas 1861*. Austin: Eakin Press, 1986.

Bradlee, Francis B. C. *Blockade Running During the Civil War, and the Effect of Land and Water Transportation on the Confederacy*. 1925. Philadelphia: Porcupine Press, 1974.

Brown, Russell K. "An Old Woman with a Broomstick: General David E. Twiggs and the U.S. Surrender in Texas, 1861." *Military Affairs*. April 1984. Manhattan, Kan.: American Military Institute, 57–61.

Buenger, Walter E. "Texas and the Riddle of Secession." *Lone Star Blue and Gray: Essays on Texas in the Civil War*. Ralph A. Wooster, ed. Austin: Texas State Historical Association, 1995, 1–26.

Catton, Bruce. *The Civil War*. Boston: Houghton Mifflin, 1960.

____. *The Coming Fury*. Garden City, N.Y.: Doubleday & Company, 1961.

Commager, Henry Steele, ed. *The Blue and the Gray*, 2 vols. New York: Bobbs-Merrill Company, 1950.

Cotham, Edward T. Jr., *Battle on the Bay: The Civil War Struggle for Galveston*. Austin: University of Texas Press, 1998.

Crook, David Paul. *The North, the South, and the Powers, 1861–1865*. New York: John Wiley & Sons, 1974.

Current, Richard N. "God and the Strongest Battalions." *Why the North Won the Civil War*. David Herbert Donald, ed. New York: Simon & Schuster–Touchstone, 1996.

Daddysman, James W. *The Matamoros Trade: Confederate Commerce, Diplomacy, and Intrigue*. Cranbury, N.J.: Associated University Presses, Inc., 1984.

Dew, Charles B. *Apostles of Disunion: Southern Secession Commissioners and the Causes of the Civil War*. Charlottesville: University Press of Virginia, 2001

Dodson, C. Marion. *Yellow Flag: The Civil War Journal of Surgeon's Steward C. Marion Dodson*. Charles Albert Earp ed. Baltimore, MD: Maryland Historical Society, 2002.

Donald, David Herbert. "Died of Democracy." *Why the North Won the Civil War*. David Herbert Donald, ed. New York: Simon & Schuster–Touchstone, 1996, 81–92.

____. *Lincoln*. New York: Simon & Schuster–Touchstone, 1996.

Eisenhower, John S. D. *Agent of Destiny: The Life and Times of General Winfield Scott*. New York: The Free Press, 1997.

Elliott, Claude. "Union Sentiment in Texas, 1861–1865." *Lone Star Blue and Gray: Essays on Texas in the Civil War*. Ralph A. Wooster, ed. Austin: Texas State Historical Association, 1995, 80–107.

Foote, Shelby. *The Civil War: A Narrative. Fort Sumter to Perryville*. New York: Random House–Vintage Books, 1986.

____. *The Civil War: A Narrative. Fredericksburg to Meridian*. New York: Random House–Vintage Books, 1986.

____. *The Civil War: A Narrative. Red River to Appomattox*. New York: Random House–Vintage Books, 1986.

Frazier, Donald S. *Cottonclads! The Battle of Galveston and the Defense of the Texas Coast*. Abilene, Tex.: McWhiney Foundation Press, 1998.

Fremantle, Arthur J. L. *Three Months in the Southern States: April–June 1863*. Introd. Gary W. Gallagher. New York: J. Bradburn, 1864; Lincoln: University of Nebraska Press, 1991.

Gallaway, B. P., ed. *Texas, The Dark Corner of the Confederacy: Contemporary Accounts of the Lone Star State in the Civil War*. 3rd ed. Lincoln: University of Nebraska Press, 1999.

Gilligan, Arthur E. "Ten Weeks in Texas as a Prisoner of War." *Texas, the Dark Corner of the Confederacy: Contemporary Accounts of the Lone Star State in the Civil War*. B. P. Gallaway, ed. 3rd ed. Lincoln: University of Nebraska Press, 1999, 192–204.

Glover, Robert Warren. *The West Gulf Blockade, 1861–1865: An Evaluation*. Diss. North Texas State U, 1974. Ann Arbor: Xerox University Microfilms, 1975.

Graebner, Norman A. "Northern Diplomacy and European Neutrality." *Why the North Won the Civil War*. David Herbert Donald, ed. New York: Simon & Schuster–Touchstone, 1996.

Grant, Mary Lee. "Researchers Dive into Ship's History," *Daytona Beach Sunday News-Journal*. July 30, 2000. 8A.

Grant, Ulysses S. *Personal Memoirs of U. S. Grant (Two Volumes in One)*. New York: Konecky & Konecky, 1886.

Heidler, Jeanne T. "'Embarrassing Situation': David E. Twiggs and the Surrender of United States Forces in Texas, 1861." *Lone Star Blue and Gray: Essays on Texas in the Civil War*. Ralph A. Wooster, ed. Austin: Texas State Historical Association, 1995. 29–44.

Horner, Dave. *The Blockade-Runners*. New York: Dodd, Mead & Company, 1968.

Irby, James Arthur. *Backdoor at Bagdad: The Civil War on the Rio Grande*. Southwestern Studies, Monograph No. 53. The University of Texas at El Paso: Texas Western Press, 1977.

____. *Line of the Rio Grande: War and Trade on the Confederate Frontier, 1861–1865*. Diss. University of Georgia, 1969. Ann Arbor: University Microfilms, Inc., 1981.

Johnson, Ludwell H. *Red River Campaign: Politics and Cotton in the Civil War*. Kent, Ohio: Kent State University Press, 1993.

Jones, Virgil Carrington. *The Civil War at Sea, January 1861–March 1862: The Blockaders*. vol. I. New York: Holt, Rinehart, Winston, 1960.

____. *The Civil War at Sea, March 1862–July 1863: The River War*. vol. II. 1961. Wilmington, NC: Broadfoot Publishing Company, 1990.

____. *The Civil War at Sea, July 1863–November 1865: The Final Effort*. vol. III. 1962. Wilmington, N.C.: Broadfoot Publishing Company, 1990.

Kerby, Robert L. *Kirby Smith's Confederacy: The Trans-Mississippi South, 1863–1865*. New York: Columbia University Press, 1972.

Lonn, Ella. *Foreigners in the Confederacy*. Gloucester, MA: Peter Smith, 1965.

Mahan, Alfred Thayer. *The Influence of Sea Power Upon History 1660–1805*. Englewood Cliffs, N.J.: Prentice-Hall, Inc., 1980.

Mahin, Dean B. *One War at a Time: The International Dimensions of the American Civil War*. Washington, D.C.: Brassey's, 1999.

McPherson, James M. *Battle Cry of Freedom: The Civil War Era*. New York: Oxford University Press–Ballantine Books, 1988.

____. "What Caused the Civil War?" *North & South*. November 2000: 12–22.

Merrill, James M. *Battle Flags South: The Story of the Civil War Navies on Western Waters.* Cranbury, N.J.: Associated University Presses, Inc., 1970.

Morison, Samuel E. *The Oxford History of the American People.* New York: Oxford University Press, 1965.

Muir, Andrew Forest. "Dick Dowling and the Battle of Sabine Pass." *Lone Star Blue and Gray: Essays on Texas in the Civil War.* Ralph A. Wooster, ed. Austin: Texas State Historical Association, 1995, 189–192.

Musicant, Ivan. *Divided Waters: The Naval History of the Civil War.* New York: Harper Collins Publishers, 1995.

Nash, Howard P., Jr. *A Naval History of the Civil War.* South Brunswick: A. S. Barnes; London: Thomas Yesloff, 1972.

Owsley, Frank Lawrence. *King Cotton Diplomacy: Foreign Relations of the Confederate States of America* (2nd ed., revised by Harriet Chappell Owsley). Chicago: The University of Chicago Press, 1959.

Potter, David M. "Jefferson Davis and the Political Factors in Confederate Defeat." *Why the North Won the Civil War.* David Herbert Donald, ed. New York: Simon & Schuster–Touchstone, 1996, 93–113.

Reed, Rowena. *Combined Operations in the Civil War.* Annapolis: Naval Institute Press, 1978.

Sandburg, Carl. *Abraham Lincoln: The Prairie Years and The War Years* (One Volume Ed.). New York: Harcourt, Brace & World, 1954.

Scharf, J. Thomas. *History of the Confederate States Navy.* 1887. New York: Random House–Gramercy Books, 1996.

Shavin, Norman. *Illustrated Stories of the Century* (4th Ed.). Atlanta: Capricorn Corporation, 1974.

Silverstone, Paul H. *Warships of the Civil War Navies.* Annapolis: Naval Institute Press, 1989.

Smith, Ralph J. "Reminiscences of Life on the Gulf Coast with the Second Texas Infantry." *Texas, The Dark Corner of the Confederacy: Contemporary Accounts of the Lone Star State in the Civil War.* B. P. Gallaway, ed., 3rd ed. Lincoln: University of Nebraska Press, 1999, 187–192.

Steers, Edward, Jr. *Blood on the Moon: The Assassination of Abraham Lincoln.* Lexington: University Press of Kentucky, 2001.

Still, William N., Jr., John M. Taylor, and Norman C. Delaney. *Raiders & Blockaders: The American Civil War Afloat.* Washington, D.C.: Brassey's, 1998.

Tyler, Ronnie C. "Cotton on the Border, 1861–1865." *Lone Star Blue and Gray: Essays on Texas in the Civil War.* Ralph A. Wooster, ed. Austin: Texas State Historical Association, 1995, 211–232.

"The Union and Confederate Navies, 'Confederate Navy' and 'U.S. Naval Academy'." Exhibits, September 5, 2001. Port Columbus National Civil War Naval Museum, Columbus, Georgia.

Watson, William. "Running the Union Blockade." *Texas, The Dark Corner of the Confederacy: Contemporary Accounts of the Lone Star State in the Civil War.* B. P. Gallaway, ed., 3rd ed. Lincoln: University of Nebraska Press, 1999, 136–145.

Welles, Edgar T. *The Diary of Gideon Welles* (3 Vols.). Boston: Houghton Mifflin Company, 1911.

Wise, Stephen R. *Lifeline of the Confederacy: Blockade Running During the Civil War.* Columbia: University of South Carolina Press, 1988.

Woodward, C. Vann, ed. *Mary Chesnut's Civil War.* New York: Quality Paperback Book Club, 1981.

Wooster, Ralph A. *Civil War Texas: A History and a Guide.* Austin: Texas State Historical Association, 1999.

____. *Texas and Texans in the Civil War.* Austin: Eakin Press, 1995.

Electronic Media

"Alleyton, Texas." *The Handbook of Texas Online.* June 23, 2000 <http://www.tsha.utexas.edu/handbook/online/articles/view/AA/hna25.html>.

Block, W. T. "Battle of Sabine Pass—Its Causes and Effects." June 25, 2000 <http://block.dynip.com/wtblockjr/battleof.htm>.

____. "The Ghostly-Silent Guns of Galveston." Extracted from East Texas Historical Journal, Vol. XXXIII, No. 2 (1995). June 7, 2001. <http://block.dynip.com/wtblockjr/ kellersbe.htm>.

_____. "The Romance of Sabine Lake." June 29, 2000 <http://block.dynip.com/wtblockjr/sabine1.html>.

_____. "Sabine Pass in the Civil War." *Civil War*. Reprinted from East Texas Historical Journal, Vol. IX, No. 2 (October, 1971, 129–136). June 25, 2000<http://block.dynip.com/wtblockjr/civilwar1.htm>.

_____. "Sabine Pass and Galveston Were Successful Blockade-Running Ports." June 25, 2000 <http://block.dynip.com/wtblockjr/blockade.htm>.

"Blockade." *The 'Lectric Law Library's Lexicon* (Lexicon on Blockade). July 13, 2000 <http://www.lectlaw.com/def.htm>.

"Brazos Santiago, Texas." *The Handbook of Texas Online*. February 2, 2000 <http://www.tsha.utexas.edu/handbook/online/articles/view/BB/rrb12.html>.

"Camp Ford." *The Handbook of Texas Online*. September 19, 2000 <http://www.tsha.utexas.edu/handbook/online/articles/view/CC/qcc15.html>.

"The Crew of the *Banshee*: A Profile," *Blockade Runners*, Archives of NARA, September 5, 2002 <http://www.archives.gov/publications/prologue/fall_1999_blockade_runners _3.html>.

"DRSC Focus: A 2000 Cinco de Mayo Primer," June 28, 2000 <http://www.cruzers.com/~cab/primer.html>.

Davis, Jefferson. "Inaugural Address." *The Papers of Jefferson Davis*. Reprinted in C.S.A. Congressional Journal 1:64–66, Lynda L. Crist and Mary S. Dix, eds. (Baton Rouge, Louisiana: LSU Press, 1992). June 21, 2000 <http://sunsite.utk.edu/civil-war/jdinaug.html>.

"The Denbigh Project: Archaeology of a Confederate Blockade-Runner." June 18, 2000 <http://nautarch.tamu.edu/projects/denbigh>.

"Dictionary of American Fighting Ships, vol. A (appendix II, and annex III)." Washington, D.C.: Navy Department, Office of the Chief of Naval Operations, Naval History Division, 1991. <http://www.ibiblio.org/pub/academichistory/marshall/military> and <http://www.hazegray.org/danfs>.

"Dubois De Saligny." *The Handbook of Texas Online*. July 26, 2000 <http://www.tsha.utexas.edu/handbook/online/articles/view/DD/fdu2.html>.

"Ford, John Salmon." *The Handbook of Texas Online*. July 7, 2000 <http://www.tsha.utexas .edu/handbook/online/articles/view/FF/ffo11.html>.

"Fort Esperanza." *The Handbook of Texas Online*. February 8, 2000 <http://www.tsha.utexas.edu/handbook/online/articles/view/FF/qcf2.html>.

"Franco-Texian Bill." *The Handbook of Texas Online*. July 1, 2000 <http://www.tsha.utexas.edu/handbook/online/articles/view/FF/ugf2.html>.

"The Franco-Texian Land Company." *The Handbook of Texas Online*. July 1, 2000. <http://www.tsha.utexas.edu/handbook/online/articles/view/FF/ugf2.html>.

"French." *The Handbook of Texas Online*. March 10, 2000 <http://www.tsha.utexas.edu/handbook/online/articles/view/FF/pmf1.html>.

"French Legation." *The Handbook of Texas Online*. May 17, 2000 <http://www.tsha.utexas.edu/handbook/online/articles/view/FF/ccf3.html>.

Gallagher, Gary W. "There Is Rancor In Our Hearts ... Which You Little Dream Of." *Civil War Times*. n. d. October 5, 2000 <http://www.thehistorynet.com/CivilWarTimes/articles/2000/0500_side2.htm>.

"Henri Castro, 'Empresario.'" June 29, 2000 <http://www.castroville.com/henricastro.htm>.

"House, Thomas William." *The Handbook of Texas Online*. August 29, 2001 <http://www.tsha.utexas.edu/handbook/articles/view/HH/fho68.html>.

Kell, John McIntosh. *Recollections of a Naval Life: Including the cruises of the Confederate States Steamers "Sumter and "Alabama."* Electronic Edition, First Ed.1998. University of North Carolina at Chapel Hill Libraries. October 10, 2000 <http://www.ibiblio.org/docsouth/kell/kell.html>.

Kiersey, Nicholas. *The Diplomats and Diplomacy of the American Civil War*. Diss. University of Ireland, Limerick, Ire., 1997. August 1, 2000 <http://www.iol.ie/~kiersey/civwar.html>.

"King Cotton." *Encyclopaedia Britannica*. July 22, 2000 <http://www.britannica.com/ bcom/eb/article/printagle/5/0,5722,46575,00.html>.

Langley, Harold D. "The Sailor's Life." The Image of War: 1861–1865, Volume IV, Fighting for Time. June 12, 2000 <http://www.civilwarhome.com/sailorlife.htm>.

Lincoln, Abraham. "First Inaugural Address of Abraham Lincoln." *The Avalon Project at the Yale Law School*. November 4, 2000 <http://www.yale.edu/lawweb/avalon/presiden/inaug/lincoln1.htm>.

____. "Proclamation of Blockade Against Southern Ports." *The History Place*. June 13, 2000 <http://www.historyplace.com/lincoln/proc-2.htm>.

____. "Second Inaugural Address of Abraham Lincoln." *The Avalon Project at the Yale Law School*. November 4, 2000 <http://www.yale.edu/lawweb/avalon/presiden/inaug/lincoln2.htm>.

Macomber, Robert N., "Yellow Fever Assaults the Fleet in Florida," Parts 1 and 2, *Civil War Interactive*. September 4, 2002 <http://www.civilwarinteractive.com/myworstfear1.htm>.

"Marshall Conferences." *The Handbook of Texas Online*. April 18, 2001 <http://www.tsha.utexas.edu/handbook/online/articles/view/MM/nhm1.html>.

"Maximilian (1832–1867)." *World Book*. June 28, 2000 <http://www.worldbook.com/fun/cinco/html/maximilian.htm>.

McNeill, Sallie. "Sallie McNeill's Diary, 1858–1867." *Levi Jordan Plantation*. September 28, 2000 <http://www.webarchaeology.com/Html/direxrpt.htm>.

"Mexican Holidays: Cinco de Mayo," June 28, 2000 <http://www.mexonline.com/cinco.htm>; "Maximilian (1832–1867)," *World Book*. June 28, 2000 <http://www.worldbook.com/fun/cinco/html/>.

Morgan, James Morris. *Recollections of a Rebel Reefer*. Electronic Edition, First Ed.1999. University of North Carolina at Chapel Hill Libraries. October 7, 2000 <http://www.ibiblio.org/docsouth/morganjames/morgan.html#morgan1>.

Murphy, David J. Colonel, USAF, *Naval Strategy During the American Civil War*. (Research Report, Air War College, Air University, Maxwell Air Force Base, Alabama, April 1999). September 5, 2002 <http://papers.maxwell.af.mil/projects/ay1999/awc/99-175.pdf>.

"O, I'm a Good Old Rebel." *Poems and Songs of the Civil War Page*. October 5, 2000 <http://www.civilwarhome.com/pooroldrebel.htm>.

"Official Records of the Union and Confederate Navies in the War of the Rebellion." 30 vols. *The Civil War CD-ROM II*. CD-ROM. Carmel, Indiana: Guild Press of Indiana, Inc., 1999.

"Oldham, Williamson Simpson." *The Handbook of Texas Online*. August 13, 2001 <http://www.tsha.utexas.edu/handbook/online/articles/view/OO/fol2.html>.

"Palmito Ranch, Battle of." *The Handbook of Texas Online*. February 8, 2000 <http://www.tsha.utexas.edu/handbook/online/articles/view/PP/qfp1.html>.

Pierce, David W. "Dick Dowling and the Battle of Sabine Pass." June 25, 2000 <http://rampages.onramp.net/~jtcreate/cofc/dowling.htm>.

Price, Marcus W. "Ships That Tested the Blockade of the Gulf Ports, 1861–1865." *American Neptune* vol. 11, no. 4 (October 1951) 262–297. July 21, 2000 <http://www.pem.org/neptune>.

____. "Ships That Tested the Blockade of the Gulf Ports, 1861–1865." *American Neptune* vol. 12, no. 2 (April 1952) 154–161. July 21, 2000 <http://www.pem.org/neptune>.

"Prize Court." *The 'Lectric Law Library's Lexicon*. June 12, 2000 <http://www.lectlaw.com/def2/p167.htm>.

Reagan, John H. "Speech of Representative John H. Reagan." September 28, 2000 <http://members.aol.com/_ht_a/jfepperson/reagan2.html>.

"Richard King." *The Handbook of Texas Online*. June 24, 2000 <http://www.tsha.utexas.edu/handbook/online/articles/view/KK/fki19.html>.

"St. Joseph Island," *The Handbook of Texas Online*. February 8, 2000 <http://www.tsha.utexas.edu/handbook/online/articles/view/SS/rrs9.html>.

"Secession Convention." *The Handbook of Texas Online*. June 3, 2000 <http://www.tsha.utexas.edu/handbook/online/articles/view/SS/mjs1.html>.

Seward, William H., to Abraham Lincoln, April 1, 1861. Available at *Abraham Lincoln Papers at the Library of Congress*, Manuscript Division (Washington, D.C.: American Memory Project, 2000–02. September 20, 2002 <http://memory.loc.gov/ammem/alhtml/malhome.html>.

"Slavery." *The Handbook of Texas Online*. May 17, 2000 <http://www.tsha.utexas.edu/handbook/online/articles/view/SS/yps1.html>.

Soley, James Russell. "The Blockade and the Cruisers," *Blockade: The Blockading of the Southern Seaports in the Civil War*) September 2, 2002. (Source: "The Blockade and the Cruisers" (Chapter 2), New York: C. Scribner's Sons, 1903.) <http://www.civilwarhome.com/blockade.htm>.

"Star of the West." *The Handbook of Texas Online*. May 13, 2000 <http://www.tsha.utexas.edu/handbook/online/articles/view/SS/qts5.html>.

Stephens, Alexander. "Cornerstone Speech, Savannah; Georgia, March 21, 1861." May 18, 2000 <http://members.aol.com/jfepperson/stephans.html>.

Surdam, David G. "The Confederate Naval Buildup: Could More Have Been Accomplished?" *Naval War College Review* (Newport, RI) vol. LIV, no. 1., Winter 2001, 107–128. May 20, 2003 <http://www.nwc.navy.mil/press/Review/2001/Winter/art7–w01.htm>

———. "The Union Navy's Blockade Reconsidered." *Naval War College Review* (Newport, RI) vol. LI, no. 4, sequence 364, Autumn 1998, 105–127. May 14, 2003 <http://www.nwc.navy.mil/press/Review/1998/autumn/art5-a98.hjtm>

"Swisher, John Milton." *The Handbook of Texas Online*. August 31, 2001 <http://www.tsha.utexas.edu/handbook/articles/view/SS/fsw20.html>.

Tans, Jochem. "The Hapless Anaconda: Union Blockade 1861–1865." *The Concord Review: Advanced Placement Essays* (Concord, Mass.). Fall 1994. June 13, 2000 <http://www.tcr.org/advpl_7.html>.

"Texas Troubles." *The Handbook of Texas Online*. June 6, 2000 <http://www.tsha.utexas.edu/handbook/online/articles/view/TT/vetbr.html>.

Theberge, Albert E., Captain, NOAA Corps (Ret.), *The Coast Survey in the Civil War 1861–1865, Volume I of the History of the Commissioned Corps of the National Oceanic and Atmospheric Administration*, "The Strategic Contribution." September 9, 2002 <http://www.lib.noaa.gov/edocs/TITLE.htm#TITLE>

Topik, Steven C. "When Mexico Had the Blues: A Transatlantic Tale of Bonds, Bankers, and Nationalists, 1862–1910." *The American Historical Review* vol. 105, no. 3 n.d., September 20, 2000 <http://www.historycooperative.org/journals/ahr/105.3/ah000714.html>.

"U. S. Navy in the Civil War." *The United States Navy Landing Party Handbook: Guide to Naval Reenacting, Section 2.2, Basic Naval History of the Civil War*. (The Navy and Marine Living History Association, Inc.) June 13, 2000 <http://nmlha.org/unit192/handbook.html>.

"The War of the Rebellion: A Compilation of the Official Records of the Union and Confederate Armies." 128 vols. *The Civil War CD-ROM*. CD-ROM v.1.0. Carmel, Indiana: Guild Press of Indiana, Inc., 1996.

Watson, William. "Running the Blockade into Galveston: A Personal Narrative." *The Denbigh Project: Archaeology of a Confederate Blockade-Runner*. June 18, 2000 <http://nautarch.tamu.edu/projects/denbigh/Watson.htm>.

Weddle, Kevin J. "There Should Be No Bungling About the Blockade:" *The Blockade Board of 1861 And The Making of Union Naval Strategy*, "International Journal of Naval History," from the U. S. Army War College, Princeton University. September 9, 2002. <http://www.ijnhonline.org/volume1_number1_Apr02/article_weddle_blockade_board.doc.htm#_ednref24>.

"The Western Gulf Blockade." *The Brown Water Navy*. May 23, 2001. <http://www.brownwaternavy.com/wg-main.htm>.

Wheeler, Joseph. "An Effort to Rescue Jefferson Davis." *The Century*. Vol. 56, Issue 1, May 1898, 85–91. September 16, 2001. American Memory, Library of Congress, The Nineteenth Century In Print: Periodicals. <http://memory.loc.gov/ammem/ndlpcoop/moahtml/title/lists/cent_V56I1.html>.

Wigfall, Louis T[rezevant]. "Cotton Is King." *Great Debates in American History*. New York: Current Literature Publishing Company, 1913. Vol. 5, 348–350. September 28, 2000 <http://www.adena.com/adena/usa/cw/cw112.htm>.

———. "The Wide Awakes." *Great Debates in American History*. New York: Current Literature Publishing Company, 1913. Vol. 5, 353–354. September 28, 2000 <http://www.adena.com/adena/usa/cw/cw116.htm>.

"Wigfall, Louis Trezevant." *The Handbook of Texas Online*. September 28, 2000 <http://www.tsha.utexas.edu/handbook/online/articles/view/WW/fwi4.html>.

Wilkinson, J. *The Narrative of a Blockade-Runner*. Electronic Edition. June 14, 2001. <http://www.civilwarancestor.com/store/files/Ebook0106.htm>.

"Woll, Adrian." *The Handbook of Texas Online*. July 3, 2000 <http://www.tsha.utexas.edu/handbook/online/articles/view/WW/fwo3.html>.

Wright, Louise Wigfall. "*A Southern Girl in '61: The War-Time Memories of a Confederate Senator's Daughter.*" Electronic Edition, First Ed.1997. University of North Carolina at Chapel Hill Libraries. September 28, 2000 <http://www.ibiblio.org/docsouth/wright/wright.html#wright221>.

Index

A. S. Rathven 78
Ad hoc committee reports 23–25; see also Blockade Strategy Board
Adams, Charles Francis 52, 130
Adams, Captain H. A. 51
Alabama 28, 45, 71, 92–96
Albatross 65
Alden, Captain James 40, 41
Alexandria, Louisiana 117
Alice 153
Alleytown, Texas 66, 71
America 36
American Neptune 157
Anaconda Plan 15, 18–20, 96, 125, 161
Anderson, Rear Admiral Bern 156
Anderson, Major Robert 12
Anglo Confederate Trading Company 57
Ann Ryan 40
Anna Taylor see *Soledad Cos*
Aransas Pass 35, 44, 78, 81, 132
Argo 39
Arizona 98
Arkansas 13, 71
Aroostook 133
Arthur 35, 79, 81
Artillery units, Texas coast 79
Ashley River, Charleston, South Carolina 50
Atlantic Blocking Squadron 25

Bache, Alexander D. 22
Back door of the Confederacy 70, 155, 166

Badger 61
Bagby, Colonel Arthur 87
Bagdad, Mexico 68, 70, 72, 73, 75; amphibious landing by French 136; neutral port 104
Bahamas 55
Bahia de Sacrificios 118
Baily, Rear Admiral Theodorous 66, 70
Banks, Major General Nathaniel P., and Galveston 87, 92; New Orleans 117, 126; Red River expedition 35; Rio Grande expedition 65, 130; Sabine pass 97, 101
Banshee (I) 55, 56
Banshee (II) 55, 56
Barnard, Major John G. 22
Barrett, Colonel Theodore H. 142
Battle Cry of Freedom 158
Baxter, Rodney (Ronald) 40, 41
Baylor University 11
Bayou City 43, 77, 87, 89
Bayou Teche 62
Bazaine, General Achille François 110
Beaumont, Texas 63, 80, 97
Beauregard, Brigadier General Pierre Gustav 12, 13, 19
Bee, General Hamilton P. 73, 117, 118, 131
Belize, British Honduras 137, 153
Bell, C. S. 155, 156

Bell, Commodore Henry H. 75, 92, 97, 102, 130
Belle Italia 81
Benjamin, Judah P. 101, 105
Bermuda 42, 51–54
Berthollet 69
Berwick Bay, Louisiana 40
Bienville 44
Blacker, Vice-Consul Louis 69
Blake, Homer C. 92
Blake Brothers & Company of Boston, Massachusetts 36, 37
Blanche 78; see also *General Rusk*
blockade: absence of legal challenge by Britain, France 152, 154, 162; as an act of war 17; activity of ship personnel 31; Atlantic and Gulf ports 19; boredom 44; consequences of remote location 65; construction of 148; definition of 147; in east Texas 103, and Galveston 60; effectiveness 45–47; efforts to strengthen 77; evasion of 63, 155, 165, 166; see also Blockade Evaluation, blockade assessment; government policies 151; illegal seizure technicalities 150; international law 70; investigative process 64; jointly with French 65; legality 18, 40, 148, 162, 175n12; Lincoln's limited goal 165; notification 148; official 16; paper 22, 39,

193

41, 42, 53, 148, 150, 154; port closures rather than blockade 21; priorities 46; procedures 51; purpose 147; respected by England 18; revised strategy 85; ships diverted to other duties 45; ships of war 19; shortage of necessities 47; strengthened throughout war 152; unintended benefit 47; Union and French 121; violation 148; Welles's expanded goal 165; in west Texas 104
blockade assessment 163; as a dynamic force 163; other factors 164, 165; probative value of documents 164; survey of opinions regarding efficacy 156–161; use of statistics and data 163, 164
blockade by Union navy 27, 31; strategic and tactical factors 128, 129; "The Union Navy's Blockade Reconsidered" 160
Blockade Evaluation 147–166 passim
Blockade Proclamation 15, 20, 21, 25, 33
The Blockade-Runners 161
Blockade Runners of the Confederacy 158
blockade running 42, 51, 60
blockade running: characteristics of vessels 54, 55; Charleston, South Carolina 150, 151; crews 55, 56; Galveston 61, 137, 184n319; high profit goods 152, 153; private cargo 153; profitability 55, 152; Sabine City 151; Southern cultural factors 152; technique 56, 57
Blockade Running During the Civil War and the Effect of Land and Water Transportation on the Confederacy 159, 160
Blockade Strategy Board 22–25, 176n23; and expanded blockade goals 161, 162
Boca Chica 69, 70
Boston Port Act 147
Bradlee, Francis B. C. 159
Bragg, General Braxton 40, 51
Brazoria, Texas 11, 79
Brazos Island 67
Brazos River 57, 65, 78, 79, 154
Brazos Santiago 65, 67–69, 78, 133, 136, 141, 143

Brazos Santiago Pass 67
bread riots in South 46, 47
Breaker 81
British *see* England
Brooklyn 40, 45, 130, 92–94
Brownsville, Texas and Cavalry of the West 136; cotton trade 60, 65, 69–72, 79, 80; General Bee's headquarters 117; history of 63; Rio Grande expedition 125; Second Texas U.S. Cavalry 143
Brussels, Belgium 106
Buchanan, President James 12
Buckner, Lieutenant General Simon 144
Budd, William Lieutenant 33
Buffalo Bayou, Brazos, and Colorado Railway 71
Buffalo Bayou, Texas 80
Bull Run, Battle of 112
Bulloch, Captain James D. 30
Bunch, British Consul 151
Burrell, Colonel Isaac S. 87
Butler, Benjamin F. 125, 127
By Sea and by River: The Naval History of the Civil War 156

C.S.A. *see* Confederate States of America, Confederacy, and Confederate
Cairo, Illinois 18, 50
Cambria 91
Camp Esperanza 79; *see also* Fort Esperanza
Camp Ford 143
Canby, General Edward R. S. 144
Caney Creek, Texas 36, 79
capacity of North and South for waging war 14
Cape Fear River, North Carolina 50
Caroline 40
Caroline Goodyear 122, 123
Castro, Henri 104
Castroville, Texas 104
Cavalry of the West 135, 136, 143
Cayuga 63
Cedar Bayou, Texas 132
The Century 139
Chamberlain, General Joshua L. 167
Charleston, South Carolina 18, 50
Charleston Harbor 11, 12, 40
Chase, Consul 153
Chase, Salmon P. 127
Chestnut, Mary 49

Chicago Journal 12
Cienfuegoes, Cuba 45
Cincinnati, Ohio 18
civil disorder 135
Clarinda 63
Cleburne, Major General Patrick R. 139
Clifton 78, 84, 85, 88, 90, 97, 98
Clinton 131
Coahuila, Mexico 108
coal for steamships 27, 55, 58
coastal packet 51
Cobos, General 72
Cochran, Hamilton 158
Columbia, Texas 79
commerce raiders 45
Committee of Public Safety (Texas) 12
Committee on Naval Affairs 28
compass corrections 121, 150
Confederacy 14; as a belligerent state 16, 20; *see also* Confederate States of America
Confederate: and army desertions 141; army ordnance bureau 52; Congress 15, 20, 123; disintegration of 140, 141
Confederate Navy: defensive role 28; non-existence at beginning 28; obtaining ships for 29; organization 29; ship crews 30, 31
"The Confederate Navy Buildup: Could More Have Been Accomplished" 160, 161
Confederate States Naval Academy 30
Confederate States of America 12; foreign policy 111; recognition of by France 119
Conklin, Lieutenant George E. 85
Continental 98
continuous voyage 149
Cook, Major Joseph J. 79, 84
Cooper River, Charleston, South Carolina 50
Corpus Christi, Texas 35, 36, 79, 81, 82, 85, 143
Corpus Christi Bay 132
Cortina, General Juan 72
Corwin, Thomas 109
Corypheus 35, 81, 82, 91
Cotham, Edward T., Jr. 154
Cotton: bales 59, 60, 69, 71, 72; collection stations 72; "Cotton, cotton everywhere!" 55; cotton lobby

pressure 130; destruction of 67, 151; dictating military strategy 103; embargo 67, 111, 112, 150, 151; export tax 72; idle textile mills 126, 128; illicit trade 73, 116, 117; pricing 59, 72; as prize of war 33, 35; regulation of 115, 116; a tangled snarl 114; thrown overboard 45; trade 60; trade profits 74; Union combined operation in Texas to interrupt flow 128; waif cotton 36
Cotton Bureau 114, 115
Cottonclads 87, 96
Court of Inquiry 144
Crescent 131
Crescent City *see* New Orleans
Crocker, Captain Frederick 82, 97, 98
Crook, David Paul 107, 148, 159
Crusader 45
Cumberland 39
Cumberland River 13
Current, Richard N. 159
customhouse 62, 85, 105

Daddysman, James 157
Dahlgren cannon 28
Dana, General Napoleon J. T. 131
Dart 40
Davis, Commander Charles H. 22
Davis, Colonel Edmund Jackson 82, 131
Davis, Jefferson: and appointment of Navy Secretary Mallory 28; defense of Texas coast 78; defensive use of navy 28, 176–177n35; Governor Lubbock forwarding Benjamin Theron's letter 106; inaugural address 66; Kirby Smith forwarding a copy of his letter to Slidell 121; letters of marque 13; president arrested 139; riot in Confederate capital 46; Trans-Mississippi Department 112
Daylight 51
Dayton, William L. 109
de facto blockade 39
de facto war 154
Delaware Farmer 39
Delta 43
Democratic Party 126, 127
Denbigh 61, 137–139, 184n321
Dennis, Isaac 140

Department of the Gulf 127
DePont, Captain Samuel F. 22
Desperate 42, 43
District Court, Southern District of New York 43
District of Texas 86
Donahue, John M. 74
Dowling, Lieutenant Richard W. 98, 99
Drewry's Bluff 30
Droege, Oetling & Co. of Matamoros 122
Dryad 118
Dunlop, Hugh 69
Duval, Captain 123

Eagle, Captain Henry 42, 83
Eagle Grove 88
Eastern Texas Railroad 83
Eighth Texas Infantry 143
Elias Pike 91
Elma 81
Emancipation Proclamation 152
Emily Ann 39
Enfield rifles 52
England: and British complaint of blockade rigidity 64; British ships at Bagdad 73; commercial ties with Confederacy 52–54; Confederate vessels manned by British crews 55, 56; construction of *Alabama* in England 92; construction of vessels for Confederacy in British shipyards 30; neutrality 13, 16, 22, 65, 68; purchaser of southern cotton 66
English blockade of American coast 147
English involvement in Bagdad smuggling 130
Era No. 3 78
Europe 73
European Trading Company 137
Evelyn 61

Falcon 40
Farragut, Rear Admiral David G.: and blockade 61, 64, 69; *Hatteras* 94; occupy Rio Grande 130; order from Lincoln 127, 128; poor condition of ships 45; Sabine pass 82; Texas coast 83; Texas incursion 126; waif cotton 36
Fernandina, Florida 23
ferryboats 27, 85

Fifth Texas Cavalry 87
First Texas Cavalry 91, 131; Union 82
First Texas Heavy Artillery: Company B. 96; Company F. 96; Davis Guards 98
Fisher (Portuguese man, casualty) 41
Florida 95, 96
Florida (state) 24, 28,
Florilda 78
Flour Bluffs 82
Ford, John S. "Rip" 68, 78, 135, 141, 143
Forrest, General Nathan Bedford 139
Fort Brown 63, 78, 136
Fort Calhoun 50
Fort Clark 78
Fort Donelson 45, 144
Fort Esperanza 129, 132
Fort Fisher 50
Fort Griffin 80, 98
Fort Jackson (ship) 138, 144
Fort Monroe 39, 50
Fort Point 84
Fort Quintana 80
Fort Sabine 82
Fort Sumter 11, 12
Fort Velasco 79, 80
Forty-second Massachusetts Infantry Regiment 87, 91
"Forward to Richmond!" 19
Fox, Gustavus V. 15, 22, 61, 125, 126
France 13, 14, 16, 65, 66, 68
Francis Marion 137
Franco-Texian Bill 104
Franklin, Major General William B. 97, 99
Fraser, John Augustus 52
Fraser, Trenholm and Company, Liverpool, England 52
freight wagon 71
Fremantle, Lieutenant Colonel Arthur J. L. 70, 71
French, Lieutenant Henry 65
French blockade of Mexico 64 122, 155
French discouraged from occupying Matamoros 133
French interest in Mexico 104–107; cotton trade 104, 108; Napoleon's dream of colonial conquest 105–107; United States reaction 104, 105, 129, 130
French invasion of Mexico 96, 107, 182n237, 108, 136, 168, 169; London convention

105; Mexican Congress, suspending interest payments on debt 104, 105; Mexico and debt to England, Spain, France 105; Mexico, civil war and political instability 104, 105; occupation of Tampico and Veracruz 105
Fullerton, acting consul 151

Gadsden Purchase 105
Galvan, Jeremiah 74
Galveston, Texas 24, 29, 47; artillery defenses at 79; blockade extended to 40, 42–44, 85; blockade running through 54, 57–59, 72, 133; insurrection at garrison 143; last deep-water port open 137, 154, 162, 163; surrender ceremony 144; Union troops arrive at 87
Galveston Bay 40, 42, 84, 138; artillery batteries at 80; Battle of 60, 89–92, 128; South Battery 40, 84
Galveston Harbor 24, 43; Bird Key Spit 138; Bolivar Point 138; Channels, main, east, and west 151; San Luis Pass, 61, 65, 151; Virginia Point 84, 88; West Bay 61
Galveston Island 61, 78, 91
Galveston News 140
Galveston Weekly News 44
General Banks 131
General Butler 81
General Miramon 130
General Order Number 3 (freeing slaves) 145, 167
General Orders No. 34 (Texas defenses) 80
General Orders No. 7 (waif cotton) 36
General Parkhill 39
General Rusk 59, 60, 86; see also *Blanche*
General T. J. Chambers 40
George G. Baker 40
Gilligan, Sergeant Arthur E. 143
Gilpin, Judge 81
Glasgow, Scotland 152
Glover, Robert Warren 61, 157
"God and the Strongest Battalions" 159
Goliad, Texas 72
Gorgas, Major Josiah C. 52
Gosport Navy Yard, Norfolk, Virginia 13, 28, 29

Graebner, Norman A. 154
Grand Bay 78
Grande Pass, Vermilion Bay, Louisiana 24
Granger, Major General Gordon 145, 167
Granite City 98
Grant, General Ulysses S. 139, 126, 168
Gray, P. W. 123
Great Britain see England
Greeley, Horace 19, 126
Green, Colonel Tom 87
Grigsby's Bluff 80
Grog 33
Gulf Blockading Squadron 25
Gulf of Mexico 19, 40, 54, 57

H. E. *Spearing* 40
Habana see *Sumter*
Halleck, General Henry W. 14, 97, 127–129, 130, 132
Hamilton, Andrew J. 127, 131
Hammond, James H. 103
Hampton Roads, Virginia 25, 39, 50, 53
Hannah 81
"The Hapless Anaconda: Union Blockade 1861–1865" 156
Harriet Lane 39, 84, 88, 89–91, 94; see also *Lavinia*
Harrington, Fred Harvey 101
Harrisburg, Texas 80
Hatteras 92–94
Havana, Cuba 45, 54, 57–59, 61, 62, 118
HBMS *Phaeton* 64, 68, 69
Hebert, General Paul O. 83
Hendley Building 40, 58
Henry Dodge see *Mary Sorley*
Henry Janes 82, 83
Herald 53, 54
Herbert, General Paul O. 80
Hill, Lieutenant Frederic S. 36, 37
Hillsborough, North Carolina 139
History of the Confederate States Navy 156
Hobby, Major Alfred M. 81, 82
Hooper, Quincy A. 82
Horner, Dave 161
House, Thomas W. 60
Houston, Texas 11, 60, 72, 97, 115
Houston Navigation Company 77
Houston Telegraph 43, 92
Hull, England 58
Hunchback 32, 33

Hunter, Lieutenant Charles 68
Hunter, Commander William W. 29, 43, 77
Huse, Captain Caleb 52
Hutchinson, William F. 44

Illinois 126
Impressment Act 114; difficulties with 115, 116
Indiana 126
Indianapolis Daily Journal 12
Indianola, Texas 60, 79, 81, 125, 132
industrial output, North and South 28
The Influence of Sea Power Upon History 1660–1805 160
infrastructure for ports 49, 50
insurrection 17
Ireland 56
Ireland, Captain John 82
Irish 55
Isabel 45

J. J. McNeil 79
J. M. Swisher and Company, Austin 60
Jackson, Governor Claiborne F. 113
Jeanette 59
John Fraser and Company, Charleston 52
John Laird, Sons & Co. of Birkenhead 137
Johnson, President Andrew 168
Johnston, General Joseph 139
Jordan, Levi 11
Josiah H. Bell 96
Juarez, Benito 64, 104
"Juneteenth" 167, 186n388

Kanawha Valley 18, 19
Keith, Captain K. D. 96
Kell, First Lieutenant John McKintosh 93, 95
Kellersberg, Captain Julius R. 80
Kenedy, Mifflin 73
Kensington 82
Key West, Florida 25, 45
Kimmey, M. M. 110
King, Richard 73
"King Cotton": as a cash crop 66, 67; as foreign policy 66, 103
King Cotton Diplomacy 156
King, Kenedy and Stillman of Brownsville 73
King Ranch 71, 131

Kinney, M. M. 130
Kirby Smith, Lieutenant General Edmund 112, 114, 116
Kirby-Smith don 112, 114, 123
Kittredge, Lieutenant John W. 81, 82
Kuhn's Wharf 87, 91

Labuan 69
Lackawanna 44, 45
Laguna de la Madre lagoon 81, 82
Lark 61, 139
Las Rucias Ranch 136
Latrille de Lorencez, General Charles Ferdinand 107
Laurel Hill 99
Lavinia 78; see also *Harriet Lane*
Law, Lieutenant Commander Richard L. 90
Lawrence and Foulkes, Brooklyn, New York 44
Lea, Commander Edward 90
Lea, Tom 70
LeCompt 79, 91
Lee, General Robert E. 139, 140
Le Tage 64
letter of marque 13
letter to Slidell 120
Lifeline of the Confederacy 158
light draft river steamers 72
lighter 119
Lincoln, Abraham 11, 13; anaconda plan 18–20; blockade 15, 20, 21, 25, 26, 33, 53, 67, 161, 162; character of 128; direct order to Farragut 127; signal French 96, 97, 128–130; Texas expedition 126, 127
listening posts 120
Liverpool, England 39, 43, 55, 61
London Times 122
Lonn, Ella 118, 122
Louisa 40
Love Bird 122, 123
Lubbock, Governor Francis R. 106, 113, 114
Lubbock, Henry 77
Lucy Gwin 78
Lunar 61
Lynn, Consul Arthur T. 41, 43, 57, 61, 67, 151
Lyons, Lord 16, 150

Maffit, Commander John 95
Magnolia 33, 123, 153
Magruder, Major George A., Jr. 121

Magruder, Major General John B. 86, 118, 121, 135; Magruder's Proclamations 57, 102
Mahan, Alfred Thayer 160
Mahin, Dean M. 150, 158
malaria 65
Mallory, Stephen R. 26, 28, 43
Manassas 13; see also Bull Run, Battle of
Manassas Junction 19
Mann, A Dudley 106
Marianao, Cuba 78
Marshall, Texas 72, 113, 142
Marshall Conference 113, 120, 142
Mary Hill 78
Mary Sorley (formerly *Henry Dodge*) 77, 78
Mary Willis 39
Matagorda, Texas 44
Matagorda Bay 65, 79, 81
Matagorda Island 78, 132
Matamoros, Mexico 36, 41, 43, 57, 58, 60; occupation by French 118–120, 129; relationship between Mexicans, French, Confederates 137; transportation difficulties 66; used to evade blockade 63, 64, 180n120, 67–69, 72, 74, 108, 110;
Maximilian, Ferdinand 107, 169
McCanfield 40
McCauley, Commander Charles 28
McClellan, Major General George B. 18, 19, 131
McClernand, Major General John A. 126
McDowell, Brigadier General Irvin 19
McHatton-Ripley, Eliza 47
McKean, William M. 69
McNeill, Sallie 11
McPherson, James M. 158
Merrick, Judge E. T. 114
Mervine, William 41
Mexican cart 71
Mexican War 112, 118, 135
Mexico City, Mexico 107
Midnight 79
Milmo, Patricio 109
Milmo and Company, Monterrey, Mexico 109
Minnesota 39, 40
Mississippi River 13, 18, 19, 50, 126
Mississippi River Defense Fleet 29

Missouri, government in exile 112
Mobile, Alabama 18, 24, 25, 50, 59, 83
Monroe, President James 168
Monroe Doctrine 66, 96, 107, 128, 133, 168
Monte Cristo 35, 81
Monterray, Mexico 72, 74
Montgomery 40, 65, 68, 78
Montgomery, Captain J. E. 29
Montgomery, Alabama 18
Monticello 149
Moore, Governor Thomas O. 117
Morell, Jose 74
Morgan, Charles 59
Morgan, James M.: aboard *Herald* 54; aboard *Patrick Henry* 30
Morning Light 96
Morse, F. H. 64
Morton, Governor 127
Murphy, David J. 161
Murrah, Governor Pendleton 114, 115
Murrah's State Plan for Cotton 116
Mustang 131
Mustang Island 132

Nancy Dawson 122, 123
Napoleon, Louis, III 105, 118, 119, 169; plans for Mexico 105–107
Narrow beamer 54
Nash, Howard P., Jr. 160, 185–186n382
Nashville, Tennessee 18
Nassau 53–55
A Naval History of the Civil War 160
Neches River 80
Neptune 78, 87, 89
neutral shipping 57
neutral waters 69, 121
neutrality 16, 53, 65
New Inlet, North Carolina 27, 50
New Orleans, Louisiana: anaconda plan 18, 19; arrival of Banks's fleet 128; battle of 45, 59, 125, 126; blockade 24, 25, 43, 44; navy yard 65; yellow fever 83
New Orleans Times 142
New Providence Island 55
New York City 27, 49, 73
New York Herald 42
New York Times 44

New York Tribune 19, 42, 126
Niagra 39, 45
Niblett's Bluff 63
Ninety-day War 19
Norfolk, U.S. Navy Yard *see*
   Gosport Navy Yard
Norfolk, Virginia 51
North Carolina 13, 16
Nueces River 66
Nuevo Leon, Mexico 108

"O, I'm a Good Old Rebel"
   167, 168
Odlum, Captain Frederick 96
Oetling, Mr. (Prussian consul)
   74
Ohio (state) 126
Ohio River 18, 50
Oldham, Williamson S. 113
One War at a Time 158
Orange, Texas 63, 80, 96
ordinance of secession (Virginia)
   13, 15
Owasco 84, 88
Owl 61
Owsley, Frank Lawrence 108,
   151, 156
oxcart 66, 67

packet boat 137
Padre Island 67
Palmito Ranch 143
Paris, France 122
Parker, William H. 30
Pass a l'outre, Mississippi 40
Pass Cavallo, 43, 78, 79, 91,
   132
Patrick Henry 30
Pelican 58
Pennington, Lewis W. 82
Pensacola, Florida 18, 27, 40,
   169
Pensacola Navy Yard 28, 65
Perkins, Lieutenant Commander G. H. 133
Perryville, Battle of 112
Peterhoff 149, 150
Philadelphia Enquirer 42
Phoenix 58
Pickett, John T. 108
Point Isabel, Texas 78
Polignac, Major General Camille
   141
Pope, General John 142
Port Lavaca 81, 85, 132
Porter, Admiral David D. 35,
   125
Portsmouth 64, 68, 69
Portsmouth, New Hampshire
   41, 42

Portsmouth Yard 45
Potter, David M. 151
Price, Leonard, Jr. 74
Price, Marcus 157
privateering 29, 45
Prize Court, Southern District
   Court of New York 33;
   defined 21,22; money 15, 35;
   ships 18, 45; system discussed 35
pro forma action 149
proclamation of blockade *see*
   Blockade Proclamation
Pryor, Roger 12
Puebla, Mexico 118; Battle of
   107

Quaker City 39
Quintero, Juan A. 108,
   183n243; relationship with
   Benito Juarez 109

Rachel Seaman 79, 82
railroad system in South 46
Ransom, General Thomas E.
   132
rebellion 17
recruiting poster 34
Red River campaign 35, 92,
   101, 132
Red River Valley, Louisiana
   133
Reindeer 35, 81
Renshaw, Commander William
   B. 83, 84, 88, 91
Republic of Texas 104, 118
Republican party 127
Reynolds, Governor Thomas
   113
Richmond, Virginia 13, 18, 30,
   78
Rio de Janeiro, Brazil 40
Rio Grande 24, 36; blockade
   40, 63–65; blockade evasion
   70, 73; neutral territory 65,
   67–70
Rio Grande City, Texas 131
Rio Grande expedition 79
   125–134 *passim*; aborted
   126–128; launched 131;
   objectives 132–133; occupation of passes 131; planning
   129
Rio Grande valley 135, 136
Rob Roy 57
Rogers, Captain W. F. 77
Romero, Mattias 168
Royal Yacht 42, 43
Ruff, Charles H. 63
Ruff, Otto 63

Ruffin, Edmund 12
Russell, Lord John (Earl) 39,
   149

Sabine 40
Sabine City, Texas 59, 62, 63,
   82, 83, 85
Sabine Lake 62, 63
Sabine Pass 59, 61–63, 78–80,
   82, 133
Sabine Pass, Battle of 97–101;
   comments by Andrew Forest
   Muir 101; joint army-navy
   expedition 97; Louisiana
   and Texas channels 98; resolution, Confederate Congress 99
Sabine River 24, 40, 72, 78,
   80
Sachem 81, 88, 98
St. George, Bermuda 54
St. Joseph Island 132
St. Lawrence 53
Saint Mary's 131
Saligny, Dubois de 104, 105,
   118
Saluria, Texas 81
Sam Houston 40, 61
San Antonio, Texas 71, 72,
   125, 135
San Antonio Herald 140
San Bernard River 80
San Jacinto River 80
Sands, Captain B. F. 62, 138
Santee 42, 43, 83
Savannah 53
Savannah, Georgia 42, 50, 53
Savoir-faire 59
Scharf, J. Thomas 156
Scherffius, Captain Henry 63
Sciota 77, 133
Scotland 56
Scott, General Winfield 11, 15,
   16, 18, 19, 25, 125
Scott's Great Snake 17
Scovel, L. L. 37
scurvy 65
secession 11, 12, 16
Second Texas U.S. Cavalry
   143
Second Vermont Battery 91
Selma, Alabama 28
Semmes, Captain Raphael 45,
   71, 92, 95
Seventh Texas Cavalry 87
Seward, William H.: and
   blockade 18, 21, 148; letter
   from London 64; loan to
   Mexico 109; North's strategy
   15; occupying line of Rio

Grande 126; plan for capturing New Orleans 125; Secretary of State, Johnson administration 168
Shark 40, 41
Shea, Major Daniel D. 79, 85
Sheridan, General Phillip 168
Shiloh, Battle of 45
Ship Island 69
ships, changing characteristics 51
Shreveport, Louisiana 115, 117, 143
Shufeldt, Consul-General R. W. 153
Sibley, Brigadier General Henry H. 87
Sibley Brigade 87, 88
Sixty-second U.S. Colored Infantry 143
Slaughter, General James 142
slave, as Confederate soldiers 139, 140
Slidell, John 120, 122, 123, 141
smallpox 59
Smith, James 74
Smith, Major Leon 87, 90
Sol Wilder 36
Soledad Cos 41
Soley, James R. 159
South Carolina (state) 11
South Carolina 40–43
South Carolina nullification crisis 147, 148
South West Pass, Mississippi River 36
Southern Steamship Company 59
Sovereign nation 148
Spear, Acting Master A. T. 91
Stanton 111, 126, 127, 130
Star 39
Star of the West 86
states' rights 29
steamships into Galveston 153, 154
Stephens, Alexander H. 13
Stevens, Thaddeus 20
Stevens, Captain W. H. 78
Stillman, Charles 73, 74
Stillman, Francis 63
strategic goals of North and South in waging war 13
straw man 74
Suffolk 98
Sumter 45
Sunflower 78
Superviele 118–122
Surdam, David G. 160

Susana 137
Swartwout, Commander Sam L. 45, 64, 65, 69
Swisher, John 60

T. W. House and Company, Houston 60
Tamaulipas, Mexico 64, 68, 108, 109, 137
Tampico, Mexico 41, 59, 63, 69, 110
Tans, Jochem H. 156
tariffs 66
Tatham, Captain Edward 64, 68, 69
Taylor, General Richard 139, 144
Taylor, Thomas E. 55
Taylor's Bayou 83
Tennessee 131
Tennessee (state) 13
Tennessee River 13
Tessier, Captain Eugene 52
Texas *see* specific towns or geographical locations
Texas: coastal fortifications 78; defenses strengthened 77; economic revival 137; gun emplacements 81, 82, 84; occupation by 50,000 U.S. troops 168; separation from Confederacy 106; Union's southwest strategy 120; western invasion route 129
Texas and Union, proposed truce 141, 142
Texas Cotton Office 115
Texas-Louisiana border 24
Texas Marine Department 29, 42, 77
Texas Secession Convention 78
Texas State Military Board 115
Texas State Penitentiary 47
"Texas Troubles" 11
Thatcher, Rear Admiral H. K. 62, 133
Theron, Benjamin 106
Third Rhode Island Volunteer Cavalry 143
Thirty-fourth Indiana Infantry 143
Thouvenel, Edouard 109
Tom Hicks 40
Topik, Steven P. 105
Trans-Mississippi Department 112, 115, 137, 142, 144, 163; as a detached province of Confederacy 124; expanded

foreign relations role 120, 123
Treaty of Guadalupe Hidalgo 64, 69
Treaty of Paris 21, 27
Tredegar Ironworks 28
Trenholm, George Alfred 52
Trinity River 24, 80
Twiggs, General David E. 12, 14, 77
Tyler, Ronnie C. 108
Tyler, Texas 47, 143

Uncle Ben 96
U.S. Coast Survey 22
U.S. Congress 18, 20, 21
United States flagged vessels 73
U.S. Naval Academy, Annapolis, Maryland 30, 31
U.S. Naval Landing Party Handbook 157

Vanderbilt 149
Velasco, Texas 43, 57, 61, 79, 133
Velocity 96
venereal disease 33
Venus 40
Veracruz, Mexico 27, 41, 69, 79, 118, 153
Vernon, Captain A. 136
Vicksburg, Battle of 45
Vicksburg, combined army-navy action 47, 48
Vidaurri, Governor Santiago 72, 108, 109
Vincennes 45
Virginia 29
Virginia (state) 13, 15, 18, 19

W. G. Anderson 36
Wainwright, Captain Jonathan M. 84, 88, 90
Wallace, General Lew 141, 142
War of 1812 15, 147
Washington, D.C. 13, 15, 27
Washington Navy Yard 27
Watson, Captain William 57, 58
Webster's Collegiate Dictionary 147
Welles, Gideon 15, 22, 23, 36, 45, 94, 125; annual report to Congress 25; blockade 39, 42, 53, 61, 62, 66, 70, 75, 133, 162; concern about Napoleon 106; importance of Rio Grande 111, 130
The West Gulf Blockade, 1861–1865: An Evaluation 157

West Gulf Blockading Squadron 36, 44, 62, 80, 97
Westfield 83–85, 88, 89, 91
Wethersford County (Texas) minutemen 141
Wheeler, Major General Joseph 139
Why the South Lost the Civil War 156

Wigfall, Louis T. 103, 144
Wilkinson, J. 55, 62
William C. Rice see *Delta*
Wilmington, North Carolina 50, 51, 55, 152
Wise, Brigadier General Henry A. 167
Wise, Stephen R. 158
Woll, Adrian 118

Wooster, Ralph 75
Wren 61
Wright, Louise Wigfall 144
writ of habeas corpus 20, 21, 123, 152

yellow fever 65, 83, 84, 95
Young America 39
Yturria, Santiago 74

www.ingramcontent.com/pod-product-compliance
Lightning Source LLC
Chambersburg PA
CBHW081557300426
44116CB00015B/2918